CHILD DEVELOPMENT
A FIRST COURSE

Child Development
a first course

Kathy Sylva and Ingrid Lunt

Basil Blackwell

First published 1982
Reprinted 1982, 1983 (twice), 1984, 1985

Basil Blackwell Publisher Ltd
108 Cowley Road, Oxford OX4 1JF, UK

British Library Cataloguing in Publication Data

Sylva, Kathy
    Child development: a first course.
    1. Child development
    I. Title   II. Lunt, Ingrid
    155.4   BF721

    ISBN 0-86216-053-7
    ISBN 0-86216-054-5 Pbk

PAGE
BROS
Printed in Great Britain by
Page Bros (Norwich) Ltd

Contents

Preface

In this book we attempt to introduce students with no knowledge of psychology to the scientific study of child development. The scholarly literature in this field is enormous, and we debated long and hard about the best means for bringing it to students at school or on professional courses. Perhaps the best way to describe our dilemma is to report the experiences of two imaginary travellers.

Travellers A and B planned a visit to a foreign land, one they wished to explore fully in the 100 days available to them. A visited 100 tourist centres – cities, towns, places of scenic beauty – and he spent one day in each place. B planned a different itinerary, going to only ten places but staying ten days in each.

Who learnt the most about the country? B, almost certainly, and it is on the basis of his advice that we have planned this book. Instead of 'covering' a wide variety of topics in a superficial, breathless way, we have concentrated on a small set and treated each in depth. For example, Chapter 5 deals at some length with the work of Sigmund Freud, describing how he slowly developed his theory and even including some case material from a child patient. Unfortunately Chapter 5 could not *also* describe the important work of later psychoanalysts who have extended or modified the theory. We have treated intellectual development in a similar way. Although Chapter 7 is an extended account of the work of Jean Piaget, there was no room to look at the work of other psychologists who study intellectual development, or indeed, to deal at all with the topic of mental handicap.

This book deals first with theories of child development and the scientific methods on which they are based (Chapters 1–9). The next section of the book (Chapters 10–15) shows how scientific understanding of children has contributed to their care, education and help with problems. The first half of the book is organized by topic, for example *perception*, whereas the applications part of the book is organized according to age of child, say *infancy*, and focuses on a variety of ways that psychology has contributed to practice within that age-range. This division into 'research' and 'practice' does not of course mean that there is no research into the practical applications of developmental psychology. As a matter of fact there has been a great deal of it, and some is reported in the second part of the book. Nor does it mean that practical applications cannot contribute to theory. It's just that, in our view, the arrangement we have chosen makes the book clearer and more convenient to use.

What has guided us in our decisions about what to include and to leave out? We wished, above all, to share with readers the nature of psychological questions and the general approach to answering them. This necessitated an in-depth treatment of classic studies, rather than a catalogue of the most recent work. In other words, we have tried to provide the most important landmarks in the new terrain, not the details of its geography. With a firm understanding of the most important ideas and methods of developmental psychology, the student is prepared for later exploration on his own.

Because the methods of psychological investigation are so essential to the discipline, they are discussed in every chapter. Summaries of the methods appear in boxes. When a method is mentioned in SMALL CAPITALS, that means that somewhere in the book (and probably within a page or two) is a box covering it. The final section of the book, Part Three, pulls together all the material on methods in a more discursive summary.

When a word is printed in **bold type**, that is intended to remind the reader that this word is defined in the glossary on page 247, along with other terms which will be useful in revision.

The book examines the development of children between birth and the age of ten. Although adolescence is a fascinating field of study we could not include it for reasons of space. Our focus has been on young children and methods devised by psychologists for studying them. No doubt we have left out much that is interesting and new. We hope that readers will rush to the libraries and bookstores as soon as they finish this book so that they can fill in the gaps we have knowingly left.

Kathy Sylva
Ingrid Lunt
August 1981

Acknowledgements

Many friends and colleagues have criticized early drafts of this book. We are especially grateful for the suggestions of Derek Blackman, Richard Cromer, Judy Dunn, Tim Horder, Eduard Marbach and David Wood. The photographs, with a few exceptions, were taken by Gavin Park who left the higher reaches of physics to roam patiently through homes, schools and nurseries with camera in hand. Finally we are pleased to thank Jacky Evans for her competence and good cheer while typing countless drafts of manuscript. The index was compiled with craft and care by Ronald Lunt.

Acknowledgements are also due for permission to reproduce text and figures as follows: Routledge & Kegan Paul Ltd for numerous passages from *Play, Dreams and Imitation* by Jean Piaget; the authors and International Universities Press Inc. for the extract on pp. 11–14 from 'An experiment in group upbringing', by Anna Freud and Sophie Dann, from *The Psychoanalytic Study of the Child*; the authors and Macmillan Press Ltd for the extract on pp. 200–203 from *Childhood Behaviour Problems* by R. and P. McAuley; the author and Victor Gollancz Ltd for the extract on pp. 205–8 from *Dibs: In Search of Self* by Virginia Axline; the Ladoca Publishing Project, William K. Frankenberg and Josiah P. Dodds, together with Harcourt Brace Jovanovich Inc. for Figure 1.2, adapted from the *Denver Developmental Screening Test*; Mr Gordon Coster for Figures 2.2, 2.4, 2.6, 2.7 and 2.8; the *Radio Times* for Figure 3.2; Michael Rutter and Open Books Publishing Ltd for Figure 3.5 from 'Parent-child separation: psychological effects on the children', in *Early Experience: Myth and Evidence* edited by A.M. and A.D.B. Clarke; Mary Evans/Sigmund Freud Copyrights for Figure 4.2. Figure 6.3 is adapted from S.W. Kuffler and J.G. Nicholls, *From Brain to Neuron*, published by Sinauer Associates Inc. Figure 6.4 is reproduced from *Eye and Camera* by George Wald © 1950 by Scientific American Inc.; all rights reserved. Figure 6.5 is adapted from Ernest R. Hilgard, Rita L. Atkinson and Richard C. Atkinson, *Introduction to Psychology* © 1979 by Harcourt Brace Jovanovich Inc.; reproduced by permission of the publishers. Acknowledgement is due to David Linton for Figures 6.8 and 6.9. Figure 6.10 is adapted from *The Origin of Form Perception* by Robert L. Fantz © 1961 by Scientific American Inc.; all rights reserved. Acknowledgement is due to the author and George Allen & Unwin Ltd for Figures 6.13 and 6.14 from *The Visual World of the Child*, by Eliane Vurpillot; Routledge & Kegan Paul Ltd for Figure 7.1. Figure 8.3 is adapted from B.F. Skinner, *The Behaviour of Organisms* © 1966; reprinted by permission of Prentice Hall Inc. Englewood Cliffs, N.J. Acknowledgement is due to the author and Oxford University Press for Figure 9.3, from J.S. Bruner, 'Learning how to do things with words', in *Human Growth and Development*, edited by J.S. Bruner and A. Garton; and to the American Psychological Association for Figure 12.3, from the *Journal of Abnormal Psychology 66* © 1963; reprinted by permission of the publishers.

Part One

The psychology of development

Figure 1.1 *At eleven months this baby can almost walk alone*

Chapter 1

Common sense and science

This book is about the ways that children grow and develop. From the moment of conception, many characteristics of the child are firmly fixed. One of these is sex, another is colour of the eyes. Characteristics such as adult height, although strongly determined from conception, are not fixed because diet and physical environment have a part to play as well. The majority of characteristics that make an individual unique are the result of the interaction between the biological 'blue-print' present in the fertilized egg and the experiences of the growing child.

Children in all parts of the world mature in roughly the same sequence. Some seem to race towards developmental 'milestones' while others amble more slowly. Still, the **genetic inheritance** of all human babies ensures that the sequence of development will be much the same. Figure 1.2 shows that all babies roll over before they sit and sit before they can stand.

Vertical marks in that figure specify the point at which half of all children have achieved each milestone. The left end of the bar shows the age at which 25 per cent of babies can perform the activity, and the right end shows the age by which 90 per cent of them have accomplished it. The diagram shows, for example, that 25 per cent of babies can sit without support when they are four and a half months old, that half of them can when they are five and a half, and that the vast majority (90 per cent) can by seven and three quarter months.

Figure 1.2 is a diagram of **maturation**, the natural growth and unfolding of skills according to a sequence that is biologically determined. The process of maturation begins when the egg is fertilized and continues throughout adulthood. Even before birth the foetus develops according to a fixed schedule. This is the reason that premature babies lag behind full-term infants in early development; their biological time-clock was set in motion at conception and they're not 'ready' to roll over as soon as babies who have had more time to develop inside the mother.

It is known that the early development of sitting, walking and so on (what psychologists call 'motor skills') proceeds according to timetables of maturation like this one. But what makes some children achieve Olympic sports standard while others sit in the stands? There's more to excellence than genes. And why do some children learn to read at four and others hardly at all? Maturational factors will not fully explain school perform-

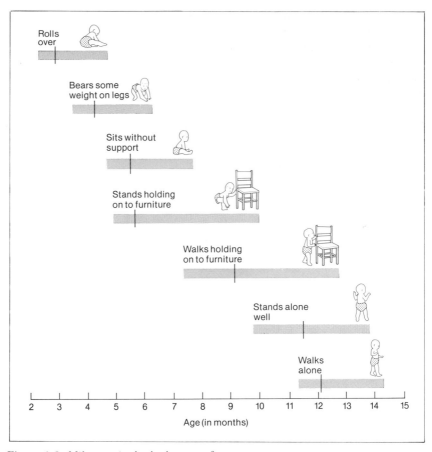

Figure 1.2 *Milestones in the development of movement*

ance or even excellence at motor skill. To answer these and related questions, we must seek information from a host of sources.

Many people are experts when it comes to children. Parents, first of all, know enough about their offspring to fill several books. Then there are doctors and teachers, each with specialized knowledge that comes from professional training and daily experience. Research scientists have another kind of knowledge, one that enables them to chart the intricacies of bone growth or hormones that bring about adolescence. Knowledge about child development ranges from common sense to science, making it different from sciences such as astrophysics, where personal experience no longer makes any contribution to serious study.

What about common sense? Common sense is a vast storehouse of knowledge about children, a whole library of anecdotes, facts, explanations and cures. Every mother knows that a 'monster face' will make her toddler laugh when she pulls it, but the same child will burst into shrieks when a stranger does the same. Every teacher knows that pupils can detect an inexperienced colleague and make his life a misery. Unfortunately common sense doesn't tell us why the baby finds his monster-mother so amusing, or what kind of logic the tyrannical pupils use in making their assessment of the hapless newcomer. These are topics for science to investigate.

One serious drawback to common sense is that it often contains contradictions. 'Spare the rod and spoil the child' suggests one course of action to a parent whereas 'an oft-beat dog turns on its master' warns against it. There are other conflicting accounts of childhood. For instance, common sense tells us that all human beings are shaped by what happens to them, yet when individuals achieve greatness in art, science or sport, we credit them *individually*, we don't credit their backgrounds. Similarly, we believe that individuals deserve praise for good moral character, while we tend to excuse the sly or dishonest because their characters have been moulded by adverse circumstances. If common sense would have us believe conflicting views, how do we decide which ones are right?

One reason why opposite 'truths' continue to live side by side is that they are never put to formal test. Consider remedies for warts. As long ago as 1627, Francis Bacon advocated the following cure.[1]

> I had, from my childhood, a Wart vpon one of my Fingers: Afterwards when I was about Sixteene Yeeres old, being then at Paris, there grew vpon both my Hands a Number of Warts, (at the least an hundred) on a Moneths Space. The English Embassadours Lady, who was a Woman farre from Superstition, told me, one day; She would helpe me away with my Warts: Whereupon she got a Peece of Lard, with the Skin on, and rubbed the Warts all ouer, with the Fat Side; and amongst the rest that Wart, which I had had from my Childhood; Then she nailed the Peece of Lard, with the Fat towards the Sunne, vpon a Poast of her Chamber Window, which was to the South. The Successe was that within fiue weekes space, all the Warts went quite away: And that Wart, which I had so long endured, for company. But at the rest I did little maruell, because they came in a Short time, and might goe away in a Short Time againe: But the Going away of that, which had staid so long, doth yet sticke with mee.

There follows an account by a contemporary schoolboy[1] written in his own words; you'll see that little has changed.

> I had warts about five months ago and I was told to cut a hazel stick about half an inch thick, cut as many notches as you have warts. Then wrap the stick in brown paper, tie with string, go for a bicycle ride and drop it somewhere in the road. Do not tell anywhone aboute it. I have not told any-whone till now. The person who picks the parcle up will have your warts. About a fortnight after my warts disapeared.

5

Did these ancient cures make the warts go away? Undoubtedly some warts disappeared, and no doubt the lucky patients were confident that the evil spirit or devil's substance had been lured out of the wart and into the lard or stick. Modern medicine now tells us that a virus causes the wart, not evil spirits, and no doctor would prescribe the remedies just described.

Must we conclude that the people who used these remedies were mentally deficient? No, it may be that firm belief can help effect a cure (but how? – there's another fascinating subject for investigation). Also warts sometimes disappear spontaneously, and no doubt each person who used a common sense remedy knew about cases like these. Then each person passed the story on to someone else. 'Do you know how Fred cured his warts? He did such-and-such.' Common sense continued to be handed down from generation to generation because no one noted failures of the remedies (and there must have been many) nor compared the success rates of different cures.

We cannot rely on common sense with any degree of certainty. We need other, more scientific ways to investigate how children grow and develop, and what is best for them – especially if we are going to use this knowledge as the foundation of our policies on education or the care of children.

Developmental psychology

The chapters that follow are written from the standpoint of developmental psychology. Psychology is the science of human behaviour, thoughts and feelings. Developmental psychology, moreover, is that branch of psychology that investigates how these develop in human beings.

Everyone reading this book has already come in contact with psychology. Although children rarely meet psychologists, every child who takes an aptitude or intelligence test has indirect contact with the discipline, as does every mother who reads articles on child care in *Woman's Own*. Teachers learn about psychology when they prepare for their profession; doctors and nurses read about its findings to help them in dealing with children. Naturally, the ways they treat or teach youngsters has been influenced by their study. Developmental psychology already influences you; learning about it will enable you to understand more about children. (For the most part, that understanding will be about children *in general*. 'Ninety per cent of children do such and such . . .' – But that doesn't tell us whether any *particular* child will be one of the 90 per cent or not. For that reason developmental psychology will not necessarily tell you anything very certain about individual children you know, or about yourself as a child.)

Although individuals can act wisely in total ignorance of psychology, it provides one way to decide amongst various common senses and recommendations. By making a serious and scientific study of children, you can put facts, fallacies and misconceptions to the test. People who use magic cures for warts do not publish success rates of their remedies, nor even the precise treatment they employ. The search for understanding requires detachment, precise description, and a willingness to accept the results of enquiry no matter how much they are at odds with intuition, or with what one would *like* to believe.

The methods of science

Science is more than the mere description of events as they occur. It is an attempt to discover order, to show that certain events stand in lawful relations to other events.

The methods of science are designed to clarify these uniformities and make them explicit.

B. F. Skinner[2]

The cornerstones of the scientific method are *observation* and *report*. Instead of relying on intuition or hearsay, the scientific investigator observes the phenomenon of interest, measures it if possible, evaluates his hypotheses about it, then makes public his observations and the methods used to obtain them. Others are then free to disagree, re-interpret, repeat or extend the investigations. In this way, each scientific investigation builds upon preceding ones. Medical scientists followed this very pro-gramme when investigating the cause and cure for warts. Different hypotheses were put forward about their cause and each one investigated. In like manner, different remedies were advanced and formal experiments conducted to see which ones worked.

The plan of this book

Some books for beginning students concentrate on the findings of psychology but give short shrift to the methods used to accumulate them. Although they transmit facts and theories, they give the student no means for criticizing the work of psychologists nor for conducting their own investigations. We have taken another tack.

There are countless means for studying child development, some better than others for specific research questions. A number of them are described in the boxes that appear throughout the text. The reader will learn to criticize each method. For which research questions is it most appropriate? What are its limitations? How certain can we be about the findings it yields? Part Three focuses squarely on these and other questions of methodology. It summarizes the basic methods of psycho-logical investigation in the boxes, commenting on their strengths and weaknesses.

Most books have a bias and ours is no exception. We have concentrated on the techniques developed by psychologists to study the intellectual, emotional and social development of children. Other, perhaps equally important, topics have had to be left out. We regret that there is no discussion of physical development, nor of the medical side to child care. Chapters 5 and 14 show where psychology touches upon psychiatry (the branch of medicine that treats children whose mental and emotional development has gone awry). Chapters 7, 13 and 15 touch upon the intersection of education and psychology. Many disciplines contribute to our understanding of children and, unfortunately, this book leaves out a lot. But then it doesn't promise an entire meal – only a 'first course'.

And now for the final confession. There are some questions that the scientific methods of psychology will never answer. *'What is morally right and wrong?' 'How will my friend Jane act tomorrow?' 'Will I be a good parent?'* The first question is beyond the scope of psychology, belonging instead to ethics or religion. Science has something to contribute to the second question about Jane's actions, but it's better at predicting how people behave in general rather than in the specific. As for the last question, developmental psychology cannot make you a good parent. Maturity, warmth, generosity, and even luck have parts to play. It's a good bet, however, that objective knowledge about the ways that children develop will also help.

Chapter 2

Do babies need mothers at all?

It's common knowledge that babies do need mothers. In *Songs of Experience*, William Blake tells us he knew this homely truth at the moment of his birth.

> My mother groan'd: My father wept.
> Into the dangerous world I leapt:
> Helpless, naked, piping loud:
> Like a fiend hid in a cloud.
>
> Struggling in my father's hands:
> Striving against my swaddling bands:
> Bound and weary I thought best
> To sulk upon my mother's breast.

Novelists and poets write about children 'from the inside', that is, from their own experiences. People who write for television or comic books do the same; they often base characters like the 'bullying schoolboy' or the 'kindly drunk' on people they know. Writers of fiction are not concerned with typicality or general truth. Their goal, instead, is to describe specific individuals in particular situations. Sometimes authors attempt to tell their audience about children in general, but they do this by describing the particular.

Scientists do not pursue imaginative insights in this way. They are interested in objective facts, in 'outside' ways to describe children and childhood. They also try to go beyond observable facts to discover the scientific laws behind them. Thus, while most people assume that mothers just *are* necessary, and perhaps look on with interest at how mothers and children they know happen to get on, psychologists go back to first principles and ask how much mothering babies *have* to have, of what kind, and when. What *exactly* is the contribution mothers make, and how does it affect the way their children develop? Answers to these questions are important: they help parents provide better and more humane care for their children. And if, for any reason, some parents cannot take care of their children, such answers help others make a better job of taking their place. Research is important for purely scientific reasons too. It tells us

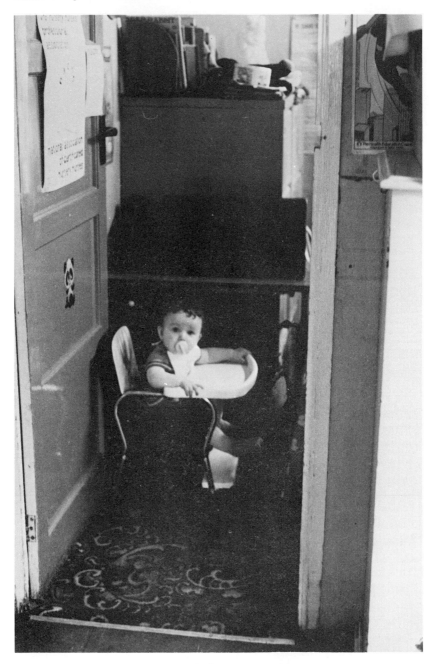

Figure 2.1 *Does this baby need a mother?*

about human emotional needs and contributes to our knowledge of development.

The answer to the question 'do babies need mothers at all?' is more subtle than one might expect. There is something – which may as well be called 'mothering' – that babies and children certainly need. But what it is and who has to provide it turn out to be very complex and interesting matters. The logical place to start exploring is with babies (thankfully rare) who have no mothers. How have they coped? What sort of people have they become? What are they like as parents themselves?

This chapter deals, then, with two studies of the motherless. One is of war orphans; the other is a much more rigorous and exact study of motherless monkeys. Both are somewhat sad, but their unfortunate subjects tell us a great deal that will benefit other children in future.

A study of war orphans

Anna Freud and Sophie Dann studied six orphans rescued from a concentration camp in Monrovia following the Second World War. Here is an excerpt from their CASE STUDY.[1]

CASE STUDY

A case study is a detailed investigation of either one individual or a small group, using careful records of past history in order to reconstruct a description of past and present. The investigator uses his subject's memories of past events as well as information from sources such as reports of physicians or relatives, and written records. Thus, information from many sources contributes to the case study, and sometimes new sources are uncovered while the investigation is in progress.

The Freud and Dann study used this method in an attempt to document the past histories and life experiences of the six young children who arrived in Bulldogs Bank. Some facts had to be surmised or reconstructed from the available information, although their experiences after arrival could be more accurately documented (see page 12).

The six young children who are involved in this [study] are German-Jewish orphans, victims of the Hitler regime . . . During their first year of life, the children's experiences differed; they were handed on from one refuge to another, until they arrived individually, at ages varying from approximately six to twelve months, in the camp of Tereszin. There they became inmates of the Ward for Motherless Children, were conscientiously cared for and medically supervised, within the limits of the current restrictions of food and living space. They had no toys and their only facility for outdoor life was a bare yard. The Ward was staffed by nurses and helpers, themselves inmates of the camp and, as such, undernourished and overworked. Since Tereszin was a transit camp, deportations were frequent. Approximately two to three years after arrival, in the spring of 1945, when liberated by the Russians, the six children, with others, were taken to a Czech castle where they were given special care and were lavishly fed. After one month's stay, the six . . . were flown to England in bombers and arrived in August 1945 in a carefully set-up reception camp in Windermere, Westmoreland, where they remained for two months. When this reception camp was cleared and the older children distributed to various hostels and training places, it was thought wise to leave the six youngest together, to remove them from the commotion which is inseparable from the life of a large centre.

The children arrived in Bulldogs Bank on 15 October 1945. The personal data of the six, so far as they could be ascertained, [included] the following:

Name	Age at arrival in Tereszin	Age at arrival in Bulldogs Bank
John	Presumably under 12 months	3 years 10 months
Ruth	Several months	3 years 6 months
Leah	Several months	3 years 5 months. Arrived 6 weeks after the others, owing to a ringworm infection.
Paul	12 months	3 years 5 months
Miriam	6 months	3 years 2 months
Peter	Under 12 months	3 years

How the children behaved on arrival

On leaving the reception camp in Windermere, the children reacted badly to the renewed change in their surroundings. They showed no pleasure in the arrangements which had been made for them and behaved in a wild, restless, and uncontrollably noisy manner. During the first days after arrival they destroyed all the toys and damaged much of the furniture. Toward the staff they behaved either with cold indifference or with active hostility, making no exception for the young assistant Maureen who had accompanied them from Windermere and was their only link with the immediate past. At times they ignored the adults so completely that they would not look up when one of them entered the room. They would turn to an adult when in some immediate need, but treat the same person as nonexistent once more when the need was fulfilled. In anger, they would hit the adults, bite or spit. Above all, they would shout, scream, and use bad language. Their speech, at the time, was German with an admixture of Czech words, and a gradual increase of English words. In a good mood, they called the staff members indiscriminately *Tante* (auntie), as they had done in Tereszin; in bad moods this changed to *blöde Tante* (silly, stupid auntie). Their favorite swearword was *blöder Ochs* (the equivalent of 'stupid fool'), a German term which they retained longer than any other.

Clinging to the group

The children's positive feelings were centered exclusively in their own group. It was evident that they cared greatly for each other and not at all for anybody or anything else. They had no other wish than to be together and became upset when they were separated from each other, even for short moments. No child would consent to remain upstairs while the others were downstairs, or *vice versa*, and no child would be taken for a walk or on an errand without the others. If anything of the kind happened, the single child would constantly ask for the other children while the group would fret for the missing child.

This insistence on being inseparable made it impossible in the beginning to treat the children as individuals or to vary their lives according to their special needs. Ruth, for instance, did not like going for walks, while the others greatly preferred walks to indoor play. But it was very difficult to induce the others to go out and let Ruth stay at home. One day, they actually left without her, but kept asking for her until, after approximately 20 minutes, John could bear it no longer and turned back to fetch her. The others joined him, they all returned home, greeted Ruth as if they had been separated for a long time and then took her for a walk, paying a great deal of special attention to her.

At night, all the children were restless sleepers, Ruth being unable to fall asleep, Paul and Peter waking up in the night crying. Whoever was awake, naturally disturbed the sleep of the others. The upset about separation was so great that, finally, children with colds were no longer kept upstairs.

When together, the children were a closely knit group of members with equal status, no child assuming leadership for any length of time, but each one exerting a strong influence on the others by virtue of individual qualities, peculiarities, or by the mere fact of belonging. At the beginning, John, as the oldest, seemed to be the undisputed leader at mealtimes. He only needed to push away his plate, for everybody else to cease eating. Peter, though the youngest, was the most imaginative of all and assumed leadership in games, which he would invent and organize. Miriam too played a major role, in a peculiar way. She was a pretty, plump child, with ginger hair, freckles and a ready smile. She behaved toward the other children as if she were a superior being, and let herself be served and spoiled by them as a matter of course. She would sometimes smile at the boys in return for their services, while accepting Leah's helpfulness toward herself without acknowledgement. But she, too, did not guide or

13

govern the group. The position was rather that she needed a special kind of attention to be paid to her and that the other children sensed this need and did their best to fulfil it.

Indoor and outdoor activities

During their first weeks in Bulldogs Bank, the children were unable to use play material. The only toys which attracted their attention from the start were the soft toys, dolls and teddy bears which were adopted as personal possessions. All the children without exception, took their dolls or teddy bears to bed with them. When a child failed to do so in the evening, it would invariably wake up in the middle of the night, crying for the missing object.

The first play activity, which the children carried out with passionate eagerness, was the pushing of furniture, the usual favourite occupation of toddlers who have just learned to walk. They began their day in the morning with pushing chairs in the nursery and returned to this activity at intervals during the day, whenever they were free to do so. After they had learned to play in the sandpit, they used sand for the same purpose, pushing a supply of it along the whole front of the veranda by means of an inverted chair. They would revert to pushing furniture even on coming home from long walks, or when tired.

Conclusions

Our material shows that the relations of the Bulldogs Bank children to each other were totally different from ordinary sibling attitudes. The children were without parents in the fullest sense of the word, i.e., not merely orphaned at the time of observation, but most of them without an early mother or father image in their minds. Consequently, their companions of the same age were their real love objects. This explains why the feelings of the six children toward each other show a warmth and spontaneity which is unheard of in ordinary relations between young contemporaries.

The six Bulldogs Bank children are, without doubt, 'rejected' infants in this sense of the term. They were deprived of mother love, stability in their relationships and their surroundings. They were passed from one hand to another during their first year, lived in an age group instead of a family during their second and third year, and were uprooted again three times during their fourth year.

Although the case of the six orphans shows that children can survive without mothers or even mother-substitutes, scholars argue about conclusions that might be drawn. On the one hand, the children fared admirably by protecting and caring for one another. Further, they eventually adjusted to a new language, new customs, and began to form emotional relationships with the adult staff. But what about their temper tantrums? Their preference for one another above all adults? Their impoverished play and poor sleep? Were the children headed towards normal lives? Unfortunately, there is no information on the adult lives of these children, or others like them, so we turn to consider another study of a different kind. It is a study of motherless monkeys on whom there are complete records from infancy to adulthood. Certainly animal studies cannot be generalized directly to human beings, but we share enough of an evolutionary history with monkeys and apes to allow them to shed some light on human lives. The fact that baby monkeys follow the same development pattern as human infants, although faster, also justifies studying their developmental experiences to give clues about our own.

ANIMAL EXPERIMENTS
Scientists interested in animals quite sensibly conduct experiments on them. However, psychologists interested in human beings often study animals because they may shed light on people. This is often done when it would be unethical to manipulate human lives. Although caution is necessary in *generalizing* results from animals to people, similarities between species sometimes allow this to be done. Formal experimental procedures are the same for all subjects – whether human or animal.

An experiment with monkeys

Whereas each of the six orphans had different experiences of loss and subsequent care, Harry Harlow[2,3] carefully arranged for a number of rhesus monkeys to have identical experiences early in life. As soon as each infant was born, it was removed from its mother's cage and placed in a special nursery. In it there were two substitute, or 'surrogate', mothers. Both were made of wire and wood, although one was covered in cloth towelling. Four monkeys were placed in cages where a nursing bottle was attached to the cloth mother, whereas a matched group of four were placed in cages where the bottle was attached to the all-wire mother. Photos of the surrogate mothers are shown in Figure 2.2.

Harlow was interested in how the babies would react. He soon found that all eight of the monkeys acted the same, spending the greater part of each day holding on to the cloth mother. When hungry, those whose bottle was attached to the wire mother nipped over to drink from the nursing bottle, but raced back to the terry-cloth figure as soon as they were through.

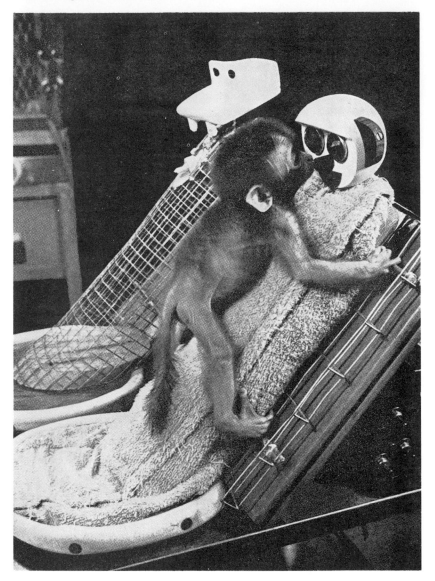

Figure 2.2 *The surrogate mothers Harry Harlow provided for his rhesus monkeys*

Figure 2.3 shows the average amount of time monkeys in each group spent clinging to the two different surrogates. Harlow concluded that baby monkeys seek something soft and cuddly to cling to. Of course, they needed milk but the fact that the wire mother provided nourishment was not enough to make her 'lovable'.

Harlow and colleagues were satisfied that infant monkeys clung in the normal way to cloth mothers but wondered if the surrogates could provide

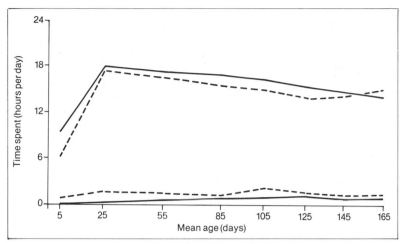

Figure 2.3 *The monkeys' preference for a cloth mother*

The vertical scale (numbers 0–24) shows the number of hours each day spent in contact with the mother. The horizontal scale shows the age (in days) of the growing monkeys.

The broken lines represent the monkeys fed on wire mothers, and the solid lines those fed on cloth. The top lines show the amount of time the monkeys spent on the cloth mothers, the bottom lines the time spent on wire mothers.

Figure 2.3 shows clearly that both groups of monkeys spent more time in contact with the cloth mother, no matter which mother 'fed' them. For example, at 25 hours of age, the monkeys fed on cloth mothers spent (on average) 18 hours a day on the cloth mothers.

comfort and safety in times of fright, as the orphan children so clearly did for one another. He formed a scientific HYPOTHESIS that *baby monkeys will seek contact with the cloth mother when they are frightened.* In order to test it, he placed a mechanical teddy bear at the entrance to each cage. It moved forward towards the monkey, beating a tin drum. All of the monkeys raced towards the cloth mother, rubbing their bodies against her and making fright sounds. Harlow says 'with its fears assuaged through intimate contact with the mother, it would turn to look at the previously terrifying bear without the slightest sign of alarm. Indeed, the infant

HYPOTHESIS
A hypothesis is a testable statement that a psychologist aims to confirm (or else prove wrong) by objective test, i.e. 'If such and such a situation is created, x will be the result.' A hypothesis is the germ of a scientific hunch translated into testable form. In the teddy bear study on this page, Harlow's hypothesis was that the monkeys would run to the cloth-covered surrogate mothers when frightened. To investigate his hypothesis, he conducted a FORMAL EXPERIMENT.

Figure 2.4 *First flight, then curious examination*

would sometimes even leave the protection of the mother and approach the object that a few minutes before had reduced it to adject terror.' Figure 2.4 shows the frightened monkey fleeing at first to its mother, then turning later to study the mechanical toy. Figure 2.5 shows the average amount of time spent on each surrogate when the teddy bear approached. These results confirm Harlow's hypothesis.

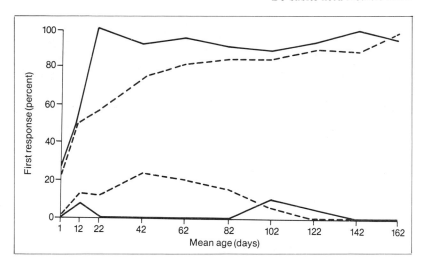

Figure 2.5 *The results of the mechanical toy test*

The vertical axis shows the percentage of first 'flight' responses to a mother. The horizontal axis is age of monkey at time of each teddy bear test.

The top lines represent the time each group spent on the cloth mother, and the bottom lines the time spent on the wire mother. The broken lines show the monkeys fed on wire mothers, and the solid lines those fed on cloth.

Figure 2.5 shows that both groups of monkeys fled to the cloth mother no matter which mother 'fed' them. For example, at 22 days, 100 per cent of the first reactions of monkeys fed on cloth mothers were to flee to the cloth mother.

After spending their childhoods isolated in cages with only two wire objects for company, all the monkeys were placed in a large compound in the company of normal monkeys. Their new peers had been reared with their mothers in family cages and allowed to play with others of their age. Had the surrogates provided adequate mothering? Sadly the orphan monkeys were not able to get on with their new, more sociable companions. They were frightened by spirited games of chase and tag and unfamiliar with the complex sounds and gestures by which they communicated. Mostly, the motherless monkeys withdrew into corners of the large, outdoor enclosure and engaged in nervous twitches.

When a little older, the motherless males were unable to mate successfully. Although the females fared somewhat better and managed to mate and produce young, they were inadequate parents to their offspring. They did not bother to nurse the young, and even cuffed them mercilessly.

Figure 2.6 shows normal and Figure 2.7 abnormal baby-care by monkeys raised with real or surrogate mothers.

Clearly something had gone wrong, but what? The inadequate monkeys had been carefully fed, allowed some degree of exercise, and kept free of disease. The adequate monkeys had been reared in identical cages, were of the same genetic stock, and after weaning, fed the same diet. The

Figure 2.6 *Normal, affectionate mothering from a mother herself reared in a normal way*

crucial difference between the normal and abnormal monkeys appeared to be the presence of the baby's mother. Harlow concluded that baby monkeys cannot grow up to be 'normal' without live mothers.

In order to compare the human orphans at Bulldogs Bank with the motherless monkeys, a distinction must be made between two types of investigation. One is the FORMAL EXPERIMENT, typified by Harlow's work.

Figure 2.7 *The monkey reared by a surrogate mother does not care for her own young as normal monkeys do*

In it, the scientist deliberately manipulates the phenomena he wishes to study before drawing conclusions about cause. Harlow arranged for two groups of monkeys to have different life experiences, one group with surrogate and the other with real mothers. All monkeys had similar breeding histories, were housed in similar cages and given identical health care. One group grew up to be as healthy and normal as laboratory animals can be, the other became decidedly peculiar in behaviour and were either incapable of mating or hopelessly inadequate as parents. What distinguished the two groups was the very factor that Harlow had manipulated – the presence or absence of real mothers. The antecedent condition, here the presence or absence of the mother, is called the independent VARIABLE: this one is deliberately manipulated. The

21

FORMAL EXPERIMENT

In a formal experiment, the psychologist looks at how two things are related by varying one of them and seeing how that affects the other. These 'things' are known as VARIABLES. It is the manipulation of variables that characterizes *experimental* method, as opposed to the various non-experimental methods of investigation.

For example, in the peer group study on page 25, Harlow wanted to find out the effects of mothers' absence on infant monkeys. So he arranged for a number of monkeys to have different life experiences. One group had real mothers with them, another had surrogate mothers, and a third had surrogate mothers and also other infants for fixed periods each day. The variable that he changed (or manipulated) was the nature of the infants' company (real mother, surrogate mother, etc.). The other variable was the behaviour that resulted.

Formal experiments normally take place in the laboratory, where the psychologist can control the environment and the conditions he wants to create. At least, he can control them more easily than in the natural setting. In this experiment, Harlow controlled genetic inheritance, health, food, type of cage, and so on, by making sure they were the same, so far as possible, for all the monkeys. By that means, he could make sure that none of these was the real cause of any difference in later behaviour.

consequent condition, normal or abnormal social behaviour, is called the dependent VARIABLE, because its nature *depends* on the independent variable.

Stated precisely, Harlow manipulated the independent variable (presence or absence of mother) to investigate its effect on the dependent variable (normality of social behaviour) in later life. He concluded that

VARIABLES

Look again at the FORMAL EXPERIMENT box on this page. The *independent variable* (or IV) is the one that the psychologist manipulates. The *dependent variable* (DV) is the one whose change he then watches. Thus in the Harlow experiment, the independent variable was the nature of the infant monkeys' company, and the dependent variable was their behaviour. In the Hess experiment on page 31, the independent variable was the age at which the duckling was exposed to the model duck, and the dependent variable was the amount of following the duckling did in the apparatus.

the relationship between the independent and dependent variables could be isolated and stated exactly. By careful laboratory control, he ruled out the influence of other factors such as differing genetic stock, differential health, and varying physical environment. Because these were the same, he concluded that lack of mothering caused later abnormalities.

Contrasting two research methods

Compare this to the study of Anna Freud and Sophie Dann. These investigators also described both antecedent and consequent conditions for the six children. They gathered information concerning each orphan's circumstances, and later treatment by authorities. They recorded in fine detail how the children acted towards one another when they finally arrived at the Bulldogs Bank house. They also documented the therapeutic treatment they received in England and how they reacted to it.

Does the work by Freud and Dann constitute an experiment? The answer is no. What distinguishes a formal experiment from an informal study is the amount of control over the independent and dependent variables. Freud and Dann did not know which, if any, of the orphans had been given affectionate care whilst living in the Ward for Motherless Children. Perhaps some of the prisoners caring for the children gave special attention to one or two of them. And because the children came to the camp when close to a year of age, some may have lived for a while with their natural mothers. For these reasons, it is impossible to define precisely how 'present' or 'absent' was each mother (or mother substitute) in each baby's life.

In addition to the mystery concerning the amount of mothering experienced by each orphan, nothing is known about their health or physical circumstances before arrival at the camp. One or two may have suffered illness or injury, perhaps to the head. Factors such as these would explain the temper tantrums, seen at Bulldogs Bank, as well as the lack of interest in toys and playthings.

In short, the Freud and Dann study is deficient as a formal experiment because the dependent variable, children's social behaviour, cannot be easily related to the independent variable, the loss of the mother. We simply do not know enough about the children. There are too many factors besides the lack of mothering that might have caused their emotional problems. Most disappointing of all is the fact that we do not know what happened to the orphans when they grew up.

Why include the study by Freud and Dann? Firstly, because it proves several points. It is known for certain that the children experienced a changing stream of caretakers, several fear-ridden journeys, and a complete change of language and culture. Despite these difficulties, they were affectionate and protective with one another and were in time able to respond warmly to the new adults who cared for them. In addition, their intellectual capacities were sufficiently intact for them to learn new speech and customs. This we know for sure. What we do not know is to what degree they were really 'motherless'. The study demonstrates that early adverse experiences can be 'overcome' at least to some extent.

There is a second reason why the study by Anna Freud is interesting. Although lacking rigorous experimental control, it is sufficiently detailed to serve as a basis for *scientific hypotheses*. During their first year of life the orphans were placed together in a small nursery in a concentration camp. Amidst the fear and poverty of a camp, they developed a deep love for one another. In these six children, diminished mothering appeared to shift to other children the feelings normally reserved for parents. This suggestive finding from Bulldogs Bank enables a prediction to be made that can be tested, at least with monkeys. If they are taken away from their mothers, the presence of other young monkeys might keep them from developing abnormal behaviour like those seen in Harlow's motherless babies.

CONTROL

Exactitude is the aim of every scientific investigation, and exactitude requires control – especially in these three areas:

(a) *Control over the gathering of information.* The investigator defines precisely the circumstances of his study. If he is carrying out a formal experiment, he lays down his procedure in great detail and makes sure he follows that same procedure every time he repeats the experiment with a new subject. If he is conducting a SURVEY, he will standardize the INTERVIEW (or questionnaire, etc.) to make sure that all the information is collected in the same way.

(b) *Control over the conditions in the experiment.* Sometimes experimenters want to find out which aspect of a situation is responsible for a given effect. For instance Bower (on page 86) wanted to discover whether – when babies duck back from a looming object – it is the sight of the object or the puff of air that is responsible. He therefore eliminated the puff by showing some babies a looming object *on film*.

(c) *Control group.* To make sure a *particular* factor is being tested, an experimenter may divide his sample into two groups, and give both groups the same experience *but for the essential factor*. For instance, in testing a new form of drug, an experimenter would give the drug to one group, and give a similar (but completely drug free) pill to the other group. He could then test the effect of the drug, rather than the effect of *taking some medicine*. The group given the drug would be the experimental group, and the other the control group.

In a subsequent experiment, Harlow tested this hypothesis. This time, the independent variable was the presence or absence of age-mates coupled with the total absence of a mother. Once again, the dependent variable was the monkey's adult social behaviour. As before, infant monkeys were removed from their mothers at birth and placed in the nursery cages with the surrogate wire and cloth mothers. This time, however, they were allowed 20 minutes each day to play with other motherless monkeys of their age. (See Figure 2.8).

When they were older these motherless, but not friendless, monkeys were introduced into a large enclosure with monkeys who had been raised

Figure 2.8 *Harlow tried an experiment to see how young monkeys with surrogate mothers would develop if they were allowed to spend some time each day with other monkeys of the same age*

with their natural mothers. In contrast to the first experiment, this new group of monkeys managed to hold their own with their new companions, despite the fact that the new peers were total strangers to them. The monkeys with cloth mothers took a while to learn the rough and tumble games of the others, and were rarely leaders of the adolescent group. Still, they were not isolates like the first lot of monkeys, and soon acquired normal skills such as mating and caring for their young. Play with peers in some way had substituted for natural mothering. Why? One reason is that live monkeys respond to the baby. Although peers and natural mothers sometimes cuff him, at least they notice his actions and reply to them in kind. Moreover, live partners can communicate by gesture and sound, signalling intentions, feelings and warnings. Surrogate mothers, although always present and often nourishing, neither respond nor communicate. This experiment provides clues to what is important in good mothering – a topic re-visited in Chapter 4.

Psychology, like other sciences, proceeds in fits and starts. It has been shown here how the findings from an informal study of war orphans can be linked to a more formal experiment with monkeys. The work of Freud and Dann employs the scientific method known as the CASE STUDY. This type of investigation uses careful records of behaviour and provides great detail. Often, it is associated with therapy or remedial help. A case study approach may be used on many individuals or just on one. There are many problems in interpreting the results of case studies because of the lack of control over independent and dependent variables. Still, case studies like the one reported here are fertile ground for hypotheses about human behaviour and can lead to more rigorous work.

The opening question 'do children need mothers?' can now be revisited. Experiments show that young monkeys cannot cope as adults if they have not had live mothers when young. Still, those deprived of mothers appear to 'get by' with twenty minutes of play each day with their peers. Although less is known about human infants deprived of mothering, the case study of Freud and Dann suggests that babies with insufficient mothering (not total absence of it) may turn their feelings towards others of their age.

Chapter 2 has looked at the minimal requirements for mothering. Happily, most children have mothers, or others filling that role. Chapter 3 looks at a theory explaining the emotional needs of babies with mothers as well as those without.

Chapter 3

The instinct that bonds

Philosophers and scientists, as well as parents of course, have been pondering the roots of infant love for centuries. What – biologically speaking – is the purpose of love? And what is the mechanism by which babies choose whom to love? Harlow's experiments show that baby monkeys spend more time clinging to 'mothers' with soft, textured surfaces than to those made of wire, even if the wire ones have nursing bottles attached. Still, one cannot equate preference for a dummy figure with human love or even monkey love. It may be that the monkeys loved neither of the surrogates. Harlow's work proves that infant monkeys choose soft rather than hard surfaces, but that preference may have little to do with 'love' as known by parents and poets. Similarly, the love of war orphans for one another provides little insight into the roots of love in normal babies reared in gentler, everyday circumstances. For a better understanding of that, we must shift attention to the work of John Bowlby, who provides a complex theory of the development of emotions.[1]

The facts to be explained

Instead of studying babies without mothers, who happily are rare, Bowlby turned to children in normal families who were separated from their mothers for reasons such as illness. The distress these children suffered, especially when their separation occurred before the age of five, was well known among nurses in hospitals and residential institutions. Even when they were hospitalized for observation or very minor treatment, children appeared to suffer greatly. No amount of kindly nursing, of toys or good food, seemed to make any difference. Bowlby wanted to pinpoint the exact reason for this obvious distress. It seemed not to be lack of care. Could it have to do with their illness? Or was it in fact that the loss of their mothers was far more disquieting than any medical malady?

It may seem odd at first that a man interested in emotional development in normal children would study those unlucky enough to be separated from their mothers. Bowlby reasoned that the importance of the mother would become apparent in cases where there was separation. In

Figure 3.1 *Is the love and presence of his mother irreplaceable?*

similar manner doctors learn about the role of the liver in normal individuals by studying patients with abnormal liver functioning.

To prove conclusively that it was *not* illness or painful medical procedures that caused separation distress one would need to study children whose mothers were absent but whose circumstances otherwise remain unchanged. Bowlby found just the evidence he was looking for in a study by René Spitz and Katherine Wolf.[2] They had looked at 123 babies whose mothers were in prison. In this particular setting, the women cared for their babies from birth to eight or nine months; they played with them, fed them and engaged in routine care when they were not needed for other prison activities. But for some administrative reason the mothers were moved elsewhere for a three-month period when the babies were nearing their first birthdays, while the babies remained behind in their special baby nursery and were cared for by others. Despite a high standard of physical care, most showed symptoms of distress, such as loss of appetite, crying, and failure to gain weight. Spitz and Wolf concluded that the babies needed the love and presence of their own mothers as much as they needed food.

John Bowlby was struck by the evidence collected by Spitz and Wolf for it agreed closely with medical observations made by James Robertson. Robertson had observed children under five who were separated from their mothers when they had to go into hospital. He described the following sequence of reactions over the course of their stay. At first children *protested* with crying and displays of anger. After this stage, which lasted less than a week, they became quiet and seemed to *despair*, crying intermittently but without the earlier force. Lastly, they became more cheerful, emotionally *detached* and appeared to have no preferences at all among their caretakers.

This sequence remained the same whatever the illness and ward routine. Further, Robertson reported an identical pattern for children who entered residential nurseries due to family illness or death. The cause, he believed, was the loss of the mother, and not the strange environment.

On the basis of the data collected by Spitz, Robertson and their colleagues, Bowlby hypothesized that a child's acute distress at separation from his mother is universal in the human species, and that the characteristic sequence of protest, followed by despair and detachment, would not vary at all among babies under five.

Bowlby next sought the psychological process that might account for a baby's suffering when separated from his mother. Research studies convinced him that 'separation anxiety', as it became known, was not a fear of losing the source of nourishment. Why, then, the distress when mothers leave for short periods, and why the apathy if the separation is protracted? Bowlby's investigation of the emotional needs of babies led him to the field of ethology. This is a science concerned with the behaviour of animals – with the action patterns that enable them to survive in the particular physical and social environment of their species. Its findings will be described in some detail because Bowlby used them to construct a theory about the emotional needs of children.

Imprinting

Ethology is the study of animal behaviour from the perspective of biology, especially the workings of evolution. It's a newer science than either psychiatry or psychology, and Bowlby drew on its recent findings when developing his theory about the infant's tie to the mother.

He had reasoned that a baby's reactions to separation from his mother are universal in the human species. But are children *born* with a biological need for their mothers, or do they *acquire* one as they first experience life? Bowlby turned to the work of Konrad Lorenz, a pioneer in ethology who investigated the origins of baby animals' attachment to their parents.[3] As

Figure 3.2 *Konrad Lorenz and his greylag geese*

it happens, interest was set off by an accidental finding at his research station in Austria. One day he noticed several greylag geese following him about, making the sounds and movements goslings usually make when they follow their parents. Lorenz guessed quickly that something had gone awry in their development. Goslings seemed to have an instinctive response to follow a moving creature. He – rather than the mother – had triggered it off.

Why? It looked as though greylag geese did not inherit genetically any information about what their parents look like. To check whether this was so Lorenz waited until a fresh batch of geese hatched. He carefully removed them from their mothers, and arranged for them to see only human beings, no mature geese. Sure enough, they began to follow the scientists exactly as the others had.

Following this up with a series of extra experiments, Lorenz found that there was a **sensitive period** during the gosling's life when it would 'fix' on a moving figure. This fixation he called imprinting. Moreover, he found that if it was imprinted on a human, a goose would later ignore other adult geese when the time came to pair up and mate.

People often assume that animals are born with all the instincts they need for survival. Ethologists have shown, though, that often it's a case of very precise and permanent learning. That learning arises from very particular events at very particular points in life. A goose, for instance, is born with no notion of what geese are like. But it does have an instinct to follow, and whatever it follows shortly after hatching will form its image both of mother and mate. In the wild, this normally works without a hitch. Its only in research stations that a goose would become attached to a scientist, or a tennis ball!

Imprinting, or something very like it, has been demonstrated in many bird species, and also in dogs, sheep and various other mammals. It's probably a very widespread phenomenon in nature. It will be examined in more detail in just one species – the mallard duckling – studied by Eckhard Hess.[4]

In pursuit of scientific exactitude, Hess constructed the apparatus shown in Figure 3.3 so that he could control precisely the ducklings'

Figure 3.3 *Eckhard Hess's imprinting apparatus*

environment. He put ducklings, whose ages he knew exactly, on the runway, where the model of a male mallard was made to move at varying speeds. The model had a built-in speaker, and gave forth duck calls. The ducklings were allowed to follow it for one hour, then returned to darkness for a short while, then replaced in the apparatus. This time, however, there were models of both male and a female mallard, each with speakers. The female gave forth recordings of the natural sounds of mother ducks, while the male made a 'gock, gock' sound, not very like the duck calls it made before. By exposing the ducklings to two models, Hess could compare their responses to the object they had first imprinted (the male model) with the more 'natural' sounding and appearing object (the female model).

The results were clear and they upheld Lorenz's original claims. Most ducklings followed the male model which they had seen first, refusing to relinquish him for a more 'natural' model. Even more interesting, Hess compared the behaviour of ducklings of different ages and found that the strength of the following response varied; in fact, newly-hatched chicks did not appear to imprint at all. There was a 'right age' for imprinting, and it is 13–16 hours after hatching (see Figure 3.4). Described in the technical language used in the last chapter, the dependent VARIABLE (i.e. the number of following actions towards the male model) varies according to the independent VARIABLE (i.e. the age of the duckling). Once imprinted to a model, the duck did not 'reverse his attachment'.

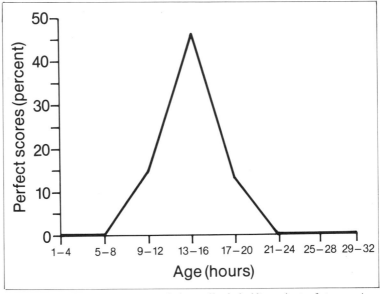

Figure 3.4 *The imprinting period for mallard ducklings (a perfect score is a completed following action)*

Imprinting is a fascinating phenomenon for several reasons. For centuries, naturalists and farmers have noticed that young ducks and geese follow their mothers soon after hatching. It was assumed that young birds were born with an instinct bonding them to their parents, a misconception that continued until some young geese began to follow Konrad Lorenz. He had the creative insight to investigate the matter further, and found a world quite different from the one suggested by common sense. Lorenz's conclusions prompted more formal studies, such as those done by Hess, and, in the end, precise relationships between the age of onset, the amount of movement, and many other factors, were discovered. What began as a casual observation was converted into a series of experiments in which the independent variables were deliberately altered to see how they affected some dependent ones . . . a journey from scientific hunch to well-established experimental fact. This is a telling instance of how science works, and how it leads down surprising paths.

Attachment in human infants

Of course, John Bowlby was not interested in how imprinting was being studied but in what it might contribute to our understanding of human babies. He wondered if the young in our own species were born with a predisposition for something akin to imprinting. Naturally, human babies cannot *follow* their mothers in the hours after birth, though they can cry, reach forward, and later follow them with their eyes. And, of course, when older they might crawl or walk towards the parent in much the same way as a duckling or a gosling.

Bowlby considered the long history of humankind. It seemed likely that during the evolution of the species it would have been the babies who were always by their mothers who would have avoided the host of predators and grown up to have children of their own. Bowlby hypothesized that both infants and mothers would have evolved a biological need to stay in constant contact with one another. A baby would not be imprinted in exactly the same way as were birds, but Bowlby believed that there was an optimal time (he called it a **sensitive period**) for them to form a bond with their mothers. They reveal this bond (termed **attachment**) by behaviour designed to bring the mother to *them* (when newborn) – or propel them (when slightly older) towards their mothers.

According to Bowlby, mothers also have a biological need to be near their babies, which is why they respond quickly both to their smiles and to their signals of distress. By focusing on the *pair*, Bowlby made a significant advance over previous theories of the baby's relation to the mother. Those were all one-sided theories which saw only the baby's part; Bowlby's was a theory of attachment that saw both parts. It assumed that for the baby to have been kept free from predators in those distant evolutionary days, it would have been necessary for the mother to want to stay by the baby, as well as the other way round. This two-way attachment is different from that of the ducks studied by Hess, but Bowlby believed there *was* a kind of human imprinting. Humans, he said, do have a sensitive period, (0–5 years), do fix on one person (usually the mother), and once fixed do stay fixed.

Furthermore, Bowlby warned emphatically that young children who do not experience a warm and continuing attachment would fail to develop healthy relationships when older. 'Mother love in infancy is as important for mental health as are vitamins and proteins for physical health', he claimed. He assumed the process of bonding (as he called it) was the basis for attachments in adult life. Woe to the child with no opportunity to form a secure attachment. If that biological need were not met, Bowlby predicted not only emotional but also intellectual problems in adulthood.

Bowlby's theory was met with much enthusiasm because it appeared to explain facts of which fond parents, worried physicians, and scientists had long been aware. But does it account for the evidence presented earlier?

(1) Consider the case of the orphans at Bulldogs Bank. Although nothing

is known for certain about their earliest histories, it is possible that none had experienced mothering as it is usually performed. During the 'sensitive period' they became attached to one another. The long-term consequences of these peculiar attachments are not reported here, so the case for peer attachments as substitute mothering must rest. But the fact that children were attached to *other children* is at odds with Bowlby's theory.

(2) In the Robertson study of children separated from their mothers and put into hospital, the same three stages of detachment were seen in all children. After release from hospital, the children were still adversely affected. The invariant sequence of stages of detachment, seen in all children, lends support to Bowlby's claim that the attachment process is an inborn part of the biological inheritance of *all* human beings. As such, it could qualify as an innate predisposition, like imprinting in animals, and support a theory that claims that a baby has an instinctive need for its mother.

(3) Then there were the children, reported by Spitz and Wolf, of mothers living in prison. As long as their mothers cared for them each day, they thrived. But when their mothers went away, despite good nursing, they were greatly distressed. Although at first glance this appears to support Bowlby's claim that early loss of the mother leads to impaired functioning, the study cannot settle the question either way as there is no information on these children when they were older.

New evidence for attachment theory

Some of the evidence above supports Bowlby's claim, but some is at odds with it. Bowlby realized that to prove that disrupting the early bond had the harmful effects on *later life*, he would need the evidence of long-term investigation. Harlow's motherless monkeys provided clues, but animal studies can never prove the facts of human development. Bowlby turned to the work of Goldfarb,[5] an American investigator who compared two groups of adolescent children, fifteen children raised by foster parents and some fifteen others who had been raised in an institution until they were over three.

Both sets of children had been separated from their mothers, for various reasons. Goldfarb believed that the only difference between them was that those in one group were placed immediately in foster homes, whereas the others lived for three or more years in residential institutions and then were fostered in families. When assessed at ages between 10 and 14 years, the institutionalized children performed more poorly on measures of intelligence, social maturity, speech, and ability to form social relationships. He ruled out the possibility that the differences in children were caused by the older children being placed in inadequate foster homes because investigation turned up few differences in the quality of care offered by parents who took the babies and those who fostered the older children.

It would seem at first that the Goldfarb study confirmed Bowlby's theory that children need to form a bond with one person, preferably in the first three years of life. It looks as though the children raised in the nursery *did* become detached and unable to form good relationships with their foster parents. But is this certain? Some critics point out that the children may have differed at the very beginning. Goldfarb had no means of knowing for sure that the children in both groups really were similar. Perhaps those who were not put forward for immediate fostering were different from the others – prone to illness, maybe, or socially withdrawn.

The Goldfarb study suffers from a classic flaw in research design, a SAMPLING flaw. Like the study of Freud and Dann, it was not an experiment. The assignment of the children to one or the other research conditions (i.e. foster family *vs.* residential institution) could not be carefully controlled – as it should have been under ideal conditions.

SAMPLES

For obvious reasons, it is usually impossible to study whole 'populations', such as all babies one week old, or all bank managers. One has to take a sample. But the sample must be characteristic of that population as a whole, and not be chosen by any biassed method. To take a fictional example, suppose one wanted to measure how satisfied people were with their local mayors, one could look at all the letters those mayors received. The sample would then be all those who had written letters. But that could be a biassed sample, because it could be that the sort of people who get up and write letters are less (or more) easily satisifed than the majority who do not. Usually, the best way to avoid bias is to select the sample at random from the population.

The same problem of possible bias arises when one divides a sample into two groups. One might, to take an unlikely example, want to discover whether a cup of coffee or a glass of beer had a better effect on people's ability at pinball. It would be necessary to ensure that there were no systematic differences between those given beer and those given coffee. One would therefore assign people randomly to the two groups. All the differences between the individuals ought then to balance out.

In his study on page 34, Goldfarb was looking at the effect of being brought up in an institution, in comparison to being adopted.

But his two groups – the adopted and the institutionalized – could of course not be assigned by chance. So any differences between them might have been just due to bias.

There's little doubt that the children *did* differ as adolescents, but it is far from certain that the difference was caused by three years of institutional (motherless) life. It may have been that the less bright children were sent to nurseries and the livelier ones placed in families. So it's possible that Goldfarb's findings did not demonstrate the pernicious effect of failure to bond; they may have demonstrated instead that children who are less bright or attractive at one year will continue to be at disadvantage later.

The research on human beings shows clearly the difficulties of investigating the long-term effects of early experiences. Take the Goldfarb study as a case in point. Scientifically, it would have been greatly improved if Goldfarb had decided by lot which babies were to be fostered immediately and which should remain in the institution. But that, obviously, would have been quite impossible. One could not assign a healthy, sociable baby to three years of institutional living because he was unlucky in the draw. Nor could one make an ill-considered placement for a child just because his number came 'up' on that day. People's needs must naturally take precedence over science's needs.

It's easier, of course, to work with animals because most people feel there are fewer ethical restrictions in performing research on them. Harlow concluded with reasonable certainty that the baby monkeys who could spend time with other baby monkeys were not harmed by being motherless, whereas the monkeys with only wire 'mothers' definitely were. This was a properly controlled experiment, and there was no difference between the kind of monkey assigned to the two groups; assignment was random. Therefore, it's safe to conclude that the differences observed in the dependent variables (mature social responses, for instance) were caused by the differences in the independent variable (access to peers or to wire dummies).

There are other advantages in working with animals. One is that they grow up more quickly – one needn't wait quite so long to see how they develop. We know for certain how Harlow's monkeys acted as parents because they were part of a LONGITUDINAL STUDY conducted for many years.

Is Bowlby's theory right?

For more than 20 years now John Bowlby has been arguing that separations of even one fortnight will lead to serious harm. Although the early research supported this claim, later, more carefully controlled studies did not. For example, Michael Rutter[6] studied a large number of boys aged 9–12 years on the Isle of Wight, and in London. He found to many people's surprise, quite a few who had been separated from their mothers when young but who seemed quite well adjusted as they entered adolescence.

Think about the many reasons why a child might be separated. His

LONGITUDINAL STUDY
In a longitudinal study the investigator studies one group of subjects at regular intervals over a long period of time, for example once a year for ten years. This method clearly takes a long time to produce results, in contrast to A CROSS SECTIONAL STUDY, which samples several groups at different ages.

Barbara Tizard carried out a longitudinal study when she followed a group of institutionalized children to see how staying in the institution, being adopted, or returning to their parents affected them. This appears on page 147.

CROSS-SECTIONAL STUDY
In a cross-sectional study, the investigator samples several groups of subjects, each of a different age. The advantage of this method is that it allows all the data to be collected much more quickly. On the other hand, it does not allow the investigator to study change in any one individual.

mother might fall seriously ill, and there might be no nearby relation to look after him while his father worked. When his mother returned home from hospital, he would return too, and family life would re-knit. But another child might be put into care because his parents' marriage was breaking down and neither mother nor father could cope with a baby's demands. Or his mother might be an alcoholic, or a heroin addict, and just not able to care for him.

It's easy to imagine that the first of these children might recover and grow to normal, happy adulthood because the early separation was something out of the ordinary in the family. But the other children might well be headed towards problems in forming relationships, later difficulties at school, or even trouble with the law. But in that case can one say that the cause was the early separation? Or could it be that the separation was just part of a chain of adversity that included foster homes, temporary family reunions, followed by further foster or residential care? If the cause of early separation were some chronic problem, then insecurity and family tension might well continue throughout childhood. Those might be the cause of later difficulty. Or the chronic problem itself – if it were for instance poor housing, unemployment, poverty, or low expectations at school – might be the cause. In real life, it's difficult to disentangle the effect of one variable, like for example maternal separation, on later behaviour. Other confounding factors (such as housing, education, continuing family strife) may contribute to, or even cause, the final result.

The Rutter survey is illuminating here because it located many boys who suffered an early separation from mother but who had no further troubles. Rutter believes that these children suffered temporary problems at the time of separation, but overcame these difficulties when family life returned to normal. There were some children in his sample, however, who were separated from their mothers early in life and who *were* maladjusted (as reported by their teachers) later on. What was the difference between the two groups? Children in the latter group were separated because of discord in the family or psychiatric illness, conditions which put heavy and continuing stress on family life. The lucky children, those who recovered from separation, were separated because of physical illness, difficulties with housing, and other problems which are not distortions of social relationships *per se*.

CORRELATIONAL STUDY

A correlation is a measure of association between two characteristics or events. Some correlational studies investigate the association between events at two different periods within the lives of many individuals. The question asked is 'which early events are associated with which later events?' Michael Rutter and his colleagues conducted a correlational study when they investigated the relation between anti-social behaviour in adolescent boys and the incidence of separation from parents in early childhood (see page 36). In their study, they found little association between the two measures, and so the correlation was low. Had they found a strong association the correlation would have been high.

Correlational studies can tell us which factors are associated with one another. They cannot, however, tell us about the cause of these events.

Rutter used a CORRELATIONAL STUDY design in which the investigator finds out whether or not there is an association between two measures. Figure 3.5 compares the occurrence of antisocial behaviour in boys with early separations due to physical illness and those due to family discord or psychiatric problems. It shows clearly that some kinds of separations are associated with later disorder while others make the child no more susceptible to antisocial behaviour than children who suffered no disruption in attachment bonds.

Although Rutter is convinced that early separation need not have lasting ill effects, he is less hopeful about the futures of children who *never* form affectional bonds. '. . . the evidence does seem to suggest that the effects of bond disruption (maternal separation) and a failure to form bonds (maternal deprivation) are different. It appears possible that a failure to form bonds in early childhood is particularly liable to lead to an initial phase of clinging, dependent behaviour, followed by attention-seeking, uninhibited, indiscriminate friendliness and finally a personality

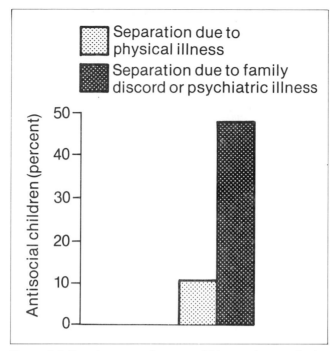

Figure 3.5 *How the* reasons *for parent-child separation are related to antisocial behaviour later*

characterized by lack of guilt, an inability to keep rules and an inability to form lasting relationships.'

Bowlby has many other opponents, but by far the most vigorous are Ann and Alan Clarke: 'We have for some twenty years been highly sceptical about this view [Bowlby's theory of attachment], and from time to time have said so. Until fairly recently, however, there has been a relative dearth of evidence. We feel that the time has now come to assemble the data and review the arguments.' Clarke and Clarke[7] have carried out this very exercise, bringing together a mass of studies that refute Bowlby's claims about the crucial significance of early attachment . . . In general, they fall into four major groups:

(1) Studies in animals showing that imprinting can be reversed. Indeed, some of Harlow's monkeys benefited from the 'therapy' administered by peers and functioned normally as adults. (With this in mind, it's no surprise that Chapter 10 shows successful adoption of children who have been institutionalized when young.)
(2) Studies of children who lack a continuing, secure attachment in early life but nonetheless attain adequate functioning later on. Included here are the Bulldogs Bank children who recovered somewhat after being rescued and placed in a warm and stimulating environment.
(3) Studies of children who have experienced temporary disruption in a

secure attachment and who have shown no ill consequences of it, for instance the Isle of Wight boys.

(4) Studies such as those of Freud and Dann showing that some babies can be attached to several people. This refutes Bowlby's claim that infants are invariably attached to only one person.

By far the most critical blow to attachment theory comes from 'reversal' studies, those investigations showing early disruption followed by complete recovery. Although Bowlby never rested his case fully on animal imprinting, *by implication* he used the framework of the early ethological studies to develop his views on the instinctual basis of love. Studies of 'reversal' in both animals and human children show them to be more flexible than Bowlby would have us believe.

Summing up

Bits of evidence, and some rather grand theories, have been discussed for the light they shed on the origins of human love.

Bowlby's theory, focusing on the biological need on the part of both mother and child to remain close together, stresses a bond to one unique female. Bowlby saw this bond as a behavioural adaptation to the dangers from predation faced by our ancestors in the distant evolutionary past. Although some studies appear to support this theory, the majority of research shows it to be simplistic and inadequate. The human baby does *not* bond to its mother with an irreversibility akin to animal imprinting. Luckily, babies are flexible and resilient creatures, capable of emotional ties to several adults – and in some cases – to other children. Luckily, too, the human mother is not biologically driven to be with her baby at all times. Many mothers arrange part-time substitute care so that they can go out to work. There is no scientific evidence that they doom their children to the developmental anomalies predicted by Bowlby.

Chapter 4

Mothering

What is mothering? The last two chapters looked at babies' needs for mothers, and at how a newborn fixes on who his mother is, and becomes attached. This chapter deals with what the process of mothering actually is, and how that too affects attachment. What are mothers for and who are they? What is special about the bond between the mother and her baby?

In a sense, everyone knows the simple answer to the question: what is mothering? Loving and caring for your child. This may seem straightforward enough, but on closer examination there is nothing simple about it. Mothers do all sorts of different things in one day, changing nappies, rocking babies to sleep, talking and cuddling, playing, offering the breast, scolding, wiping noses, loving children in spite of or because of everything. Yet many of these activities can be and are increasingly carried out by other adults, for example fathers. So what is so special about mothers?

Weekly magazines and baby books abound with advice on mothering and how to bring up children. Fashions change and experts swing from 'feed on demand' to 'feed at four-hourly intervals' and from 'always pick him up when he cries' to 'leave him crying and he'll learn to stop'. Common sense and personal prejudice contribute widely to the literature on child care, but it is only through scientific studies that we can learn objective truths about mothering and pick our way around rival common senses. Psychologists have therefore increasingly turned their research towards careful and detailed studies of the mother–baby pair in order to establish what is so special about the way they relate to each other.

Attachment

In Chapter 3 we looked at the notion of attachment and concluded that the human baby does not bond irreversibly to its mother, and that he is capable of attachments to several adults. However, although there is a universal predisposition and tendency (some would say instinct) for a mother and her baby to become attached to each other, there are wide differences between individuals in how this is achieved. A major goal of research is therefore to study the factors affecting the formation of attachment in order to better inform parents and others in the field of

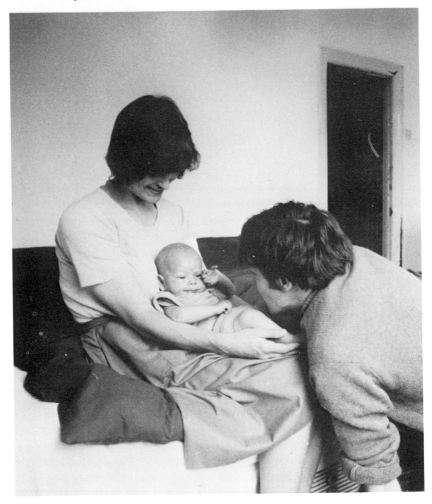

Figure 4.1 *Both parents mothering their three-month-old son*

early child care. One of the most interesting aspects of the relationship is its mutual reciprocity from a very early age. (Reciprocity is Rudolph Schaffer's word for the way in which the mother responds to the behaviour of her baby and is influenced by it, and the baby in turn is influenced by his mother's behaviour.[1] Schaffer's ideas appear a page or two further on.)

Reciprocity between mother and child

Recently, several researchers have devoted hundreds of hours to making detailed NATURALISTIC OBSERVATION studies of mothers and their young babies, and have shown on videotape the unspoken 'dialogues' carried on

NATURALISTIC OBSERVATION
A method of describing and analysing the behaviour of people or animals in their natural setting. It is derived from the ethological work of Konrad Lorenz. The investigator intervenes as little as he can and may try to remain unobserved. His main task is to record in as objective a way as possible, keeping to what he sees rather than what he infers: thus, 'X laughs for 8·4 seconds,' rather than 'X thinks that joke was great.'

from very early on in the babies' lives: mother and infant can be seen to be drawn to each other and to respond to one another's needs and activities. Colwyn Trevarthen and Martin Richards have made naturalistic studies of young babies' 'conversations'.[2] In an early study they filmed five babies once a week from birth until they were six months old, either with small toys hanging in front of them, or with their mothers. Each mother was simply asked to 'chat with her baby'. Trevarthen and Richards found 'highly elaborate activity' and 'indications that infants of a few weeks of age were showing signs of intentions to speak and that soon after this they were entering into well-organized, sometimes even witty or humorous, conversation-like exchanges with adults'. These young babies were responding to adult stimulation and conversation in a very sensitive way and seemed at this early age to be well aware of the 'dialogue'. Their responding then influenced their mothers' chatting and sustained their interest, so that each responded sensitively to the other. This is 'reciprocity' in full flight.

Daniel Stern has also analysed hundreds of hours of videotape and film in great detail to show the pattern of interaction between mother and child.[3] He found that three-month-old babies and their mothers, looking at each other face-to-face, move their heads in time with one another. As mother approaches, the baby turns his head away for a split second, and then turns back towards her as she withdraws her gaze. (Direct eye-to-eye gaze is very stimulating and even adults tend not to look eye-to-eye when close up.) 'The infant is a virtuoso performer in his attempts to regulate both the level of stimulation from the caregiver and the internal level of stimulation in himself. The mother is also a virtuoso in her moment-by-moment regulation of the interaction. Together they evolve some exquisitely intricate dyadic [i.e. pair] patterns. It takes two to create these patterns'. Daniel Stern emphasizes that this mothering is *purely* social. 'The immediate goal of a face-to-face interaction is to have fun, to interest and delight and be with one another. During these stretches of purely social play between mother and infant, there are no tasks to be accomplished, no feeding or changing or bathing on the immediate agenda . . . We are dealing with a human happening, conducted solely with interpersonal 'moves', with no other end in mind than to be with and enjoy somebody else. There is no way to overstress the importance of such a

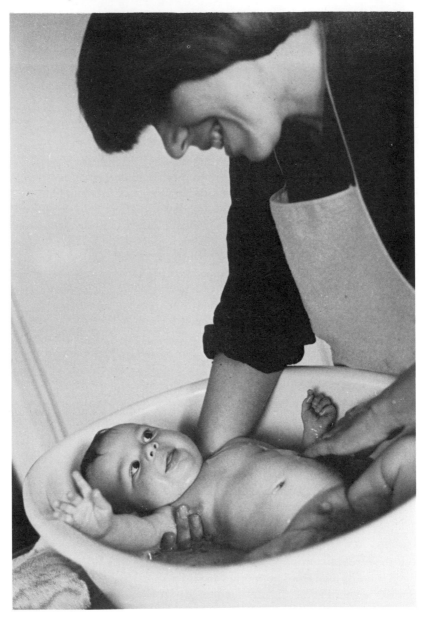

Figure 4.2 *Dialogue between mother and baby continues in the bath-tub*

seemingly effortless endeavour . . . The infant first has to learn to be with someone and to create and share the experiences that a relationship is built on. Besides the gratification of feeding and warmth, these involve the mutual creation of shared pleasure, joy, interest, curiosity, thrills, awe, fright, boredom, laughter, surprise, delight, peaceful moments, silences resolving distress, and many other such elusive phenomena and experiences that make up the stuff of friendship and love.'

The young child's communications

There is much evidence now to suggest that the baby seeks attachment almost as soon as he is born, that he is potentially 'social' from birth. Early on he is attracted to the sight and sound of humans rather than other objects and noises (and Chapter 6 will show the very young infant's preference for visual complexity and particularly the human face). From a young age he gives out strong signals (particularly crying and smiling but also grasping and gazing) which draw adults, and particularly his mother, to him and make them respond. One of the earliest baby observers was Charles Darwin, who observed of one of his own children: 'This infant smiled when 45 days, a second infant when 46 days old; and these were true smiles, indicative of pleasure, for their eyes brightened and eyelids tightly closed. The smiles arose chiefly when looking at their mother, and were therefore probably of mental origin.' More recent studies have shown that babies smile from the first week of life (although these smiles are probably not directed at anyone). When Aidan Macfarlane asked mothers of two-month-old first babies, the question 'What sort of thing do you enjoy most about your baby?', 75 per cent of the mothers included 'smiling' in their replies.[4] Smiling is clearly a powerful social signal for the child.

The other powerful early signal, crying, was studied by Silvia Bell and Mary Ainsworth.[5] They were interested in exploring the relationship between the mothers' responses to their babies' crying (i.e. the number of cries a mother ignored; the length of time the baby cried without obtaining a response from her; and what finally ended the crying) and changes in those babies' crying during the first year. They observed 26 mothers and babies in their own homes for four-hour periods at three-week intervals throughout the first year, and found that maternal responsiveness was the main factor which affected the amount a baby cried. During the first three months of life, a baby was more likely to cry when he was alone than when he was near his mother, and least likely to cry when he was actually being held by her. In fact the single most important factor which reduced crying over the first year was the promptness with which a mother responded (usually by picking up or cuddling). The mother's early responsiveness and sensitivity to her baby's needs appeared to lay the foundations for the child's later social and emotional development.

The mother's sensitivity

Mary Ainsworth has described the sensitive mother as one who

> is able to see things from her baby's point of view. She is tuned-in to receive her baby's signals: she interprets them correctly, and she responds to them promptly and appropriately. Although she nearly always gives the baby what he seems to want, when she does not she is tactful in acknowledging his communication and in offering an acceptable alternative. She makes her responses temporally contingent upon the baby's signals and communications. The sensitive mother, by definition, cannot be rejecting, interfering, or ignoring.
>
> The insensitive mother, on the other hand, gears her interventions and initiations of interactions almost exclusively in terms of her own wishes, moods, and activities. She tends either to distort the implications of her baby's communications, interpreting them in the light of her own wishes or defences, or not to respond to them at all.

The sensitive mother's responsiveness looks very like readiness for the reciprocity described earlier in this chapter.

Mary Ainsworth found that mothers who responded sensitively in this way tended to have children who cried less, were happier to explore new situations, and were less worried by brief separations from them. Furthermore, they found that mothers who gave relatively more physical contact (cuddling, picking up) to their children in early months, had children who enjoyed interaction with adults and were also happy to be put down and to turn cheerfully to exploration or play.

> To have been given the contact that a baby seems programmed to promote does not make him into a clingy and dependent one-year-old; on the contrary, it facilitates the gradual growth of independence. It is infants who have had relatively brief episodes of being held who tend to protest at being put down, and who do not turn readily to independent play; indeed they seem highly ambivalent about physical contact – they may seek it, but they do not respond positively to it when they get it, and yet when put down they protest.

The importance of physical contact between mother and child shows up again though less clearly, in the work of Marshall Klaus and John Kennel.[6] They looked at babies immediately after birth in the hospital and compared mothers who had routine hospital care with those who had extra contact with their babies. They randomly allocated 14 mothers to CONTROL group and 14 to experimental group; the control-group mothers received the routine hospital care, according to which the baby was separated from his mother immediately after birth, briefly seen for inspection six to eight hours later, then returned for 20 minutes feeding every four hours. The experimental 'high contact' mothers, on the other hand, were together with their babies for most of the time from birth, except for very brief periods; they were thus given the opportunity for close physical contact, stroking, caressing, exploring, touching for most of the time. Klaus and Kennel found interesting differences between the groups of mothers; the experimental group mothers looked at their babies eye to eye, kissed and caressed their babies significantly more than the control group and they were more likely to want to stay at home with them. By the end of a year, though, it was clear that the babies who had had the ordinary hospital routine had 'caught up', showing that the effect, though marked, was short-term.

Overall, it appears that the emotional bond and development of the child depends on qualities in the early reciprocity and sensitivity of the relationship between mother and child. But is it necessarily the biological mother to whom a baby forms this attachment or relationship? Bowlby's early theory suggested not only that the baby needed the continuous presence of a mother but also that he was unable initially to form attachments to more than one person. However, recent studies have shown that this is not the case.

More than one attachment

Rudolph Schaffer and Peggy Emerson[7] studied a sample of 60 Glasgow children for the first 12 months of their lives to look at some of the ways in which a baby forms his first attachment to another person. Again, they used the method of NATURALISTIC OBSERVATION and made four-weekly visits to the babies, and their families, over the first year of life. This time the criterion for attachment was 'separation upset' (for example, protests made when the baby was left alone in a room, left with other people, put down after being on mother's knee, or left outside in a pram) and Schaffer and Emerson found that attachment to a specific person tended to occur around the age of seven months. They also found that most infants formed attachments to several people, including fathers, brothers and sisters, grandparents and sometimes even neighbours; in fact, three months after the onset of attachment behaviour (at approximately 10 months old) only 41 per cent of the sample had only one 'attachment object,' while at 18 months this percentage had decreased to only 13 per cent of the sample. By 18 months, 75 per cent of these babies had also formed an attachment to their fathers. There appeared to be a hierarchy of attachment objects, with mother usually at the top and several others also eliciting attachment responses.

Schaffer writes 'there is . . . nothing to suggest that mothering cannot be shared by several people . . . being attached to several people does not necessarily imply a shallower feeling towards each one, for an infant's capacity for attachment is not like a cake that has to be shared out. Love, even in babies, has no limits'. These findings are important since 'the changing nature of family life is forcing us to take note of other figures who play a part even early on, particularly fathers whose involvement in child care is gradually becoming much greater than it used to be. And, once we are willing to take these figures into account and realize that infants can form attachments to them too, it becomes very much easier to distinguish the factors that after all play little, if any, part in bond formation (the 'blood' relationship, the provision of good, constant availability), and concentrate on the particular qualities in the adults' behaviour that result in love relationship'.

What are these particular qualities? One important finding emerges from the Schaffer and Emerson Study. How strongly a baby is 'attached' does not seem to be related to the amount of time spent with him nor to

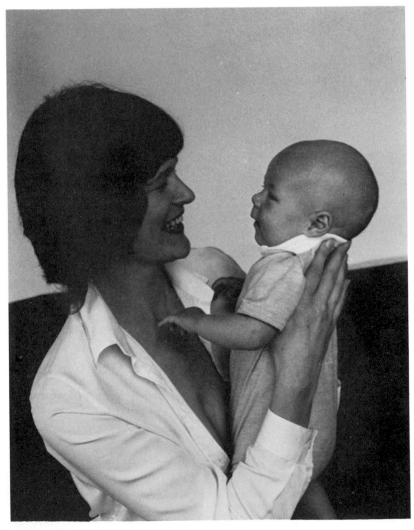

Figure 4.3 *Feeding ends with a game – as much a part of mothering as the feed itself*

the basic caretaking functions (feeding, washing, dressing) but rather to the quality and intensity of the interaction between adult and child. Babies whose mothers play a lot with them, and give them plenty of stimulation and undivided attention, develop stronger attachments than those whose mothers simply give basic physical care; similarly, babies whose fathers are particularly attentive and stimulating may develop a stronger attachment to their father than to their mother if she 'only' feeds them. Again attachment is a 'two-way process' and depends on the quality of the interaction and on the sensitivity and responsiveness between adult and child; there is a subtle balance for both mother and child of sensitivity to each other's needs; the child is influenced by the mother who, in turn, is influenced by the child. At first, the mother follows the child and is guided by his movements and inclinations; she elaborates, repeats, expands on these. Later, the child follows the adult and so a mutually satisfying relationship develops.

Cross-cultural studies

CROSS-CULTURAL STUDIES (such as comparing babies in Israel with infants in England) may tell us about human infants and their potential for relationships; however, we have to be careful to separate out what is common to infancy and what is specific to the cultural situation, in this case communal or collective living on an Israeli kibbutz. In a typical kibbutz, the child is brought up jointly by a *metapelet* and his parents while living mainly in the Children's House. A mother usually spends about six weeks with her new born baby, thus forming the primary attachment, and thereafter gradually resumes work until by the end of the infant's first year, she is working full-time and the *metapelet* is caring for the child. Children spend a long 'Children's Hour' daily with their parents in the parental home in the early evening, when the parents have time and energy to devote themselves actively and completely to their children. The *metapelet*, on the other hand, plays a knowledgeable and affectionate caring role which does not disrupt the primary attachment, and yet provides the children with physical and emotional care for a large part of the day. Kibbutz practice is based on the evidence that children can thrive with multiple caretakers without losing their primary attachments to their own

> CROSS-CULTURAL STUDY
> Cross-cultural studies make comparisons between societies or cultures. What are tested are the cultural differences in behaviour – whether physical, intellectual, emotional, or social. Cross-cultural studies may use different types of research method. FORMAL EXPERIMENTS, NATURALISTIC OBSERVATION, CASE STUDIES, or whatever may be appropriate.

families, and that it is the quality and mutual responsiveness of parent–child interaction rather than its length and 24-hour continuity which are important to the maintenance of the parent–child attachment relationship. In fact, the parents maintain their roles as primary attachment figures though they only spend a small proportion of each day with their children. It is the quality and intensity of this period (two or three hours) which is important and which enables the parents to keep their primary position in their children's affection.

A second cross-cultural study was carried out by Mary Ainsworth, who was interested in mother–infant relationships among the Ganda people of Uganda in East Africa.[8] She wanted to compare the 'attachment behaviour' of two cultures, the Ganda and the American. Ainsworth made a LONGITUDINAL STUDY over nine months of 28 babies between 0 and 24 months, paying each household a two-hour visit every fortnight and interviewing the mother with her child (*via* an interpreter) and observing the mother with her child. It is clearly difficult to measure 'attachment' and Ainsworth devised a number of factors which she used to determine its strength. These were factors such as smiling at the mother, crying when she left the room, turning towards her, clinging to her, clapping hands in greeting her. These children had regular contact with several other adults, and most of them seemed able to form an attachment simultaneously to several; their behaviour was not affected by the number of adults to whom they had to respond.

Nevertheless, care is needed when drawing conclusions from cross-cultural studies. Some of the most informative cross-cultural literature is presented as detailed description. The formulation of research questions, the isolation of variables and the allocation of suitable controls pose such formidable problems that researchers have concentrated their efforts in other directions. Accounts for instance of kibbutz life are largely anecdotal and descriptive, for how could one carry out a controlled study? Which aspects of such a very different society are significant? What is the independent variable? Type of mothering, type of caretaking or extent of communal life? What are the dependent measures? Attachment, intelligence, independence, social adjustment? A host of variables in the environment contribute to a host of different effects and it is impossible to isolate them. The cross-cultural researcher aims therefore to provide a detailed and structured description usually on selected aspects of the culture under observation, and attempts to draw comparisons and conclusions within and between cultures.

Studies such as these, which show that young babies are capable of forming attachments to several adults, have important implications, particularly in a society in which there is an increasing trend both for mothers to go out to work (and therefore share the mothering) and for fathers to play an important or sometimes exclusive part in the mothering relationship. There is no scientific foundation for the myth of the 'blood bond' or the belief that the biological mother alone is uniquely capable of caring for her child. This loving relationship may be carried out or shared by one or several other adults provided that they show certain qualities. What are these qualities? Sensitivity, consistency, stimulation and responsiveness are some of the qualities important to the early relationships in a young child's life.

In fact, a child's ability to thrive with several 'caretakers' is likely to be advantageous, since he gains additional social and intellectual stimulation, and experiences less distress during periods when his mother *is* absent. In addition is the fact of which there is growing awareness that it may also benefit the mother to have some rest from the child (and the chores) and thus gain increased enjoyment from the child.

To sum up

Do babies need mothers or do they need mothering? What they do need is physical care and a loving relationship. These are usually provided by the mother, but in fact they could be provided by someone else – not the mother, not necessarily female. It doesn't have even to be one person – it could be several. Nonetheless, as Rudolph Schaffer writes:

> Mothers are without doubt in an excellent (and usually the best) position to influence their child's development, but the older sibling and the woman next door may well leave their mark too . . . mothers go out to work, fathers bathe babies, people decide to live in communes or kibbutzim, and society's involvement in the child-rearing process – by the way of care provision and education – is constantly being extended. But children will always need mothering, whatever the social milieu in which they live, and to understand in precise detail the emotions, functions and effects involved in this process remains one of our more urgent tasks if we are to improve the conditions under which early development takes place.[9]

The research described in this chapter is very recent, and it points in a number of exciting directions. We turn next to another theory of emotional development: the work of Freud. Freud's views belong to a rather different tradition from the kind of science described so far. In fact, as will become plain, a problem with Freud's theories is that one cannot test whether they are true, or compare them directly with other theories. Nonetheless, they continue to influence the thinking, not just of psychologists but of everyone, to such an extent that the next chapter will be devoted to them.

Figure 5.1 *Sigmund Freud, near the age at which he gave his famous lecture on the seduction of children by their parents*

Chapter 5

Freud: love in the family drama

In Vienna before the turn of the century a sober, almost puritanical doctor startled the scholarly world by proclaiming the origin of love in children to be sexual attraction. Imagine the setting. Before an august audience composed of Victorian physicians, young Sigmund Freud held forth a complicated theory that claimed children in ordinary families were often seduced by their parents. The chairman of the meetings declared it 'a scientific fairy tale' and Freud wrote to a friend several days later describing the lecture: 'the donkeys gave it an icy reception'.

The events leading to Freud's lecture in 1896 read like a detective story and they will be traced here. What prompted such a startling view?

While a young neurologist (a medical specialist in the nervous system) Freud, with his colleague Josef Breuer, encountered many patients suffering from a disease with no apparent cause. Patients with the illness, known as hysteria, were afflicted with various symptoms including blindness, loss of memory, and paralysis. Little was known about the disease except that the affliction, although real, was at odds with neurological evidence. For instance, a patient would report a pattern of body paralysis that was physiologically impossible. When this happened, the form of the mysterious illness conformed to a layman's view of bodily functioning but not a doctor's. As Freud pointed out, hysteria 'behaves as though anatomy did not exist or as though it had no knowledge of it'. A hysterical affliction is different from one deliberately feigned because a pretender's symptoms will disappear if he thinks he is not observed, whereas the hysteric's remain.

While tracking down the causes of hysteria, Freud and his colleagues began formal investigation into that domain of the human mind that is not ordinarily accessible – the **unconscious**.

Investigating the unconscious

Freud and his colleague Josef Breuer believed that hysterical symptoms were often preceded by great fear. One patient who convinced them of this

Figure 5.2 *Bertha Pappenheim, the original 'Anna O'*

was a woman called Fraulein Anna O who began treatment with Breuer at the age of 21. Immediately before treatment she had undertaken the task of nursing her father through a grave illness. One of Anna's symptoms was paralysis in the right arm and Breuer believed that he had found the cause. It was a fright that she did not remember.

He described the case like this. Late one night while tending her father, Anna sat in a chair near his bedside with her right arm thrown across its back. She was anxiously waiting for the doctor, but in her exhausted state she 'saw' a great black snake moving forward to bite the sick man. She attempted to save him from the 'attack' but the arm she tried to use, her right one, had 'gone to sleep' and she could not move. Breuer discovered this sequence of frightening events while conducting what Anna called the 'talking cure'. In it, she recounted to Breuer her thoughts, dreams and imaginings. For each symptom, and she had many, Breuer was able to trace the origin in a fright or some other strong emotion that was not expressed when first aroused. When the triggering event was identified and the pent-up feeling released, the symptoms disappeared.

Breuer and Freud published their theory in *Studies in Hysteria*, claiming that hysteria was always the consequence of intolerable emotions which could not be expressed when they were aroused. They continued in an internal, almost strangulated state. Therapy consisted of helping the patient to bring the event into conscious awareness and express the full strength of feeling. The arm paralysis of Anna O, for instance, disappeared when in the consulting room she expressed the terror that she could not release in the sickroom of her sleeping father.

Although giving patients opportunity to talk about a pent-up emotion often proved therapeutic, as in Anna's case, there were other patients who could not easily remember the precipitating trauma (literally 'wound') that caused the problem, and it was to these that Freud turned next.

At first, he used hypnosis to help the patient recall previous events that were associated with their hysterical symptom. In many cases, although not all, recovering the memory of a long-forgotten crisis fully erased the symptom. Freud parted from Breuer and continued working on a technique for recovering the past which he called 'free association'. In it, the patient rested comfortably, often lying down on the now-traditional couch, and let his thoughts flow spontaneously along any path that came to mind. The cardinal rule was to allow each thought to lead naturally to the next, no matter how surprising or repugnant. Freud soon learned that thoughts are not organized in random fashion, nor do they appear in strict logical order. Although the patterns of association are unique to each individual, Freud found many universal **symbols** as well as common **chains of thought**. (Symbol here means words, pictures or events standing for something else.) Using symbols and chains of thought, Freud began to devise a theory of how the mind works.

Many patients visited Freud's consulting rooms and he listened to countless hours of talk. Often the stream of ideas and events led to the patient's past and it was here that Freud made his surprising discovery. Many of the early memories concerned sexual activities that shocked the hapless patient and, it seems likely, Freud too. In most cases Freud found that respectable adults harboured inside them memories of childhood lust and incest, and it was the scholarly report of this that stunned Freud's staid audience in 1896. Using evidence from his patients' thoughts and dreams, Freud concluded that the origin of hysterical disorders was the incestuous seduction of young children. Moreover he claimed such a crime was common in the Austria of his day. The children's emotions froze and so turned into hysterical symptoms in adulthood. Through Freud's new therapeutic technique of thought and dream analysis, many patients were surprised to discover how much they had desired and enjoyed the incestuous relations. And, Freud further told his audience that hysterical symptoms evaporated magically when the childish feelings of lust (and fear of detection) were allowed expression during therapy.

For some time Freud continued with this theory. One after another the experiences of eighteen of his early patients seemed to confirm it. Despite the cries of disbelief from all his distinguished colleagues, he did not shrink from what he considered the unpleasant truth about family life in Austria.

Suddenly, however, he changed his mind. There is much speculation about why Freud recanted his theory of infant seduction but one likely conjecture is that Freud's investigations into his own childhood caused him to alter the theory. In the summer of 1897 he told a colleague that he was 'tortured with grave doubts' about the seduction theory of hysteria. It was at the same time that he embarked on the 'talking cure' himself, using dreams and free associations to explore his own unconscious. No doubt Freud dredged up childhood memories of lustful feelings for the mother, perhaps even images of childhood seduction. Yet Freud was convinced that no *actual seduction* had occurred in his childhood. Perhaps the patients who revealed childhood seductions through memories and dreams were innocent in reality.

Through analysis of his own dreams and pattern of thought associations, Freud came to the conclusion that sexuality in childhood consists of the *wish* to sexually possess the parent – not really the act itself. This erotic wish he believed to be present in all children, not just those destined to become hysterical in later life.

> One feature of the popular view of the sexual instinct is that it is absent in childhood and only awakens in the period of life described as puberty. This, however, is not merely a simple error but one that has had grave consequences, for it is mainly to this idea that we owe our present ignorance of the fundamental conditions of sexual life.

Why are adults unaware of the strong sexual desires they felt as children? In *Three Essays on the Theory of Sexuality*[1], Freud described:

> the peculiar amnesia which in the case of most people . . . hides the earliest beginnings of their childhood up to their sixth or eighth year . . . during these years, of which at a later date we retain nothing in our memory but a few unintelligible and fragmentary recollections, we reacted in a lively manner to impressions, . . . we were capable of expressing pain and joy in a human fashion, . . . we gave evidence of love, jealousy and other passionate feelings . . .

'Clinical' research

Thence began several decades of clinical work in which Freud continued to develop his theories concerning the origin of love in children. Whereas the research evidence presented in Chapters 1–3 was derived from direct study of young animals and children, Freud's investigations were focused on the dreams and thoughts of adult patients. They flocked to his consulting rooms with a variety of mental disorders, and for each he prescribed the 'talking cure', so named by Anna O. Bit by bit, he pieced together the childhood histories of each, for it was here that he believed their development had 'gone wrong', giving rise to their physical and emotional problems in adult life.

In tracing the course of normal functioning by the examination of abnormal cases, Freud followed standard procedures of medical science. For centuries doctors had made important discoveries about the functioning of physiological systems by studying people with abnormalities. The medical treatment of patients, say with diabetes, sheds light on the normal functioning of the pancreas and blood sugar. Freud argued that the mental anomalies in his patients were merely exaggerations or distortions of normal mental functions. He was quite firm in his belief that the dreams and thoughts of his patients were suitable evidence for a theory about ordinary people in everyday circumstances.

Armed with the conviction that many of man's wishes and memories are inaccessible to them – that they have gone 'underground' – he looked for examples in normal people of the unconscious.

How the unconscious intervenes in everyday life

Freud's new source of data was 'slips of the tongue' made by normal people, including himself, his family and acquaintances, or reported in the news. He collected errors of speech with a passion, then pored over his list with great pains, using each slip as a clue to the workings of the unconscious:[2]

> A substitution takes place when a poor woman says she has an 'incurable *infernal* disease', or in Mrs Malaprop's mind when she says, for instance, 'few gentlemen know how to value the *ineffectual* qualities in a woman'.

Freud believed that such slips came about when the second, unconscious meaning surfaces.

> . . . when a lady, appearing to compliment another, says 'I am sure you must have thrown this delightful hat together' instead of '*sewn* it together' no [thing] can prevent us from seeing in her slip the thought that the hat is an amateur production. Or when the lady who is well known for her determined character says: 'My husband asked his doctor what sort of diet ought to be provided for him. But the doctor said he needed no special diet, he can eat and drink whatever *I* choose,' the slip appears clearly as the unmistakable expression of a consistent scheme.

In each of the examples, the speaker would be horrified to be told that his or her 'real' (i.e. unconscious) intentions had leaked to the surface. Freud recounts the chilling case of a famous slip of the pen.

> You may recall the case of the murderer H. who managed, by asserting himself to be a bacteriologist, to obtain cultures of highly dangerous disease-germs from scientific institutions, but used them

for the purpose of doing away in this most modern fashion with people connected with him. This man once complained to the authorities of one of these institutions about the ineffectiveness of the cultures sent him, but committed a slip of the pen and, instead of the words 'in my experiments on mice and guinea-pigs (*Mäusen und Meerschweinchen*)', the words 'in my experiments on people (*Menschen*)' were plainly legible. This slip even attracted the attention of the doctors at the institute but, so far as I know, they drew no conclusion from it. Now, what do you think? Would it not have been better if the doctors had taken the slip of the pen as a confession and started an investigation so that the murderer's proceedings might have been arrested in time? In this case, does not ignorance of our conception of errors result in neglect which, in actuality, may be very important?

In addition to slips of the tongue, Freud found many apparent errors in action which could easily be attributed to the underlying motivation of the unconscious. 'They are not accidents, they are serious mental acts, they have their meaning – they arise through the concurrence – perhaps better, the mutual interference – of two different intentions.'

Let us turn to a particularly ambiguous and obscure form of error, that of losing and mislaying objects. It will certainly seem incredible to you that the person himself could have any purpose in losing things which is often such a painful accident. But there are innumerable instances of this kind: A young man loses a pencil to which he was much attached. A few days before he had had a letter from his brother-in-law which concluded with these words: 'I have neither time nor inclination at present to encourage you in your frivolity and idleness.' Now the pencil was a present from this brother-in-law. Had it not been for this coincidence we could not of course have maintained that the loss involved any intention to get rid of the gift.

The book on slips of the tongue and other 'Freudian errors' was published in 1901. It was Freud's last work on ordinary behaviour, and it satisfied him that the thoughts and feelings of which normal people are directly aware are but the tip of the iceberg. Underneath is the unconscious with a host of other thoughts, some repugnant, some erotic, some merely faded. Freud sometimes spoke of 'the unconscious' as though it were a place in the mind, but of course, it's not. He used it as a convenient metaphor for material not in our awareness but which, nonetheless, influences daily emotions and actions.

Freud's theory of infantile sexuality

According to Freud personality is the pattern of thoughts, emotions and intellectual skills that makes a person unique. He believed that much of personality is unconscious and these hidden parts are responsible for the 'errors' and 'slips' discussed earlier. Although personality is what prompts each of us to act in characteristic ways, scientists cannot directly observe it because it is internal. This didn't daunt Freud, however, who was confident that he could uncover patients' personalities by listening to their thought associations and dreams. Using this kind of evidence, Freud pieced together what he thought were the crucial childhood experiences that shaped the personalities of his patients.

A key concept in understanding how personality develops is **libido**, an instinctual source of energy. Libido is present from earliest childhood and motivates all action. Libido is sexual energy, but do not take this in its narrow sense. Libido is a life force, the kind of energy that propels individuals to act in ways that reproduce the species. Naturally, this includes sexual intercourse and events associated with it, but it also includes affectionate play between the generations. When Freud describes the tender caresses exchanged by child and parent as 'sexual', he does not mean that they include actual sexual arousal – only that the excitement behind body games comes from the same source as adult love.

This broader definition of 'sexual' activity can be extended to adults as well. Who would deny that the pleasure felt by romantic couples sharing the same glass is sexual in origin? In adults and adolescents these activities produce genital sensation, but in children, they are not integrated into a coherent set of sexual feelings and so Freud called them pre-genital sexual drives. Whether adult or child, however, Freud firmly believed that sexual energy was what prompted people to care for one another, even if the caring did not appear 'sexual' on the surface.

While growing up, children learn to direct their sexual energy away from their parents and towards goals that are socially acceptable, such as sport or scholarship. The uniqueness of individual personality stems from the particular channelling of sexual energy away from their parents, the first sexual-love-objects, and towards other non-reproductive activity.

How do the instinctual drives motivate action? Freud likened personality to an engine with several interconnected parts. The steam necessary to run the engine is likened to the instinctual drives of libido. The form of the engine, and the working relations between its parts, changes as the child grows older. Freud stressed the fact that the instinctual drives were the same throughout life and always sexual, but that their goals change with age.

Freud's theory apparently compares human beings with locomotives, pushed along certain courses of action by hot, seething drives. The drives arise somewhere in the body and their goal is to reduce the tension or pressure they create. Throughout life, the source of all actions is libido, and the aim is always to relieve tension. The way in which instinctual drives are satisfied changes as the child grows older, as his love-objects change, but the source of energy is always the same.

Freud was convinced that libido had evolved in us to ensure reproduction. Some scholars believe that Darwin's book *The Origin of Species* prompted Freud towards insistence on sex as life's motivating energy. Others point to the similarity between the steam technology of the time (Freud was born in 1856) and Freud's theory of the driving, pushing libido and the pressures it creates. In any case, the Freudian theory of libido – well-spring of all activity – owes much to the thoughts and technology of the historical period in which he lived.

Three parts of personality

Freud thought that personality consisted of three parts. The most primitive, and the only one present in the newborn baby, is the **id**. This is the centre of the instinctual drive, libido. The task of the id is to find a way to satisfy the instinctual needs *immediately*, and *at all costs*. In other words, libido energy makes the infant restless and the id must find a means of satisfaction.

One way the id may satisfy the instinctual drive is to conjure up an image of an object that will relieve the tension. An example of this is the baby's fantasizing the mother's breast. This tactic will not satisfy for long, of course, but the id does not distinguish between the internal and external world and thus cannot know that a daydream is different from the real thing. Freud claims that the id is characterized by the **pleasure principle**, a mental operation that relieves tension without recourse to reality.

The id continues to function throughout life and its job is always the immediate and unrealistic satisfaction of an instinctual need. Freud points out that wish fulfilment seen in dreams (the boy who becomes a football hero overnight, the man whose rival suddenly dies of malaria) is brought about by the pleasure principle.

As the child grows up, a new structure known as the **ego** takes shape in his personality. The ego operates according to **reality principle**, which consists of rational activities directed towards satisfying the needs of the instincts. Learning, thinking, perceiving and evaluating, topics discussed later in this book, all take place in the ego and operate on the reality principle. Although infants can survive with only the id part of their personality working, older children need ego functions to live in a realistic manner in which fantasy is distinguished from reality.

The ego has its own instincts, whose goal is the daily maintenance of the body. These 'ego instincts' include hunger, thirst, and the drive to escape pain. Freud provides little information about these drives because he thought they contributed little to the uniqueness of personality. He believed that the ego instincts were similar in everyone, unlike the patterning of libido which did make individual differences.

The third personality structure to emerge in development is the **superego**, a moral watch-dog over the entire personality. This is the centre of individual conscience, as well as a model of what people *ought to* be like (sometimes called the ego ideal). Both the conscience and the ego ideal are formed by parental teachings. Although the superego is not dominated by the need for satisfaction here and now, it is not as rational as the ego and – by keeping the individual in tight moral check – can be the cause of much anxiety and irrational behaviour.

From years of clinical experience, Freud pieced together a theory of personality development showing how early experiences affect adult life. Their theory pointed to the importance of different areas of the body, called 'erogenous zones', as the child progressed through successive developmental stages. Moreover, the way that each child negotiated the developmental stages would determine his later personality.

Stages of psycho-sexual development

For the first two years of life, babies find great sensual pleasure from sucking and putting things in their mouths. Freud believed that the sexual pleasure derived from sucking, followed later by biting, was proved by the obvious pleasure infants gained from sucking almost anything they could carry to the mouth, and also the fact that they continued sucking when there was no nourishment to be got. Freud further substantiated his theory of sexual satisfaction in sucking by memories and fantasies of his patients.

According to Freud, the child in the **oral stage** (first two years) has no conception of the external world, nor any distinction between himself and his mother. It is as though his whole being is centred around his mouth and he believes that he, himself, brings about the pleasure that comes from sucking. The infant cannot differentiate the pleasurable effects he brings about himself from those brought by his mother. This gives the baby a sense of childish omnipotence.

It must be clear from the baby's confusions about reality that the ego is not yet present. Until it is, the infant is totally dependent on the nurture and care of his mother. Although *he* may feel omnipotent, he requires constant care because he cannot act rationally in the real world. If his mother cares tenderly for him, he will acquire a sense of trust and optimism that lasts him through life. On the other hand, if his needs are not met or satisfaction is consistently delayed, he will cry and rage, unable to bring about a realistic change. When this occurs, Freud warns us, the child will grow up to become pessimistic and mistrusting in adulthood.

Recall that the id operates according to the pleasure principle, the irrational mode of thought which cannot distinguish wish from reality, the body's inside from its outside, or the mother from the baby. It's easy to see why Freud believed that the baby does not love the mother in a tender, *personal* way. Instead, the infant loves the breast that gives the most satisfaction to his need for oral pleasure. Because the baby does not distinguish his own body – his own hands and arms and feet – from his

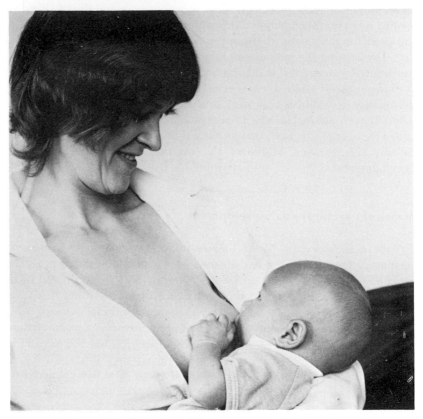

Figure 5.3 *Babies in Freud's 'oral stage' derive great sensual pleasure from sucking*

mother's, he cannot love her as a distinct person. Further, if infants are not satisfied or secure during the oral stage, they will not progress to the more mature stages that follow. When this happens, Freud says they are 'fixated' or arrested in psychological development. Despite later sexual maturity, Freud claims, fixated individuals will be incapable of *personal* love for other people. Instead, they will go through life seeking oral satisfaction and treating people as objects – not real persons distinct from them.

The oral stage is followed by a shift in the primary source of sensual pleasure towards the anus. Beginning around two years of age, Freud claims that the infant experiences pleasurable feelings from retaining faeces and also from stimulating bowel movements. This is the **anal stage**.

At first glance, the theory seems far-fetched. Although commonsense tells us that babies get pleasure from sucking and biting, it is not immediately apparent that they enjoy those sensations associated with bowel movements. What prompted Freud to this view? As always, his source of evidence was the dreams and associations of adult patients. During psychotherapy (the talking treatment he invented for psychological disorders), they recovered childhood memories of sexual pleasure during elimination. In addition to patients' memories, the association between contemporary thoughts showed how close were events associated with the anus and feelings of sexual excitement.

The period of life (two to three years) that Freud calls the anal stage coincides with that time when parents in many cultures toilet-train their children. They reward them for eliminating at the right time and place, and punish them when they soil themselves. In all cultures children fail to comply completely with the demands of training. Do they do this, as Freud says, because they enjoy the bodily sensations of 'holding back'? Others, such as Erik Erikson, have suggested that they might soil themselves in order to show their independence. Or, just as likely, they might not fully understand the 'right time, right place' rule. Lastly, soiling might occur because children were not sufficiently skilled at detecting the inner urge. Clearly, there are many hypotheses about toilet training different from Freud's, and the theory of sensual pleasure at with-holding and eliminating is merely one view. Freud extends the theory by saying that the child loves his own faeces because they are associated with pleasurable sensations in the anal region. This explains why a young child might smear his cot and beam a smile at his exasperated mother.

Just as difficulties during the oral stage can lead to emotional problems in later life, children who become fixated during the anal stage are also headed for problems in the future. Because a child loves and takes pleasure in holding and giving forth his faeces, he may have difficulty when he's older at keeping and giving objects such as money or other valuables. Over-possessiveness is a consequence of his parents having forced him too violently to give up his 'treasure'. Or, if the parents have been too harsh about punctuality of toileting, he may become compulsive later in life about time and infuriate his acquaintances by over-attachment to his watch. Lastly, the child who is trained too harshly may become overly fastidious himself, putting everything in its 'proper place' with a vengeance that is no longer rational.

During the anal stage, the ego makes its appearance. The child could never learn the do's and don'ts of toileting without realistic demarcation between himself and the rest of the world. Further, he must get himself to the toilet, negotiating obstacles that lie in his path. Luckily these early demands on the child to be a socialized and civilized little creature come at a time when his brain is sufficiently developed to cope with them.

Somewhere around the age of three or four, the area of intense sexual pleasure shifts to the genitals. Freud makes it clear that the three zones of erotic pleasure (mouth, anus, genitals) do not lose their pleasurable potential as the child matures – only that the locus of *most intense pleasure* shifts with age. During this period, the child is curious about his genitals and those of others as well. 'What is this for?' 'Why don't you have one too?' and of course, 'Where do babies come from?' These are common questions of this age and, once again, are found in all cultures and signify an awakening interest in sex.

Children at this **phallic stage** (four to six years) have intense emotions, usually directed towards the parent of the opposite sex. Now, the child is capable of tender, excited love for another person. When a baby, he loved the breast; when a little older, he loved his faeces and his own activities associated with them. In the phallic stage, he is mentally mature enough to appreciate the unique characteristics of the parents. In fact, the child longs for exclusive intimacy with one parent.

Whereas boys and girls have identical feelings and goals during the first two psychosexual stages, they diverge sharply at the third. Mental maturity, coupled with a shift of sensitivity towards the genitals, make the anatomical difference between the sexes more important. According to Freud, the penis becomes highly valued and little boys find theirs small compared to their fathers'. Girls discover that they lack one altogether. No wonder that Freud believed that boys and girls felt inadequate or cheated.

Masculine development will be examined first because Freud was more explicit about it; you will notice he gave the name of the male sex organ to this developmental period.

The young boy begins to desire his mother, often his most constant companion and the one who has satisfied earlier needs for oral pleasure. He is now mature enough to see that the mother–father relationship is characterized by the same tenderness that he enjoys in the mother–son pair. He becomes intensely jealous of the fact that his father shares his mother's bed because he has reached the age where he feels genital excitement. The mother sees the boy's new-found interest in his own genitals, along with an interest in hers as well. Some mothers gently turn their sons from these preoccupations, but others scold and blame them as 'naughty boys'.

Whichever course of action is followed by the mother, the child senses a rebuff from the object of his love (mother) as well as a threat from his rival (father). According to Freud, the boy studies his rival only to discover, to his dismay, that father has a bigger penis as well as being taller and stronger. Moreover, this bigger and more successful lover appears annoyed at signs of the awakening sexual interest in his son. Father tells his son to stop being a mummy's boy, to stop clinging to mum's apron strings. Freud believes that the boy fears that his father will punish him – or even castrate him – for his 'naughty desires'.

The boy is now in a fearful situation. His mother refuses his clumsy attempts at childish love-play, and his father appears angry with his clinging to mum. Freud believes that boys resolve this painful and frightening dilemma by **identifying** with the father. The boy notes that they are both male, that someday he too will be a father, and that his father actively encourages him in 'manly' pursuits. Identification with the father (the imagined aggressor) is the means by which young boys outgrow dependence on their mothers and come to seek masculine activities and interests outside the family. Part and parcel of the identification is the acquiring of an ego ideal, that moral standard that the father has set.

The case for girls must be different. Like their brothers, they long for the parent of the opposite sex. However, fathers are usually more tolerant of flirtation from daughters and both parents may encourage their daughters to be 'cuddly' or 'attractive'. Still, the girl notices that she does not have breasts like her mother and begins to feel an inadequate rival to her mother, just as the boy felt about his father. She also notices that she does not have a penis like father or brother, and Freud thinks that little girls leap to the conclusion that their penises have been cut off as punishment for naughty desires.

The girl is in a painful predicament; she loves the father with sensual, tender feelings yet feels rejected because of his obvious preference for her mother. Moreover, she feels that she has been castrated as punishment, imagining that the same dreadful event occurred to her mother as well when she was young. The little girl also identifies with her rival – the mother – in hopes that she will someday have a husband who will give her babies. Along with this identification comes an ego ideal, that moral standard which the boy acquires from his father.

It's clear that the description of masculine development in the phallic stage is more convincing than Freud's feminine theory. Although the boy might perhaps identify with men out of fear of castration, there is much less reason for the girl to identify with her rival because she sees herself as *already* punished.

Freud named the child's part in this family drama the **Oedipus complex**, after the hero in a Greek play who killed his father and married his mother, supposedly every boy's fantasy wish. As a consequence of identification with the same-sex parent, he thought, the superego begins to take shape. The child assumes the mannerisms as well as the moral values of the parent. In this very interesting theory of Oedipal love, Freud invented a mechanism by which the parents' morality becomes planted in the young. Of course, the ego must have sufficient maturity to recognize the adult's views. Despite the fact that moral thinking and planning are carried out by the ego, the strong desire to be like the parent and the emotional need to be a 'good' child arise in the superego.

Once the child has internalized parental standards, he or she is sufficiently socialized to move outside the family and join other children at school. Once having successfully negotiated the first three psychosexual stages, the child will have achieved the following:

(1) a secure trust that needs for nourishment and care will be met
(2) ability to imagine/fantasize the object of libido's desire by the operation of the pleasure principle of the id
(3) reality principle (rational) skills of the ego such as planning, problem-solving and delaying the impulsive actions dictated by the id

Figure 5.4 *When boys identify with their fathers, they tend to copy their actions . . .*

Figure 5.5 . . . *as do girls their mothers'. By this means, traditional sex roles tend to get perpetuated*

(4) regulation of bladder and bowels in a way that does not stifle feelings of autonomy
(5) a sexual identity based on the ideal of the same-sex parent
(6) a superego acquired through identification. This moral watchdog will change according to the teaching of parents and others, but its origin is firmly established before school age.

Having achieved all these skills and personality structures, the child enters a period of dormant sexuality known as the **latency stage**, which lasts from six until puberty. True adult genitality begins at adolescence. This last, mature, period is called the **genital stage**.

A case study

Many people respond with disbelief when first confronted by Freudian theory. Intuitively, it seems likely that all persons are occasionally moved by unconscious forces, but is there really something inside us that fits Freud's description of the id? Many people think not. Moreover, it's easy to see some sexuality in young children, but do they really fear that their fathers will castrate them? One way to test Freudian theory is to apply it to a real child, and Freud provides material for just this in the case of Little Hans.[3]

Hans was born in Vienna in 1903. Although Freud was not a close family friend, he knew quite a bit about the development of young Hans because the father was a doctor who greatly admired Freud's work and sent him written reports on Hans's development. Like other adherents of the revolutionary new theory, Hans's father (and presumably his mother) reared Hans in a comparatively permissive way in hopes that he would not develop the neuroses Freud found in adult patients whose parents had rejected or frightened them when they were young.

But when Hans was five he developed a phobia, an irrational fear. Hans was desperately afraid that horses would bite him. Hans's father wrote in distress to Freud, describing the boy's symptoms and asking for guidance. Here is a summary of the case.

Because he was afraid that horses would bite him, Hans would not go out in the streets of Vienna – filled as they were at that time with horses drawing carts, trams and carriages. Hans said that he was especially afraid of *white* horses with *black around the mouth* who were wearing *blinkers*. After many letters were exchanged between father and Freud, Freud concluded that the boy was afraid that the father would castrate him for desiring his mother. Freud interpreted that the horses in the phobia symbolized the father, and the little boy feared that the horse (father) would bite (castrate) him as punishment for his incestuous desires for the mother.

Roger Brown[4] examines the case in considerable detail and gives the following evidence in support of Freud's interpretation of the phobia.

(a) In one instance, Hans said to his father as he got up from the table 'Daddy, don't *trot* away from me.'

(b) The father's skin resembled *white* horses rather than dark ones. In fact, Hans once said 'Daddy, you are lovely. *You're so white*'.

(c) Hans feared horses with black around the mouth and Hans' father had a *moustache*.

(d) Hans feared horses with blinkers on, and Freud noted that the father wore *spectacles* resembling them.

(e) The boy and his father had played 'horses' together and in the game the father often played the role of horse and son that of rider.

Summing the evidence presented gives some support to Freud's claim that Hans associated his father with the kind of horses he feared most. But how much evidence is there that Hans feared castration at the hands of his father? Only if one assumes that biting symbolizes castration, a far-fetched notion, can one conclude that there is some evidence that Hans feared castration, although it appears that he may have associated his father with the feared horses.

What has the Freudian interpretation added to the facts of the case? The Freudian techniques allow us to get beneath the surface of conscious material (the fear of horses) to the unconscious emotion underneath (the fear of the father). It seems likely that a five-year-old boy may have feared his father, especially in nineteenth century Vienna where even liberal fathers were stern disciplinarians by today's standards. It is hoped that this brief presentation of case material shows clearly Freud's dramatic leap from *observed actions and talk* to the *deeper interpretation*. He used this case to support his theory about castration anxiety and the development of the superego. There is no doubt that something had gone wrong in the life of Hans because most children are not terrified of horses. However, castration anxiety is but one of the factors that could lead to this fear, the others being more everyday explanations such as witnessing *someone else* being bitten followed by a horse, followed later by a fear that it could happen to him.

Was Freud right?

The first question to be asked is *did Hans recover from the phobia?* The answer is that he did, after his father had a heart-to-heart talk with him to assure the little boy that he was not planning to cut off his penis. Freud claims that Hans' cure is proof for his interpretation of the problem as Oedipal fear of castration. Still, one wonders whether the little boy might have recovered even without his father's assurance that he would not cut off his penis. Many children outgrow childish fears without strange chats with their parents.

Freud's theory of personality and its related therapeutic treatments have been used by countless clinicians all over the world for dealing with patients suffering psychological abnormality. Many cases of successful treatment have been reported in medical journals. On the face of it, the therapy appears to work. Or so the therapists tell us. But what can this tell us about the development of normal children? A main criticism of Freud's work is that his theory of emotional development is derived largely from the study of adults with emotional disorders. (In fact, Hans was the only child studied by Freud.) Even if Hans *did* suffer fear of castration, and there's a great deal of doubt about it, it might tell us little about normal boys and girls.

There is still another problem in the Freudian work. The evidence Freud used to support his theory of the unconscious, the three-part personality, and the psychosexual stages of development all came from dreams and associations of patients. How can these be used to establish certain important *facts* about the childhood experiences of individuals? Or their early feeding and toilet-training? The process of psychoanalysis (analysing the psychological organization of the personality through therapeutic talking sessions) works backwards. In other words, Freud and his followers never predict individual behaviour; they analyse it afterwards. And, as everyone knows, it's easier to 'explain' a team's performance after the final football score has been announced.

Perhaps the greatest difficulty in assessing Freud's theory is that it uses evidence from thoughts, memories and feelings to prove *internal* structures like the id, ego, superego, and libido. This is enormously difficult because the external evidence for internal structures comes from a variety of symptoms, ideas and dreams. Thus, Freud tells us that biting symbolized castration for poor little Hans but that another action might serve the identical function in another child. It's difficult to know what external fact (a sentence, dream, or fear) signifies what hypothesized internal state.

Some formal research studies (not individual case studies presented by psychotherapists) have tried to test parts of the Freudian theory of development. One was conducted by Leon Yarrow.[5] He hypothesized that children who received inadequate satisfaction in feeding during the oral stage would become 'fixated' (Freud's word for stuck) at this developmental stage. He further hypothesized that they would suck their thumbs when older, seeking the oral gratification they had not received at the appropriate stage.

Yarrow studied 66 children, asking their mothers about early feeding and also later thumb-sucking. The Freudian theory received some support because the children who spent relatively little time at each feed when they were babies were more likely to be thumbsuckers when older. But does this constitute proof that there is an 'oral stage' of development? Or that libido is centred around the mouth? Perhaps babies who were constitutionally nervous sucked less and later turned to thumbs. In other words, it may have been their highly strung temperaments that led them to thumb-sucking, not a frustrated libido drive. The case can never be decided, because Freud's personality structure and psycho-sexual stages cannot be studied directly. Although Yarrow's study fails to prove that Freud is right, it is difficult to devise a study that would prove the opposite.

Why is a theory of such dubious scientific value presented at great length in this book? The answer is complicated. For one, Freud's theory explains how and why individuals are different. Most of the other theories in this book are devoted to groups of children at various ages and stages. Freud is unique in keeping the *individual* paramount (due, perhaps, to his CASE STUDY method). Freud's theory has eluded scientific investigation for decades because it is so difficult to prove or disprove. Although we concluded that Freud's theory about Hans is not demonstrated in the facts, it is impossible to claim the reverse – that it is proved wrong by the facts.

Thoughtful students of child development have pondered long and hard about Freud's insights into human nature. There is no doubt that some memories, wishes and thoughts are not accessible to conscious awareness. Further, Freud pointed out that children love their parents with a passionate force that appears sexual at times. No one argues against these parts of Freudian theory because they are compatible with personal intuition and observation. There is no scientific support however, for the three-part personality or the psychosexual stages of development. Indeed there could never be scientific support for these, because they are completely invisible and unique to each individual. Thus, though we all think of ourselves differently as a result of what Freud wrote, his work has an uneasy perch in the field of psychological *science*.

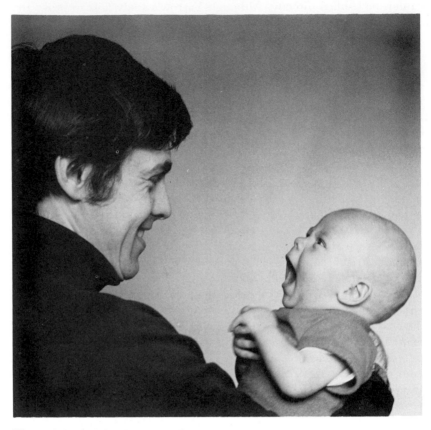

Figure 6.1 *Are babies 'programmed' to pay attention to human faces?*

Chapter 6

Perceptual development

All development is a process of continuous change, sometimes fast-paced and obvious, other times slow and difficult to see. Developmental change is not haphazard but proceeds in an orderly fashion, and throughout life. In fact childhood is just one stage in a life cycle of development that culminates in old age and death.

Think of a child at the start of his second year; he is beginning to walk and explore the environment on his own. He makes known his desires by single words and gestures, recognizes his parents, and cries with anger and passion when they go away. This child can act in an effective way on objects in the household and remember what happened yesterday.

How has this one-year-old changed since birth? He is now firmly attached to his parents, although not in so rigid an emotional way as Bowlby would have us think. Then too his body has matured in size, strength and skill. He's still a novice at language, but his intellect has grown by leaps and bounds in just one year. Although these domains of development – physical size and skill, emotions, language and intellect – are intertwined, for the purposes of this book they will at first be considered as separate entities. The preceding chapters investigated the development of the baby's relations with his parents and the beginnings of his personality. This chapter and those that follow look instead at the perceptual and intellectual side of the child. Although baby, child and even adult are developing all the time with changes that are synchronized, it's easier to look at each 'slice' of development in order to see its intricacies and the scientific methods that have been devised for studying them. We turn now to perception.

The newly born baby opens his eyes and stares at a world that is fresh and strange. If he is born in hospital, there are plastic and metal objects nearby; there is a bed with white and dark green cloth, and drab walls in the distance. Against this stationary backdrop are moving figures, nurses and midwives wrapping him warmly, and his mother's face anxiously peering at him. What does the baby see? Does he notice that his mother's eyes are brown, or that the cot has sharply angled corners? Thanks to ingenious experiments performed by psychologists interested in the development of perception, questions like these can now be answered.

Before going further into what babies can see, it might be helpful to consider what the adult's visual sense can do. Figure 6.2 shows how an opening door looks to us. Despite the varying images impinging on the eyes, we perceive it as rectangular. In other words, our psychological experience is of a rectangle, and not the trapezoid or vertical line that the drawings show. We do not always 'see' what is there.

A second example will show even more subtlety. As I sit at my desk I have a cup in front of me. And as I look at it, it is in a sense just a pattern of light reflected into my eyes. Yet I see far more than that. I can see that the cup rests on a saucer, that it is three dimensional, that it is a particular distance from me, that it is a particular size, and so on. If I get up and look at it from across the room, it appears to be the same size, though of course the pattern of colour and contour reflected into my eye will now be smaller. As I move about the room, the pattern changes and moves too, yet I see the cup as completely still. And I see it as the same shape and colour, though I look from different angles or place it in a darkened corner.

All sensory perception is a miraculously complex process. But there's more to it than that. Our visual senses are coordinated to our other senses, and those to each other. If I touch the cup, my sense of touch tells me it is rounded, as my eyes have already done by different means. If the cup falls to the floor while my face is turned, my ears will tell me where the crash happened, and I can turn to look in that direction. These abilities, which we take for granted in everyday life, show the marvellous powers of perceptual organization. Some perceptual process must organize the diverse arrays of stimulation that reach our eyes, ears, etc. into meaningful objects and events, ones that appear stable despite momentary fluctuations in that sensory information.

Philosophers have been debating for centuries whether babies come into the world with their senses already organized as adults' are. *Nativists* believe that they do. On the other hand, the *Empiricists* believe they face a chaotic jumble of colours, shapes, sounds, and smells and have to learn to make sense of them. Returning to the cup, the empiricists would claim that the newborn baby does not know that it is three dimensional or located at a certain distance from him. The nativists claim the opposite.

Developmental psychologists have settled this issue now, but it has taken some very cunning and subtle experiments to do it. Babies are not easy subjects for experimenting: they cry or sleep a great deal, they can't talk, and naturally they aren't very interested in what psychologists are interested in. It turns out that the nativists are largely right; babies are born with far greater perceptual ability than was ever thought. On the other hand, some learning is also involved and it will be described later. So the empiricists are not completely wrong. Perhaps the mistake was to talk in terms of either/or. That mistake though, produced some fascinating research.

74

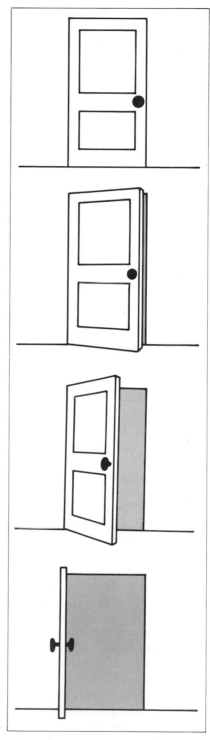

Figure 6.2 *The images of a door that impinge on the eye can vary a good deal, yet we always perceive it as rectangular*

Perception and the senses

All the baby's knowledge about the world must come through his senses. There are six of these, and they include sight, hearing, taste, smell and touch. Through these the baby comes to know the colour of his mother's hair, the smell and taste of milk, the sound of the bells suspended over his cot, and the feel of his coverlet against his cheek. The sixth sense, called proprioception, tells him the location of the mobile parts of his body, say his legs, in relation to the rest of him.

Perception is the process by which each of us gains *direct* awareness through the senses of the world around us. The key word here is 'direct'. If someone tells me that it is raining outside, I have gained knowledge through the sense of hearing but it is not direct knowledge; instead, the information has been carried in language. If I were to stroll outside and feel the raindrops on my head or watch them make patterns in a pool, I would perceive the rain directly.

Most of the information that comes through our senses is concerned with difference and changes in the environment. Everything that we hear, whether a radio or the wind in the trees, has sent out sound waves. The waves consist of regions of compression and expansion which travel outwards from their source through the air, and cause the pressure on our ears to go up and down and our ear drums to vibrate. Specialized receptors pick up different frequencies. Receptors for smell line the nose; those for taste (sweet, sour, salty, and bitter) line the tongue. There are touch receptors in the skin, and vision receptors in the eye. Lastly, there are receptors in the joints that tell us the angles of the bones coming together there.

Of course, none of the receptors convey to the brain an exact replica of what is being 'perceived'. A tuning fork does not magically appear inside the brain, nor does a realistic picture of the mother's face. Instead, the receptors pass coded messages along a network of nerves to the brain, which itself consists entirely of other nerves, called neurons (see Figure 6.3), interconnected almost more intricately than we can conceive. Neurons produce bursts of minute electrical pulses when they fire. The presence (or absence) of pulses, the patterns in which they fire and the way they make other nerves fire, creates the code by which messages are transmitted to the brain.

To what kinds of sights, sounds, and so forth is the newborn sensitive? Do all the baby's receptors function at birth, and do sensory messages get transmitted to the brain just as with adults? J. B. Watson conducted an early experiment with one newborn baby shortly after birth. He placed a mild irritant on the baby's nose and watched what happened next. The baby's hand came quickly to his nose as though to remove the unpleasant substance. Watson concluded that a baby's touch receptors do work, and moreover, that his proprioceptive sense is good enough to guide his hand to his nose rather than somewhere else. You will notice also, that babies

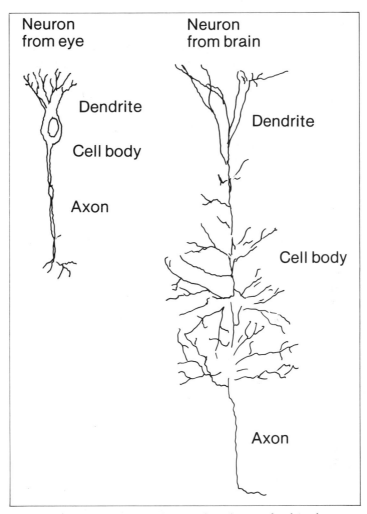

Figure 6.3 *Neurons vary according to where they are found in the nervous system. In this figure are neurons from the eye (left) and the brain. Both carry messages in the same way*

are born with a simple coordination of the senses, so this baby could use touch and proprioception together.

Similarly, Michael Wertheimer also tested the perceptual abilities of a newborn baby, only minutes old, by studying his reactions to sounds coming from various places in the room. He and others have shown that babies as young as one day look in the direction – although clumsily – of each sound. Obviously, a newborn *is* aware of sounds and has some means of locating them in space.

Although all six human senses are complex and fascinating to study, we will confine ourselves from now on to babies' and children's vision; a discussion of *all* the senses would take up most of the book!

Light and the eye

Light consists of electromagnetic waves in the range of frequencies to which our eyes are sensitive. X-rays, Gamma rays and ultra-violet radiation are waves of the same kind but higher frequency; infra-red radiation (which we perceive as heat) and radio waves have lower frequency. Most of the electromagnetic spectrum is invisible. The eye selects a narrow band of frequencies from the whole spectrum just as the ear selects sounds from a limited range of frequencies. The physiology of the senses makes all perception – not just vision – selective. This important characteristic of perception will be discussed later because it occurs at all stages of perception.

The eye is often compared to a camera. Both consist of a chamber with an opening for gathering light and a lens for projecting an image onto a light-sensitive surface on the back of the chamber. In both cases this chamber is coated with a black material for absorbing stray light that might otherwise be reflected back and forth. In both eye and camera the projected image is far smaller than the 'real' one. For example, if you look now at a nearby person who is close to six feet tall, the image on your retina is less than half an inch long. It is also upside down.

But here the differences start: light in the eye is focused on the retina, a sheet of living cells, rather than on film. The two 'instruments' are different in another way: a camera is focused by moving the lens closer to or further from the film. In the eye, however, the distance between the lens and retina is fixed and the focusing achieved by changing the shape of the lens and hence its focal length. (See Figure 6.4.)

In a camera, of course, once the film is exposed to light, the 'seeing' is over. But with human beings the retina is just the first link in the perceptual chain and is connected to the brain by a complex pathway of nerves. The living retina is a far cry from film. It consists of photosensitive cells, called rods and cones. It is here that the process of coding and selecting begins.

The rods and cones lead to the bipolar cells, which lead to the ganglion cells. Many rods or cones connect to each bipolar, and usually many bipolars to each ganglion cell (see Figure 6.5). In the end, some 150 million rods and 7 million cones feed about 1 million ganglion cells. That is necessary to save the brain from overload. 157 million rods and cones could bombard the brain with 100,000,000 bits of information every second – far more than it could digest. From this brief description it will be clear that perception has to organize information as well as select it. Yet this selection cannot be haphazard, since then it would certainly miss information essential to survival.

The bipolars, which are in the retina, lead to the ganglion cells whose axons (see Figure 6.3) make up the optic nerve. The optic nerve leads to that area of the brain which deals with vision, the striate area of the occipital lobe.

This gives a brief glance at the human visual system. It's amazing that

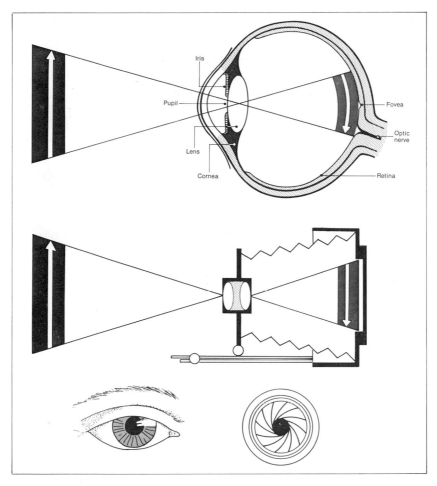

Figure 6.4 *The similarities of eye and camera are clear from their cross-sections. Both use a lens to focus an inverted image onto a light-sensitive surface. And both have an iris, to adapt to the varying intensity of light*

babies, after nine months in the womb and no visual experience, are born with this system practically in full working order. Figures 6.6 and 6.7 shows the brain's gross anatomy, and a schematic diagram of how perception works.

A good deal of selection and organization of information occurs in the sense organs themselves (i.e. looking at it diagramatially, in the box to the left of Figure 6.7) because of their complex physiology. More happens also in the box to the right, as will be discussed on p. 90.

The newborn visual system

There are some differences between the newborn and the adult, however. The baby's lens cannot yet change its shape, so quite a lot of what he sees

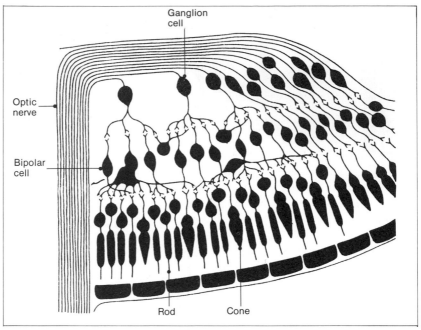

Figure 6.5 *This cross-section of the retina shows its three main layers: the rods and cones, the bipolar cells, and the ganglion cells. The ganglion cells receive messages from one or more bipolars, which receive messages from one or more rods or cones*

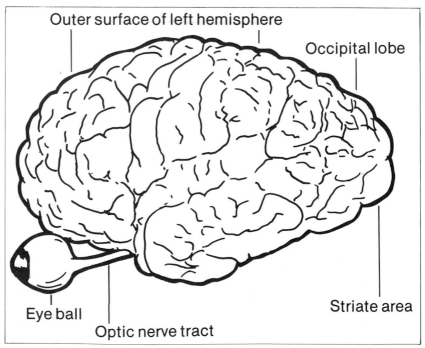

Figure 6.6 *The anatomy of the brain, slowing the striate area, part of the occipital lobe*

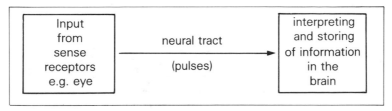

Figure 6.7 *Figure 6.6 in diagram form*

is blurred. In fact, he focuses best at about ten inches – a distance whose importance will become clear in a page or two.

In addition to changes in the eye itself, the baby's nerve cells grow and increase in number. The nerve fibres themselves thicken, allowing information to be carried with more speed. By the end of the first half year of life, the baby's visual system functions much like that of any adult. But does he 'see' as we do?

Form perception

Doctors were puzzled for years about what babies could see. They knew for certain that one-week-old infants could turn their gaze when a shiny object, say a watch, was swung before their eyes. But did they notice the thin chain attached to the larger round watch? Of course they wouldn't recognize the numerals, but did the black figures look different from the white watchface? Or was the entire event a light-show of indistinct colours and shapes in haphazard array? How could psychologists investigate vision in a creature who cannot talk, never follows instructions, and spends much of his time either crying or asleep?

Robert Fantz[1] was a pioneer in this field, with a simple invention he called the 'visual preference apparatus'. He reasoned that if a baby was shown two patterns together, and consistently preferred one to the other, he *must* be able to discriminate between them. He designed a cot for the baby, called a 'looking chamber', above which could be displayed two different card patterns (see Figures 6.8 and 6.9). He measured how long each baby looked at each of the patterns.

For his first experiment, Fantz tested 30 babies aged between one and 15 weeks, at weekly intervals. He showed them four pairs of patterns, and found that where one pattern was markedly more complex than the other the babies showed a clear preference for it no matter whether it appeared on the left or the right. Babies showed this preference as young as one week old, so it was likely that they didn't learn it. This experiment, summarized in Figure 6.10, shows that young babies can tell the difference between various patterns and that their skill at visual discrimination is present as early as one week. 'Some degree of form perception', Fantz concluded, 'is innate'.

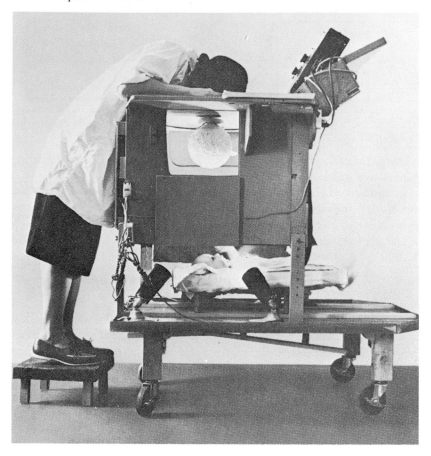

Figure 6.8 *Robert Fantz's 'looking chamber'*

What about babies' acuity, – their ability to see fine detail? Fantz devised further experiments (see Figure 6.11) to study this question. To see how much acuity babies are born with, and how it develops, he presented them with patterned cards alongside grey ones, knowing that since they preferred patterns they would tend to go for stripes if they could distinguish them. He found that six-month-old babies could distinguish 1/64 inch stripes at 10 inches. Even at less than a month, they could see 1/8 inch stripes at that distance. This is by no means adult 20/20 vision, but it shows considerable acuity nonetheless.

Next, Fantz turned his attention to what might be called social meaning in visual perception. If babies see best at about 10 inches, prefer patterns, and grow increasingly good at seeing detail, could it be that they are 'programmed', as it were, to prefer the human face peering at them during feeding?

We tested infants with three flat objects the size and shape of a head.

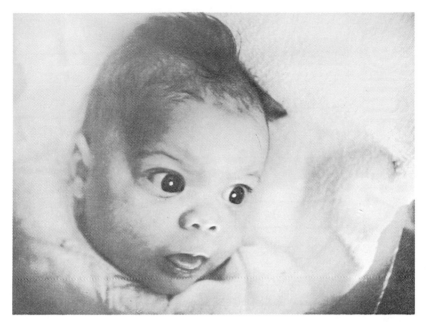

Figure 6.9 *A baby photographed inside the 'looking chamber'*

On one we painted a stylized face in black on a pink background, on the second we rearranged the features in a scrambled pattern, and on the third we painted a solid patch of black at one end with an area equal to that covered by all the features.

Fantz showed these three objects to 49 babies, from four days to six months. He found they all looked mostly at the 'real' face, and somewhat less at the scrambled one, and largely ignored the last. This suggests fairly strongly that babies *are* born with a preference for face-like patterns. As far as form and pattern are concerned, babies certainly do not have to learn to see.

Perception of depth and distance

Exciting experiments often have commonplace histories. A good example is the apparatus known as the 'visual cliff'. Eleanor Gibson,[2] so the story goes, was picnicking one day close to the rim of the Grand Canyon. She wondered whether a baby would fall off the edge, or like her, be frightened of the abrupt drop and so remain safely far from it. Gibson returned to the psychology laboratory to design a miniature Grand Canyon, shown in Figure 6.12, for testing whether or not babies are afraid of what appears to be a sharp drop.

A baby is placed on a central bridge with a normal, solid floor to one

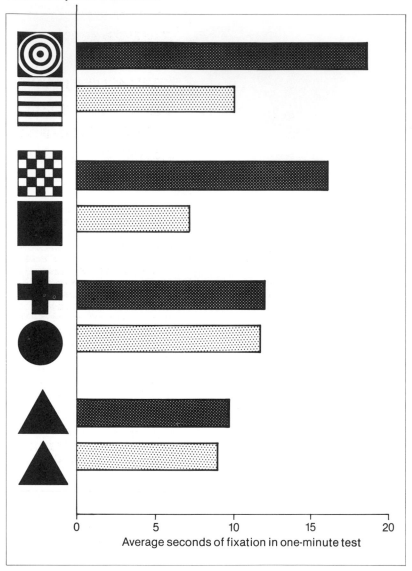

Figure 6.10 *Babies prefer more complicated patterns. Fantz showed four pairs of pattern to babies as young as one week old; even they showed a distinct preference. The bars on the right of the figure show the amount of time devoted to each pattern*

side and a deep drop to the other. The genius of the apparatus is that the drop is covered by clear glass. The floor below is covered with checkered linoleum, which makes it look all the more (at least, to an adult) as if the floor is a good distance below the baby on the bridge. Gibson, and her colleague Richard Walk, found that babies of nine months refused to crawl on the 'deep' side of the bridge, despite their mothers calling to them from the other side and shaking their rattles. Gibson's guess about

Figure 6.11 *To discover how acute babies'*
vision is, Fantz showed some these striped
patterns – each one paired with a plain grey
square. He knew that if a baby could detect a
pattern, he would look at it in preference. It
turns out that babies under a month can see the
⅛-inch stripes at the top, and that by six months
they can see the 1/32-inch stripes at the bottom

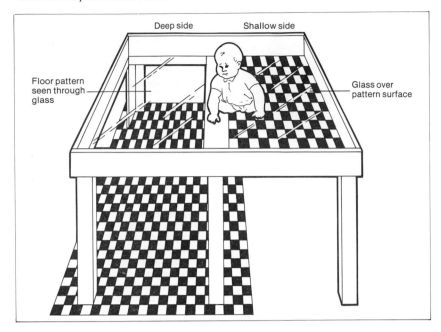

Figure 6.12 *Eleanor Gibson's 'visual cliff'*

the Grand Canyon turned out to be correct, at least for babies with nine months' experience of life. They perceived the depth and avoided it.

Other animals were placed on the visual cliff, including newly hatched chicks, and they too avoided the deep side. This proved, at least for chicks, that depth perception must be innate because they had no opportunity for learning. However, for all its neatness, the Gibson and Walk experiment could not prove that depth perception is **innate** for humans, because of course they cannot crawl until they are several months old and have had plenty of opportunity for learning. It was left to Tom Bower to devise another test of depth perception, one suitable to very young babies.

Doctors had known for years that normal babies would make defensive responses (widening their eyes, retracting their heads, and putting their hands before their faces) when objects were moved rapidly towards them. This simple test will discriminate blind from sighted babies. The difference between blind and sighted babies must be due to visual abilities alone, because both could feel the rush of air as the object approached. In order to know that an object is moving dangerously close, babies must estimate the rapidly diminishing distance between themselves and something 'out there' as it gets closer to them.

Bower decided to explore this clinical observation and devised three laboratory settings, requiring some ingenious experimental control, to do so.[3] Results of the three experiments described below enabled Bower to conclude that 'the baby must be capable of detecting the changing positions of visible objects moving in space' and that this *ability* rests on

Experiment	Conditions	Results (normal babies)
1	object movement and air movement	defence reaction
2	object movement alone	defence reaction (slightly less than Exp. (2)
3	air movement alone	no defence reaction

Table 6.1

visual information and not tactile. Further, he organizes fluctuating light patterns into a whole object.

What clue might babies use to determine that the object they see before them is on a collision course? Bower designed another experiment and found that babies as young as 10 days respond by 'defending' themselves when an image on the retina gets bigger and bigger, which is of course what happens when something approaches the viewer.

Earlier in this chapter we stressed that *selection* and *organization* are the keys to understanding perception. Selection begins at so basic a physiological level that the senses do not provide an 'open window' to the outside world. Instead, they select certain kinds of information and transmit it in coded form to the brain. Organization also begins in the physiology of the visual system with the funnelling of information from rods/cones to bipolars to ganglion cells. Further, some information, such as that from the fovea (the part of the eye on which light falls if we look directly at an object), gets priority over information from the periphery.

Most of the studies reported have taken pains to show that the visual system of a newborn (or at least the very young) baby is capable of both selection and organization. Is there no development, then? There is. With many visual tasks it appears that the older the child, the better his performance. Why?

Development of perceptual judgements

Eliane Vurpillot[4] has studied children between the ages of three-and-a-half and seven-and-a-half to investigate the development of their perceptual abilities. She is not interested in the acuity of visual functioning, nor indeed in the ability to discriminate clues such as depth or pattern. Instead she is interested in· the way that children *use the perceptual skills they have.*

Vurpillot showed children a drawing of a landscape that included a *house*, a *shrub*, a small *pond* and the *sun* in the sky. There were some other things in the landscape, like a path and a large tree. Along with this drawing, children were shown a second drawing similar to it and asked to spot the differences between the two. The original drawing, called the standard, is shown in Figure 6.13; so also are four of the comparison drawings. There were many changes in the comparisons; sometimes something would be missing from it altogether, such as the house. Other times, something would have changed in form, as when the originally

87

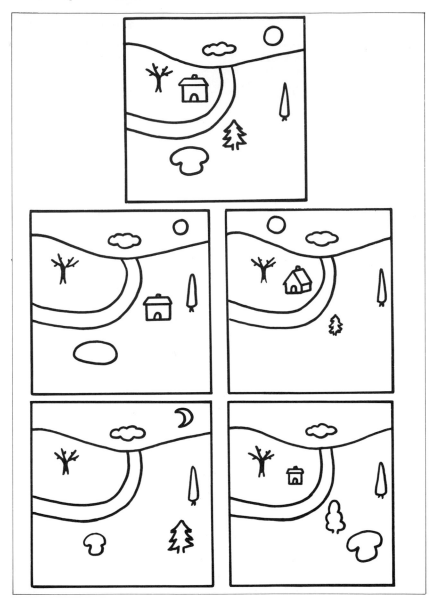

Figure 6.13 *The Vurpillot standard drawing (top) plus four comparisons*

round sun is replaced by a crescent-shaped one. Sometimes an object would be reduced in size, as when the shrub that appeared in the standard is reduced to half its size. The fourth difference concerned change of position, as for example when the sun which originally appeared at the right was switched to the left.

Vurpillot found that children as young as three-and-a-half are quick to perceive differences in *form* (when a round sun is changed into a crescent

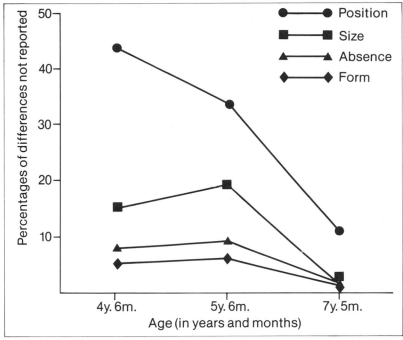

Figure 6.14 *The number of children at different ages who do not notice the differences between the Vurpillot drawings*

one) and also when parts of the drawing are *absent*. By seven-and-a-half they are skilful at reporting changes in *size*, but still not proficient at detecting changes of *location*. Figure 6.14 shows the proportion of children at each age who cannot yet detect these different kinds of disparity between the standard and the comparison.

Why did the younger children so blithely assume the drawing to be similar when an important element was moved to another location? Or reduced in size? Vurpillot argues that all children could discriminate these differences; their vision was certainly good enough. When discussing the greater skill of the older children she writes: 'as a general rule it seems that change in performance expresses . . . the adoption of a new decision criterion . . .'. In deciding whether or not the drawings were similar the younger children did not bother to compare size or location. For them, a yes/no decision hinged on form being the same in each drawing and also the sheer presence or absence of something. Vurpillot says that response to this task is determined by an understanding of what makes visual events similar. As long as the parts are present and in identical form, the young child is satisfied they are similar. The older child requires something more – that the components of the drawing be of the same size and in the same location. His understanding of perceptual similarity includes size and location as well as presence and form. This kind of perceptual selection belongs to the right-hand box in Figure 6.7.

In sum, the younger child is not limited by lack of visual discrimination but by his capacity for gathering, recording and thinking about perceptual information. He relies on a few simple criteria for making perceptual judgements. What matures with age are decision rules for making visual comparison and strategies for selecting from a wealth of information. These are part of the mind's structure for deciding which visual information in the environment is necessary or important. To understand more about intellectual development, we must leave perception and turn to the study of children's minds.

Chapter 7

Piaget's research into the minds of children

Ask a four-year-old to tell you the capital of France and he'll laugh and run away. Or ask a five-year old the change he should get after paying 50 pence for sweets worth only 22. He'll look at you in surprise, as would a six-year-old asked to spell *obfuscate*. It's no wonder that young children are ignorant of geography, subtraction and spelling because these intellectual feats are mastered through lessons in school.

Now consider another case. A four-year-old falls off his bicycle and announces 'I fell off because it was Marie's birthday'. While it seems obvious to us that the birthday did not *cause* the accident, the child appears to think it did. Three years later, however, the same boy will say 'I fell off my bicycle because the front wheel skidded in a puddle and I went over the top'. Clearly children acquire sophisticated notions about cause and effect which they don't learn in class.

Teachers concentrate on numbers, letters and historical facts, paying little attention to the learning that occurs 'naturally'. But in fact the most comprehensive theory about the development of thinking focuses on 'spontaneous' rather than 'book' learning. It's the work of a Swiss psychologist, Jean Piaget. Like Freud, he did not begin his research by studying children; that was to come later.

Piaget was born in Neuchatel in 1896. He had a schoolboy passion for biology and his first nature report, published when he was 11, concerned an albino sparrow seen in the park. Between the ages of 15 and 18 he studied shellfish known as molluscs, writing several scientific papers on them while assisting the curator at a nearby museum to classify zoological specimens. As a young biologist, Piaget was concerned with the kinds of structures easily seen in the living mollusc, such as its protective shell. He was curious about various anatomical structures that helped animals cope with the environment in which they lived. Piaget was especially fascinated by evolution: how did *this* particular species come to have *this* particular structure enabling it to adapt to *this* particular environment?

After completing his zoological studies at Neuchatel, Piaget turned to other kinds of 'structures', *mental* ones, which are just as crucial for adaptation as those he studied earlier. In order to survive animals need

Figure 7.1 *Jean Piaget*

knowledge *about* things and events (which berries are poisonous; when the sun sets) as well as knowledge about *how to do* things (how to build a nest). Mental structures consist of these two types of knowledge and Piaget was fascinated by them. Although anatomical structures are inherited through the genes, he wondered if mental ones were as well. Of course human beings have mental structures that are complex, such as the notion of 'honesty' or the ability to perform arithmetic subtraction. Are these inherited? Where do they come from?

Mental structures are more difficult to describe than anatomical ones because they do not correspond to known parts of the body. In order to investigate them, Piaget had to depart from the methods of biology.

Piaget's first attempt at the study of mental structures took place in the

Paris laboratory of Binet and Simon, the birthplace of IQ testing. The assignment given the young Swiss was to standardize the French version of an English test, a tedious job but an important one since such tests must naturally present children of different nationalities with identical tasks.

While trying out his questions on children, Piaget showed immediately his unorthodox approach to intelligence. Instead of noting 'incorrect' on a wrong answer and continuing to the next question, he paused to reflect. He found himself wishing to enquire further when a child made a mistake, probing the child's mind to see why, for him, something other than the 'standard' answer was appropriate. Of course, this is exactly what examiners at the lab were not permitted, and Piaget decided that intelligence testing was not for him.

But he did, luckily, catalogue enough wrong answers to conclude that children did not think at all like adults. Children's minds, it seemed, were organized differently from those of older people. In fact, children appeared to solve problems on an entirely different level; the difference between older and younger children was less a case of the older children having *more* knowledge than of their knowledge being of a different sort. With this discovery, Piaget began the study of the development of mental structures.

He began to think that what distinguished children's thought from that of adults was not the sheer amount of knowledge but its complexity. On the basis of children's 'mistakes' on intelligence tests, he guessed that there were dramatic shifts, during infancy and childhood, from one type of thinking to another.

Piaget returned to Switzerland to begin research of his own design. Its goals have remained constant from that time: the discovery and description of the mental structures (he calls them **schemas**) of children as they grow from infancy to adulthood. Piaget considered his lifetime's work a natural outgrowth of his early biological studies. Intelligence enables complex animals, including man, to adapt to their environments. Fundamental to intelligence are schemas consisting of knowledge *about* things/events and knowledge of *how to do* things.

Piaget began by studying children before entry into school; he asked them all manner of questions. 'Can a plant feel the prick of a pin?', 'Why does it rain?', 'Who were the first people to play marbles?' His method of interview was a far cry from ones used in intelligence testing because he gently explored the child's view of the world, tailoring his questions to the particular child he was talking to. If a child gave an interesting answer Piaget pursued it. If the child did not understand the question, Piaget clarified it. The aim of this method, called the 'clinical INTERVIEW' by Piagetians, was to follow the child's thoughts without distorting them. Although Piaget called this method 'clinical', it is quite different from the method used by Freud, and has nothing to do with psychiatry. But both of them studied one person at a time, rejecting a rigidly programmed list of questions so that they could follow the individual's thoughts. However,

> INTERVIEW
> An interview is a means of gathering information about an individual by asking him questions.
> (a) *Predetermined* interviews have precisely set questions which are asked in a rigid sequence.
> (b) *Clinical* interviews do not have a predetermined list of questions. In them, the interviewer has an overall goal but varies the questions according to the circumstances. Piaget used the clinical interview to find out about children's notions concerning nature and morality.

Piaget's interest was not in the uniqueness of individual children but rather in the similarities between children of roughly equivalent age. Like Freud, he wanted to unravel the immature mind, but unlike Freud, he attempted this by studying children who are perfectly normal.

In these early studies, Piaget did not manipulate variables in the manner of FORMAL EXPERIMENTATION. Instead, his early research programme attempted to *describe* the kinds of thinking characteristic of children before adolescence. He used a CROSS-SECTIONAL technique meaning that he interviewed many different children at several different ages.

> CROSS-SECTIONAL STUDY
> In a cross-sectional study, the investigator samples several groups of subjects, each of a different age. The advantage of this method is that it allows all the data to be collected much more quickly. On the other hand, it does not allow the investigator to study change in any one individual.

Piaget questioned hundreds of children[1] between the ages of 3 and 12 to discover how they thought about things as disparate as natural phenomena (the sun, moon, living creatures) and morality. He found that at first a child's thinking is characterized by **animism**, meaning that he considers natural phenomena to be alive just as human beings are. The sun began because 'it knew that life (i.e. people) had begun'. Lakes and pebbles act in intentional ways and all living creatures have the same feelings as we do. A little later, the child believes that some agent, either human or divine, created natural events. 'What makes the sun shine?' '. . . a big light, it is someone in Heaven who has set fire to it.'

That children have peculiar conceptions of natural events was not a new discovery. What made Piaget's research interesting was his going beyond isolated 'misconceptions' to find the systematic ways of thinking characteristic of children at various ages. One of these is *egocentrism*, the child's inability to consider events from the point of view of another. Egocentrism explains, to some extent, early animism because the child cannot conceive that natural phenomena are different from him and therefore imbues them with feelings and intentions like his own. Another is his inability to deal with *several aspects* of a situation at one time. But above all, Piaget tells us that the child before the age of six or seven is incapable of thinking logically. (Recall the little boy who fell off his bike on Marie's birthday.)

The development of logical thinking mystified Piaget. Just listening to people could account for some changes in the child's view of the world. For example, parents teach children that it doesn't hurt the log to be burnt and teachers struggle to explain the formation of rain clouds or the origin of the sun. However, logical thinking seems to develop quite spontaneously and it was to this that Piaget turned next. What are the roots of logic?

A radical and very fruitful change in method occurred in the years in which Piaget's three children were born. He turned his attention to their development, thinking that the precursors to logic might occur earlier than the years three to twelve he had studied so intensively. The clinical interview was not a useful technique with babies, so instead he had to rely on NATURALISTIC OBSERVATION – watching, but intervening as little as possible. Piaget watched his own three children, two girls and a boy, as they turned towards a finger stroking the cheek, looked at toys dangled before them, and attempted to solve 'puzzles' such as procuring a watch chain placed inside a matchbox. Such activities are commonplace in households with young children but Piaget saw them as indications of the development of intelligence. (Remember that for Piaget intelligence is not a score on a standardized test; it is that kind of mental activity that enables adaptation to the environment.)

Piaget worked out a theory that logical thinking develops in steps, broken at roughly two, and roughly seven years of age. Children, he showed, are not like vessels waiting to be filled up with knowledge. They actively construct their understanding of the world by interacting with it. At different periods of their development, they are capable of different kinds of interaction, and arrive at different kinds of understanding. The period before two (or so) he called the *sensory-motor period*, that from two to seven the *pre-operational period*, and that from seven on the *operational period* (which he subdivided into two – the *period of concrete operations* (seven to eleven years), and the *period of formal operations* (eleven to adulthood). We will now take a closer look at these periods, to see what happens in which, and how each leads on to the next.

The sensory-motor period

Think about the baby's early experiences of the breast, certainly an important object in his life. First he nestles in the crook of the mother's arm, looking towards the nipple several inches from his eyes. He makes incipient suckling actions, then his mother moves him closer so that he may take the nipple. Of course, the breast appears quite different now, and also much larger. Does the baby know that this is the same object he examined several seconds ago? Piaget says not. But the baby responds to many different images (including a finger) with sucking action. Piaget would say he has a 'simple functional category'; that means he has a rough category of things to which he reacts in the same way – in this case by sucking. Of course, he doesn't recognize the breast in the sense of having a name for it, but he does in the sense of having a response to it, an **action pattern** for it.

Action patterns are the key to the **sensory-motor period**, since it is through the combination of sensation and movement that the baby builds a permanent picture of the world. There follow several excerpts from Piaget's diary account[2] of the development in Laurent of the action pattern, *striking objects*. Note that they begin when the boy was 0 years; 4 months (7) days old, and extended over one month.

> With regard to Laurent . . . striking arose in the following way. At 0;4(7) Laurent looks at a paper knife attached to the strings of a hanging doll. He tries to grasp the doll or the paper knife, but, at each attempt, the clumsiness of his movements results in causing him to knock these objects. He then looks at them with interest and recommences.
>
> The next day, at 0;4(8) same reaction. Laurent still does not strike intentionally but, trying to grasp the paper knife, and noting that he fails each time, he only outlines the gesture of grasping and thus limits himself to knocking one of the extremities of the object.
>
> At 0;4(9), the next day, Laurent tries to grasp the doll hanging in front of him; but he only succeeds in swinging it without holding it. He then shakes it altogether, while waving his arms. But he thus happens to strike the doll: he then begins again intentionally a series of times. A quarter of an hour later, as soon as he is confronted by the same doll in the same circumstances he begins to hit it again.
>
> At 0;4(15), faced by another hanging doll, Laurent tries to grasp it, then he shakes himself in order to make it swing, happens to knock it, and then tries to strike it.
>
> At 0;4(18) Laurent strikes my hands without trying to grasp them, but he has begun by simply waving his arms in the air and only 'hit' subsequently.
>
> At 0;4(19), at last, Laurent directly strikes a hanging doll. At 0:4(21) he strikes the hanging toys in the same way and thus swings them as much as possible. Same reaction on the following days.
>
> From 0;5(2) Laurent strikes the objects with one hand while holding them with the other. Thus he holds a rubber doll in the left hand and strikes it with his right. At 0;5(6) he grasps a rattle with a handle and strikes it immediately. At 0;5(7) I hand him different objects which are new to him (a wooden penguin, etc.): he hardly looks at them but strikes them systematically.

In the first three days Laurent develops a striking routine when the paper knife and doll hang above him. Piaget reminds us that the baby has acquired something more than a series of actions (locating the toy in space, raising hand to be ready to strike, executing the swiping movement, then stopping his hand's forward motion while continuing to observe the movement of the toy). He has constructed a mental structure, called an *action schema*, that guides the various steps in hitting a toy, and toy of the same sort of size. A week later at 0;4(15) he is confronted by a different doll and does not strike at it, until, by chance he happens to knock it. The sight of it swinging triggers his 'striking schema' and he deliberately strikes the new doll.

In Piaget's terminology, the schema developed with the paper knife *takes in, or* **assimilates** a new object. The schema itself changes little but it now includes the possibility of a new object.

In his fifth month, Laurent encounters a new situation – the toy in the hand rather than dangling above him. Whereas he could easily assimilate a new object into the schema if it dangled before him, he must now change the schema if he wishes to strike the hand-held toy. This he does, and Piaget would say that the striking schema adapts itself, or **accommodates** to the new situation. In this instance, accommodation involves coordination of two hands because now the baby must use *both* left and right whereas before he used but one.

Piaget says that a baby is born with simple schemas for sucking, grasping and the like. The process of assimilation enables him to 'take in' information about all sorts of objects he acts upon. For example, he learns about the breast, his own fingers, and a variety of toys by sucking on them. Very early in life, these things have no meaning to him except as part of his action schemas. Later, as seen in the case of Laurent in the excerpt above, some actions in the world require schemas to be adapted to suit new circumstances. As a result of this kind of accommodation, his schemas become differentiated and more complex, and so the process goes on.

In summary, Piaget began his study of children in search of mental structures that enable intelligent adaptation to the complicated world of events and people. He called these structures 'schemas' and he found that the simplest kind were present at birth. As the baby acts on the world, he assimilates objects and events to the schemas, thereby building a store of knowledge. Further, his schemas accommodate to new experiences – they become more differentiated and complex, and assimilate a wider range of objects in a wider range of ways. In a sense, the baby constructs more complex schemas by using his simple ones.

The development of the *object concept* during the sensory-motor period

By the time a child is two, the end of the sensory-motor period of intellectual development, he has an effective repertoire of coordinated schemas for dealing at the practical level with the world. These early schemas are the precursors to later ones that include **logical operations.** During the first two years he learns much about objects, time, space and causality. We turn to the first as it has been studied extensively by Piaget as well as others. There follow observations of the three Piaget children learning about objects. At first, if you recall Laurent and the striking schema, objects exist in the child's world only as part of his actions. Later, as you will see, they take on an interest in their own right.[2]

> At 0;8(30) Laurent, for the first time, examines a wooden hen from which hangs a ball which activates the animal's head by its movements. First he sees the hen, touches it, etc., then examines the ball, feels it and, seeing it move, strikes it immediately; he then attentively watches it swing and then studies it for its own sake; he simply sets it in motion, more and more gently. Then his attention is brought to bear on the accompanying movement of the hen and he swings the ball while watching the hen.
> Lucienne, at 0;8(10), likewise, examines a new doll which I hang from the hood of her bassinet. She looks at it for a long time, touches it, then feels it by touching its feet, clothes, head, etc. She then ventures to grasp it, which makes the hood sway. She then pulls the doll while watching the effects of this movement. Then she returns to the doll, holds it in one hand while striking it with the other, sucks it and shakes it while holding it above her and finally shakes it by moving its legs.
> Afterwards she strikes it without holding it, then grasps the string by which it hangs and gently swings it with the other hand. She then becomes very much interested in this slight swinging movement which is new to her and repeats it indefinitely.
> At 0;8(9) Jacqueline looks at a hanging necktie which she has never seen. Her hands move around it and touch it very warily. She grasps it and feels its surface. At a certain moment part of the necktie escapes her grasp: visible anxiety, then, when the phenomenon is repeated, satisfaction and, almost immediately after, something which resembles an experience of letting go and recapturing.

There is a considerable difference between the way children of four or five months act when they come across a new object, and the way the same children do four months later. The eight-month-old examines it as though it presented a problem to his mind – as though he were trying to understand it. Not only does he look at it for far longer before starting to act on it (strike it, suck it, or whatever), he also feels it, explores its surface and edges, turning it over and around. All this shows a completely new attitude: the unfamiliar represents for him an external reality – he has to adapt himself to it. It is not simply part of his action schema. He does, after taking a good look, try his schemas on it. But in doing so he gives the impression that he's trying an experiment rather than just assimilating yet another object to his schema. Piaget says '. . . it is as though the child said to himself when confronted by the new object: "What is this thing? I see it, hear it, grasp it, feel it, turn it over, . . . what more can I do with it?" '

But although children at about eight months show an active interest in *objects for their own sake*, they show no knowledge of the fact that objects continue to exist regardless of whether they are exploring and acting on them or not. Consider the following observation on Jacqueline, just coming up to her eight month 'birthday'.[2]

> At 0;7(28) Jacqueline tries to grasp a celluloid duck on top of her quilt. She almost catches it, shakes herself, and the duck slides down beside her. It falls very close to her hand but behind a fold in the sheet. Jacqueline's eyes have followed the movement, she has even followed it with her outstretched hand. But as soon as the duck has disappeared – nothing more! It does not occur to her to search behind the fold of the sheet, which would be very easy to do (she twists it mechanically without searching at all) . . . I try showing it to her a few times. Each time she tries to grasp it, but when she is about to touch it I replace it very obviously under the sheet. Jacqueline immediately withdraws her hand and gives up. The second and third times I make her grasp the duck through the sheet and she shakes if for a brief moment but it does not occur to her to raise the cloth.
>
> Everything occurs as though the child believed that the object is alternately made and unmade . . .

The observations of Laurent, Lucienne and Jacqueline demonstrate clearly the method of NATURALISTIC OBSERVATION in which the researcher does not intervene with the children he studies. But remember that Piaget was a father as well as a scientist and the informal 'experiments' he performed on his children, such as hiding a doll, were no more than familiar games played by all parents. They constituted a deliberate manipulation of the child's experiences little different from that performed by most parents. What distinguished Piaget from other parents was the theory he slowly constructed as a consequence of watching and playing with his children.

The observations also demonstrate that children during their first year change in their actions towards objects. At first they seem to use them simply as material (Piaget called it **aliment** or food) for their action patterns, and only towards eight months and beyond do they seem to be truly curious about them. In other words, at first they appear to ask 'Can I *strike* (or *rub* or *suck*, etc.) this thing?' with little concern for what the thing really is. By eight months, however, they appear to ask themselves 'what is this unique object? how can I act upon it to tell me more about its characteristics?' Finally, at nine months or thereabouts, babies do search

Figure 7.2 *A baby, before he understands object permanence, will reach for an object he can see . . . and ignore it when it disappears from view*

for hidden objects, demonstrating that they know that objects exist in definite locations despite the fact that they are out of sight.

The *pre-operational period*, sometimes called the intuitive period

Sometime during the second year of life children begin to talk. At first they use single words, like 'milk' when they want a drink. Later, they string several words into sentences such as 'Daddy go bye-bye'. Before language appears, children's intelligence is practical in nature – they know *how* to act in the immediate environment. With language, their mental schemas are transformed into symbolic ones. They are no longer trapped in the here and now but can discuss events that occurred in the past and those that will occur in the future 'snow on tree' and 'Granny come'.

Because the two-year-old has words for objects and events in his daily routine, he can think about the world without acting on it. However, despite a rapidly expanding vocabulary, the child between two and seven does not think like an adult or use language in the same way. Piaget reports on one of his daughters:[3]

> At about 2:6, she [Jacqueline] used the term 'the slug' for the slugs we went to see every morning along a certain road. At 2:7(2) she cried: 'There it is,' on seeing one and when we saw another ten yards further on she said 'There is the slug again.' I answered, 'But isn't it another one?' I went back to see the first one. 'Is it the same one?' 'Yes,' she answered. 'Another slug?' 'Yes,' she answered again. The question obviously had no meaning.

During the years between two and seven the child learns much about the physical world. He learns that inanimate objects need an outside force to set them in motion. He learns about the social world too, such as when to share and when to defend property. Some of this learning is spontaneous, while other is deliberately taught by parents and teachers. Despite the many intellectual feats of the period, children do not reason in a logical or a fully mathematical way. The girl of four will tell you that 'my sister doesn't have a sister' with no clue that the statement is logically impossible.

According to Piaget, this little girl reveals her incomplete understanding of the concept 'sister' because she fails to see the necessary reversibility between female siblings. Although she uses the same word as the adult, she has an incomplete concept rather than a mature concept.

In interviews with scores of children, Piaget found more instances of immature reasoning in young children. One child told him that the moon was alive.[1]

'Why?'
'Because we are alive.'

This answer reveals both the **animism** (attributing life to inanimate objects) and the **egocentrism** (the inability to take into account the point of view of someone else) discussed earlier in the chapter.

Further examples of egocentrism appear in the answers of two little boys to questions about the game of marbles. These boys, who often played together, told Piaget about the rules which they followed. Much to his surprise, Piaget discovered that they followed very different rules –

despite their frequent playing 'together'. Each boy played an individual game, showing that his understanding was egocentric. Children do not lose egocentricity in games before seven or eight, at which ages they can, at last, de-centre.

Children's thinking in the **pre-operational period** is characterized by what Piaget called **moral realism** as well as by animism and egocentrism. To learn about children's conceptions of morality, Piaget modified the clinical INTERVIEW somewhat. He told stories of good and naughty deeds, and followed them with questions. The stories were usually of two types: in one, the central character performed an unintentional act which resulted in a great deal of damage. In the other, the character caused a small amount of damage while acting in an intentionally naughty way. Here are two examples:[4]

> A little boy who was called Augustus once noticed that his father's inkpot was empty. One day while his father was away he thought of filling the inkpot so as to help his father, and so that he should find it full when he came home. But while he was opening the ink bottle he made a big blot on the table cloth.

The corresponding story involving minor damage is as follows:

> There was a little boy called Julian. His father had gone out and Julian thought it would be fun to play with his father's inkpot. First he played with the pen, and then he made a little blot on the tablecloth.

After telling the stories, Piaget asked whether the children were equally guilty, or was one child the naughtier. Here are the replies from a girl of seven.

> 'Which is the most naughty,'
> 'The one who made the big blot.'
> 'Why?'
> 'Because it was big.'
> 'Why did he make a big blot.'
> 'To be helpful.'
> 'And why did the other one make a little blot?'
> 'Because he was always touching things. He made a little blot.'
> 'Then which one of them is the naughtiest?'
> 'The one who made a big blot.'

The child's morality speaks for itself; to cause a great deal of damage is to be naughty. Piaget claims that answers of this kind demonstrate moral realism because intentions are ignored while assigning guilt, and attention is focused on the realities of physical damage.

How can we summarize children's thinking in the pre-operational stage? The clinical interview allowed Piaget to conclude that it is characterized by animism, egocentrism, and moral realism. At first, these may seem disparate characteristics but they are alike in one way; they demonstrate a failure to deal simultaneously with several aspects of a situation. Animism is the failure to adopt one stance towards inanimate objects and another towards oneself. Similarly, moral realism is the consequence of viewing morality in one sense only, that concerned with damage. The young moral realist ignores intention as a contributor to guilt because he cannot consider damage and intention at the same time. And lastly, egocentrism is the consequence of the child's taking only one perspective, in games as well as in assigning kinship. The child achieves the next stage of intellectual development when at last he can consider a situation from several different aspects – in other words, he can de-centre.

> The newborn acts as if the world is centred about himself and must learn to behave in a more adaptive way. Similarly, the young child thinks from a limited perspective and must widen it. Both infant and young child must de-centre – the former, his action and the latter, his thought.[5]

The *operational period* (sub-period of *concrete operations*)

At six or seven years, the child passes an important milestone when his thinking becomes logical. This does not happen overnight, of course, but in the space of a year or two the child can think on an entirely new plane. Recall that Piaget devoted his life to finding the roots of logical thinking. He discovered the early mental structures, or **schemas**, that underlie babies' sensory and motor abilities. Later, he saw how language enabled a child to represent his knowledge symbolically and to conceive of yesterday and tomorrow. But for all his apparent sophistication, the **pre-operational** child was seen to be limited in his thinking. Now consider the following scenario showing the kind of logic that *older children and adults* use every day.

The adult arranges six sweets in a row, then asks a child of seven to make a row which will be 'the same' as the original. The child carefully takes sweets from a saucer and makes a new row, parallel to the adult's and also containing six. When asked if they are the 'same amount' the child answers 'yes'. Then the adult re-arranges his row by decreasing the distance between each sweet and making his row shorter in length. He asks the child to consider the number of sweets in each row. 'Are they the same now?' The child looks at the adult in amazement, and answers 'yes' without glancing at the sweets. Any reasonable person, *if he is logical*, knows that the rows must be the same because no sweets have been added or taken away. But that is precisely the point! A younger child is tricked by his perception; he would 'fail' the task.

Here is Piaget's report on a pre-operational child of five years, seven months named Per.[6] He

> . . . had no difficulty in making a row of six sweets corresponding to the model. (Piaget uses 'model' to refer to row A, the row to be copied, and 'copy' to refer to row B.) The model was then closed up:
> 'I've got more.'
> 'Why?'
> 'Because it's a longer line.'
> (The process was then reversed.)
> 'Now there are more there, because it's a big line.'
> But a moment later, Per said the opposite:
> 'Are there more here?' (referring to the longer row).
> 'No'
> 'Why not?'
> 'Because it's long.'
> 'And there?' (the shorter row).
> 'There are more there, because there's a little bundle.' (The child meant that the shorter row was denser.)
> 'Then there are more in a little bundle than in a big line?'
> 'Yes.'
> After this, Per went back to using length as the criterion, made the two rows the same length again, and said:
> 'Now they're both the same.'

In Figure 7.3, Part 2, Per is 'tricked' by the appearance of things and so fails the task. Piaget calls this an experiment in **conservation** because it requires the child to conserve the number of items despite transformation in its appearance.

Note that the word 'experiment' has crept back into the text. To investigate the development of logical and mathematical abilities, Piaget had to abandon both NATURALISTIC OBSERVATION and the clinical INTERVIEW. He thought the latter depended too much on what the children actually said. Perhaps children knew more than they could express – perhaps his questions 'led them' to conclusions that were not theirs. He turned instead to formal experiments in which all children were presented with identical objects and events. In some instances the children were asked to manipulate the objects, such as in the following experiment (Figure 7.5).

The child and adult sit at a table and before them are three beakers, B1, B2 and B3. Beaker B1 is filled with milk, and the adult asks the child to fill the identical beaker B2 with milk from the jug so that it has 'the same amount' as the model. The child complies, carefully lining up the two beakers so that he can see when the height of the milk is the same in them.

Next the adult produces a third beaker, B3, which is taller and thinner than B1 and B2. He asks the child to pour the contents of B2 into B3. 'Is there the same amount in this beaker (B3) as in this one (B1)?' Older

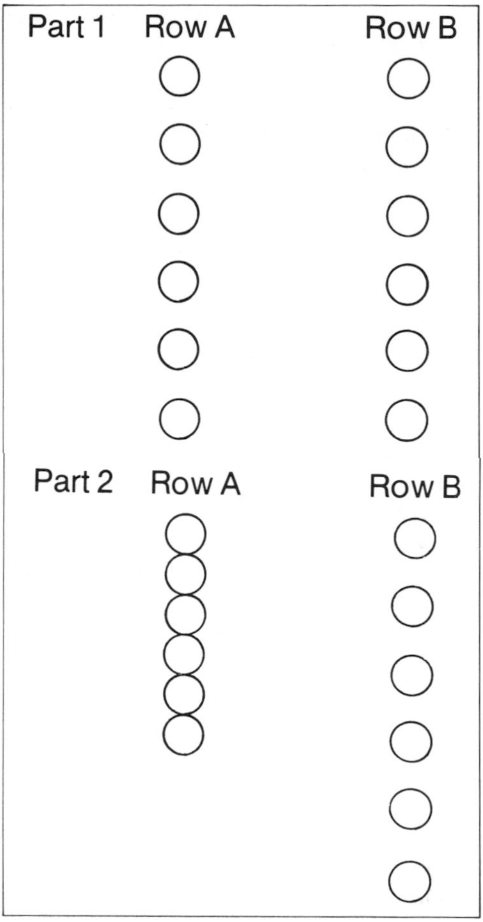

Figure 7.3 *Piaget's experiment on the conservation of number. Part 1 shows the sweets at the start of the experiment, and Part 2 the same sweets after transformation*

children are not fooled by the task, just as they were not in the experiment with sweets. 'They are the same.'

Can younger children solve the problem? Piaget has shown that children younger than six or seven *are* fooled by the pouring and claim that B3 has 'more'. Why? Because they are fooled by the greater height in the third beaker. To them, 'lower' indicates less and 'higher' more. Of course, this rule will work with identical beakers but not with those whose shapes vary. Occasionally Piaget varied the task, pouring the milk from Beaker B2 into a B3 that was short and fat instead of tall and thin. Now, the pre-operational child would say that the third beaker had 'less' in it.

Conservation of quantity can be studied with substances other than fluids, as for instance, with plasticine. The adult rolls two identical balls in his fingers. Next, he transforms the appearance of one ball by rolling it

Figure 7.4 *The number conservation experiment actually happening. The girl on the left (who is just six) first decides the two rows have the same number of bricks – which is right. When the experimenter spreads one row out, she is misled into thinking the longer row has more*

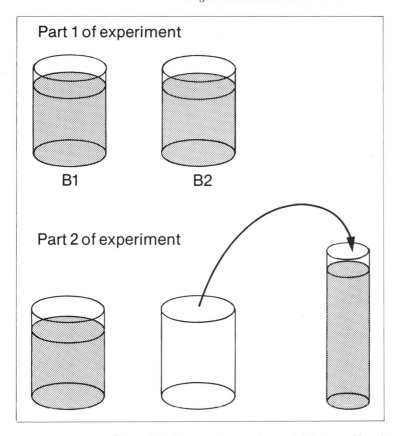

Figure 7.5 *Conservation experiment with beakers of liquid*

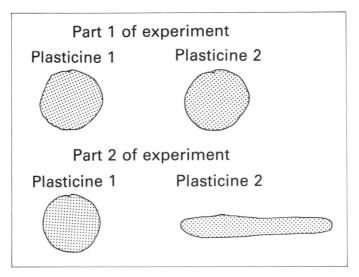

Fig. 7.6 *Conservation experiment with plasticine*

into a sausage shape. If he compares it with the first lump of plasticine (the model), the older child will say it's the 'same amount'. A younger child will be fooled, as with the beakers, and say that the new sausage shape is 'more' (if he focuses on length) or 'less' (if he focuses on width). In either event, the younger child says that the amount of plasticine has changed because it appears different (Figure 7.6).

Piaget performed many other experiments on **conservation** involving weight and volume, but the results of these were not much different from experiments on conservation of number, liquid quantity, and substance. All these conservation experiments are similar because they involve first a phase in which the child judges that two similar things are equal. Most children above four can get this far. Then a visible transformation is performed. While the child watches, one of the entities is transformed in appearance by being changed in shape or transferred to another recepta- cle. It is quite clear that no new quantity is added to the one that has been transformed, but it now looks very different from the entity first encoun- tered. Each experiment requires that the child must judge whether the two things are still the same or are different.

After many experiments, Piaget and his colleagues concluded that there is a sequence of development for each of the conservations. First, children do not conserve at all. They blithely tell the experimenter that 'it's more now' or 'less'. When finally capable of conservation, children are able to make the following arguments as to why the number (or liquid, volume, etc.) is still the same. 'If it were returned to the original beaker, it would still be equal.' (This is called the *negation* argument.) Another is that 'of course it is equal; it is still the same water'. (This is the *identity* argument.) Or lastly 'although it's higher now, it's also thinner and so must be the same amount'. (This is the *compensation* argument.)

Oddly enough, children do not achieve conservation all at once. Some of the problems are 'easier' than others. In fact, children usually master conservation of continuous quantity (as with the water) and substance (plasticine) at 6 or 7, weight at 9 or 10, volume at 11 or 12. In each case, the arguments are roughly the same but the child's reasoning seems tied to particular situations and objects.

Why do school aged children succeed at conservation tasks? For one, their thought is *reversible*. Take the task with pouring of liquid amounts. The operational child can mentally reverse the pouring procedure, and so doing, realizes that the liquid is the same amount as before. The same with the plasticine; the child can mentally reverse the moulding of the sausage. Moreover, the child succeeds at conservation tasks because he is attentive to several kinds of information at the same time. He considers the height of the beaker (or the length of the row) as well as the additional information concerning width.

Children new to concrete operations may study the objects in the experiments. 'The beaker is taller now, but it's more narrow.' This is the essence of compensation. But older children, those firmly established in logical reasoning, do not bother with examination of the objects after the transformation has been performed. For them, the question 'Are they the same?' seems silly. '*Of course*, they are the same.' These children do not believe that the question requires perceptual judgment; instead, they know that questions of logical necessity do not need verification in this way. Number or quantity remains the same despite changed visual appearance, just as the essential identity of an object remains despite its visual disappearance.

So far it has been shown that children in the period of **concrete operations** can perform the mental operation of *reversibility* and can attend to *several aspects* of a situation at once. This second skill should enable them to look at an object from the point of view of someone else – and so overcome their earlier egocentrism. This is precisely what happens.

Another experiment of Piaget's will illustrate the ability to de-centre of children over eight. A child sits at a table on which is placed a papier maché model of three mountains (Figure 7.7). Each mountain looks different; on top of one is a large cross, another is snow-covered, and the third is green pasture-land. The child is asked to describe what he sees and can do a good job at this task. Next, a doll is placed on the other side of the table and the child is asked 'What does the doll see?' He is shown several drawings of the mountains, and the child of eight can readily choose the view the doll sees (how the mountains look from the other side of the table). He realizes that the three mountains look different from different perspectives.

As might be expected, children in the pre-operational period think the doll sees exactly what they see themselves.

In sum, children's thinking in the period of concrete operations is logical and mathematical. It is characterized by mental actions of reversibility, ability to take into account several aspects of a situation, and de-centring. Piaget studied the further development of logical thinking in adolescence (the period of **formal operations**), and 'reflective abstraction', that very human capacity to be aware of one's own thoughts and strategies. But those are beyond the scope of this book.

Summing up the theory

Recall that Piaget was interested in the kinds of structures that enable an organism, be it man or mollusc, to adapt to its particular environment. Some are physical structures, such as the elephant's trunk or the tortoise's shell, while others are mental ones. Piaget called the mental ones **schemas**, and they are as important to adaptation as the ones clearly visible. Piaget devoted a lifetime to describing the various stages of mental organization, each more complex than the preceding one. The basic unit of mental organization is always the schema; in infancy, schemas are

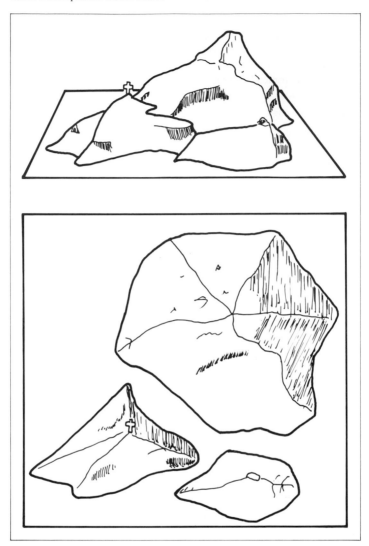

Figure 7.7 *Piaget's model mountains, which he used to demonstrate the 'egocentrism' of young children, viewed from the front and from the top*

simple and practical, whereas later they become differentiated and complex. Examples of complicated schemas include symbolic ones such as notions of 'infinity' and mental operations such as algebra.

Where do schemas come from and how do they change? Piaget is quite explicit about this: the infant is born with rudimentary schemas, such as sucking and grasping, and these he calls *action schemas*. Through the process of **assimilation** the child uses early schemas to take in information about the world, including people, objects and events. Through the complementary process of **accommodation**, the earliest schemas become modified to fit the child's experiences. Thus, as a consequence of both processes, the infant's schemas become more complex to keep pace with his action in the world.

The twin processes of assimilation and accommodation continue throughout life. Assimilation is always the process that enables an individual to deal with new situations and new problems by using the current stock of schemas. Accommodation, on the other hand, is always the process where the individual undergoes a mental change in order to manage problems that were at first too difficult to solve.

Piaget believes that thinking is an active process. Children and adults are not creatures who passively ingest information; they actively organize experience and this activity modifies the schemas they already have. Just as an organism ingests food so that the body may be restored and grow, so does the child ingest information so that his mental structures may develop further.

Although Piaget is explicit in describing the complementary processes of assimilation and accommodation, he is less clear as to *why* a child bothers to acquire new knowledge. Piaget stresses that the child is naturally curious about the world and explores it with no prompting or reward from others. But why does he progress beyond sensory-motor intelligence? Couldn't he go on with sensory-motor exploration forever? Piaget describes a push towards cognitive development called **equilibriation**. This is a self-righting system whereby conflicts in the child's thinking are resolved by mental reorganization towards coherent system. For instance a child might know that 'daytime' comes about when the sun rises while at the same time believe that day comes because he wishes it. Seeing the contradiction will prompt the child toward a new, more mature understanding.

Central to Piagetian theory are the concepts of **stage** (each period is a stage), **sequence**, and **invariance**. Piaget divides the child's intellectual development into three main periods (one subdivided) and for this reason he is said to have devised a stage theory. A developmental period is characterized by the complexity of its schemas as well as by how coordinated they are with one another. The first stage (sensory-motor period) is characterized by practical schemas, whereas the following stage (pre-operational period) is characterized by symbolic ones. The next stage (concrete operational period) is also characterized by symbolic schemes but these are organized into a coherent network to form a logical system.

The exact ages at which children typically enter or leave a stage are only approximate, and Piaget tells us, for instance, that children may enter into the concrete operational period as early as five or as late as eight.

Although the precise ages are not important, what matters is that the sequence of stages is *invariant* – the same for each child. The invariant sequence of stages shows a progression from simplicity to mature, logical intelligence. The progression begins with the infant's sensory-motor schemas without which he could not develop symbolic ones. And without symbolic schemas, the child could not develop a coordinated network of logical, mathematical ones. In a very real sense each period depends on the one before it and this dependence is the essence of a stage theory of development.

Development can proceed in two ways. One of them, characterized by the life cycle of the butterfly, is in stages. First a caterpillar, then a chrysalis, then a sudden metamorphosis, and the butterfly appears. In a sense, it is the same creature, although in a radically different form. Mussen and Kagan have likened a *stage theory* such as Piaget's to this kind of development. Its opposite, characterized by the gradual development of a kitten into a cat, is called a *continuity theory*. Does the mind really develop like a butterfly, distinctly different at each age? Or does it slowly grow and differentiate without sudden reorganizations? This kind of problem wakes a psychologist in the middle of the night because of its vitality and our ignorance of the answer.

There is an age-old argument between those who claim intelligence to be innate, or inherited, and those who argue that intelligence is acquired through experience. Piagetian theory straddles the two camps by claiming that early schemas are present at birth, yet stressing that mature, logical schemas are the consequence of the child's self-initiated activity on the world. Is there innate intelligence? Piaget answers *yes* because simple schemas are present at birth. Does mature intelligence require experience in the world? That answer is *yes* as well because complex schemas cannot be constructed without acting on the world.

But was Piaget right?

No other theory of intellectual growth is as broad in scope or as detailed as Piaget's. Ask any psychologist who has made the greatest contribution to our understanding of cognitive development and the answer will invariably be 'Piaget'.

But was he right about everything? Did he tell us all there is to be known about intellectual development? Of course not. Much is left to be discovered; indeed, some of Piaget's 'discoveries' are clearly wrong. We will evaluate Piaget's work here in some detail for two reasons: first, he has had great influence in education, linguistics, anthropology and medicine, as well as other fields. If he is wrong, there are practical consequences. Secondly, Piaget's work provides an interesting example of how arguments go on in science.

Some important areas are not touched by Piaget's work

Piaget is often accused of being too relentless in his pursuit of logic and with being totally unconcerned with children's emotions. The first may be true, but Piaget certainly did appreciate the complicated interaction between thought and feelings. That is implied for instance in these observations:[3]

> At 2;6(3), and on the following days, the child pretended to suck at his mother's breast after seeing a baby being suckled. This game was repeated at about 2;9.
> At 5;8(5), being for the moment on bad terms with her father, the child charged one of her imaginary characters with the task of avenging her: 'Zoubab cut off her daddy's head. But she has some very strong glue and partly stuck it on again. But it's not very firm now.'

Piaget was familiar with the work of Freud on the development of emotions and thought it provided valuable clues to the content of children's thinking. Piaget tells us at which *intellectual level* a child can think whereas Freud suggests what *kinds of things* (attraction for the parent, fear of castration) he thinks about.

Methodological problems

There are other problems with Piaget's work which have to do with methodology. For instance, his reliance on the clinical INTERVIEW is somewhat doubtful. Piaget himself tells us that it takes a year of daily practice to conduct clinical interviews skilfully with children. Because there are no set questions or set order of presentation, the interviewer might 'lead' the young child to views he does not possess. Piaget saw problems with this technique, however, and most of his later work was more rigorous in design.

Even the experiments with fixed materials and questioning have methodological problems. Some critics, such as Peter Bryant,[7] claim that Piaget designed his tasks in such a way as to make it maximally difficult for a child to give correct answers. In a series of ingenious experiments, Bryant has shown that children are capable of logical thinking well before their fifth birthdays. Where Piaget insists that even the cleverest children at this age are lost in the illogicality of the pre-operational period, Bryant believes that he is too pessimistic about their abilities and that supposed 'failures' could be due to many things – memory deficiencies, for example, or the child's not realizing that logic is called for in a particular task.

Still another critic of Piaget's methods is Margaret Donaldson[8] who, like Peter Bryant, believes that children can solve logical problems well before Piaget thinks they can. Whereas Bryant modified Piaget's experimental tasks to make them somewhat easier, Donaldson and her colleagues retained the form of the Piagetian tasks while changing the context in which they appeared. McGarrigle and Donaldson followed

Piaget's procedure with rows of sweets – but with one important difference. Instead of having an experimenter alter the two rows, a 'naughty teddy' entered the scene (contrived by the experimenters, of course) and re-arranged the objects while making comic mayhem. Needless to say, the children looked with great interest at the antics of the teddy bear. When later questioned about the number of objects in the rows thrown about by the teddy bear, they easily gave the correct answer (i.e. that the number was 'still the same'). Something in the antics of the disgraceful teddy bear helped children to conserve number, despite the altered appearance of the rows.

McGarrigle and Donaldson argued that their task, identical to Piaget's except for the alteration being performed by an accomplice, was easier for children because it made sense for them to count carefully the items after wicked mayhem, whereas when the experimenter did the re-arranging they didn't realize that their perceptual judgments might be wrong. Thus, argues Donaldson, children may appear to fail Piagetian tasks because of deficiencies in logic when actually they are *quite capable* of correct solutions under different circumstances.

The 'naughty teddy' experiment shows a great flaw in Piaget's work; he fails to take sufficient notice of the effect of the *context of the task* he sets before children. By concentrating on a limited number of tasks, he underestimates children's abilities. Bryant makes this point forcefully.

> How does Piaget's theory stand today? Though every psychologist will agree that he raised some marvellous questions, many doubt that his answers are the right ones. His conclusion that children simply lack the ability to be logical for a large chunk of their childhood was surprisingly pessimistic for someone who, as a brilliantly precocious boy, published his first scientific paper at the age of 11.

Are the periods psychologically 'real'?

The criticisms from Bryant and Donaldson point in the same direction: Piaget's stages of development are based on children's inability to perform certain tasks at certain ages. When they fail his tasks, he claims it is because they have not reached the appropriate stage and lack the requisite mental structures. But Bryant and Donaldson have shown that, at least in certain instances, children fail Piaget's tasks because they do not realize that it is appropriate to apply skills (such as conservation) that they already possess. No one would argue that children are born with the capacity to conserve or to de-centre – it is rather that the steps between the periods, which Piaget says are extremely clear-cut, are really blurred. A step-wise sequence of development may be a consequence of particular tasks chosen for study, rather than biological patterns of child development.

Still, no one would argue that the minds of babies are organized in the same way as those of schoolchildren. And many would agree with Piaget's description of characteristic thought patterns of children (egocentrism, moral realism, and the like). Perhaps it's best to conclude that intellectual development consists of sequential stages of structural organization, but that the 'stages' blend into one another rather than comprising a stair-like pattern.

Piaget's concepts are rather vague

The abstractness of concepts such as 'schema', 'assimilation' or 'accommodation' is at once a strength and a weakness. On the positive side, Piaget looked at apparently quite different actions and sequences of behaviour to find what they had in common beneath the surface. This is easy to see in infancy, as for example the baby's underlying striking schema which is the basis of different actions in keeping with the object being struck, its location, whether it is motionless or swinging, and so on.

It is more difficult to discover underlying structures as the child grows older. Piaget found a similarity between the child's moral reasoning at four and his failure to take into account the perceptual view of another person. Beneath both moral and perceptual judgments is the child's prevailing egocentrism – his inability to see things from the viewpoint of someone else. Instead of concluding that children 'say funny things' or that they 'make mistakes', Piaget described the kind of thinking common to both events.

By focusing on the structure of thought rather than momentary actions or words, Piaget was able to describe the characteristic thought patterns of children at different ages. This stage theory allows us to see the essential changes in intellectual development, the sequence from simple action schemas to symbolic and then logical ones. Only a notion as abstract as the *schema* could be applied to the thinking of both infants and adults. If one term is used to describe very different things, it is bound to be abstract – even vague. Piaget was in fact courageous to insist on looking for deep, underlying similarities between all sorts of logical (or less logical) behaviour, at a time when other psychologists thought it unscientific and quite unpardonable to stray from behaviour that could be seen and measured on the spot.

On the negative side, abstractness and vagueness are undeniably a problem. Piaget, and others since, have verified that children all over the world do indeed learn about the permanence of objects, and about conservation (to name a few) according to the sequence he described. And his way of explaining developing intelligence seems a good one. But whether there *really* is a process like for instance 'equilibration' one can never really prove. We must infer its existence from children's performance on simple tasks such as searching for hidden keys or answering questions about amounts of liquid. The sequence in which children acquire notions of object permanence and conservation has been verified again and again on countless children all over the world.

Chapter 1 outlined some milestones in motor development, a timetable found all over the world. One can think of Piaget's work as providing 'intellectual milestones', a developmental timetable that gives approximate dates to cognitive achievements. Why does object permanence appear when it does? Why does conservation of discrete quantity (sweets) precede continuous quantity (water)? Why do children learn about logic on their own? Piaget's theory explains the observable facts of intellectual development. Although its weaknesses have been summarized here, *in general* it is substantiated by scientific research. The task for younger psychologists now is to build on Piaget's work, eliminating the methodological flaws and working to remedy the vagueness of concepts. This is the way that science progresses.

Stage	approximate age	nature of the schemas	typical adaptations
sensory-motor	birth to 2 years	practical action	can act intentionally on the world, object permanence.
pre-operational	2 to 6 or 7 years	symbolic (but not logical)	can symbolize, talk about past and future, judgments showing egocentrism and moral realism
concrete operational	6 or 7 to about 11 years	logical and mathematical	can deal with two or more aspects of a situation at the same time, can decentre and conserve
formal operational	11 years (or so) onwards.	logical and mathematical abstractions	formalism of physics and higher maths, morality based on intentions

Figure 7.8 *A summary of the Piagetian stages*

Chapter 8

How do children learn?

Learning is often associated with school and the very word brings to mind boring classes and weekly tests. But people also learn the rules of cricket, not an arduous task, as well as the hit records in the top twenty. In fact, more learning goes on outside school than in it. Babies learn the distinct sounds of their mother tongue and the meaning of its words. Older children learn about nature and logic in an effortless way. Even the elderly learn to cope with retirement, by taking on sports and hobbies.

Piaget's work bears directly on learning, although there are important differences between the Piagetian view and the one presented below. These will be discussed near the end of the chapter.

Why do people learn? it is clear that children spontaneously learn to recognize their mothers and that they learn about objects and language without special prodding from the family. An especially good example of spontaneous learning is the baby's struggle to walk. The desire to stand up and toddle is unmistakable. Although parents may sometimes hold childrens' hands and often praise the first few steps, it is unlikely that parental reward is what motivates babies to pull themselves erect, struggle forward and bravely pick themselves up when they fall. Babies do this when no one is watching and in families where adults never appear to notice. Psychologists now agree that the human need for *mastery* prompts much early learning. Walking is a consequence of it, arising on schedule as the baby's legs strengthen and muscles achieve the necessary control.

Some other achievements – arithmetic, the Ten Commandments, labouring in the fields – do not arise spontaneously. Left to our own devices, most of us would lounge about, cheat, count on our fingers and read comic books. What prompts hard work and diligence? In many instances, reward and punishment take over where self-mastery leaves off.

Instrumental learning

Edward Thorndike started experimenting on the behaviour of cats, chickens and dogs while still a student. He invented a puzzle box in order to study how ordinary animals come to learn about the environment. In a typical experiment, he placed a hungry cat inside the box. Outside, the cat

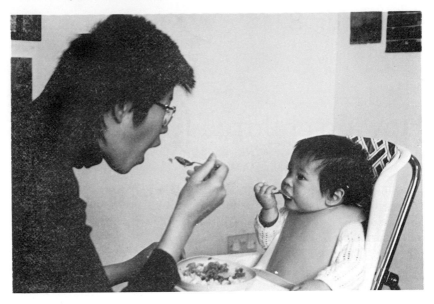

Figure 8.1 *Observational learning: a baby watches, then imitates, his mother's action*

could see some food but the door to both freedom and sustenance was blocked by a wooden bar. To open it, he had to pull two strings, which would, in turn, lift several weights and move the bar holding the door shut. How long would it take cats to learn the trick?

On average, they learned to escape in 10 minutes. At first they scratched, clawed, and paced about. This activity usually led to their pulling one rope, then the other. By chance, all the cats escaped, although some were quicker than others.

Thorndike's contribution to psychology is that he put the cats back in the box on subsequent days and carefully recorded how long it took them to escape. Not surprisingly, he found that the escape took a shorter and shorter time, until finally they began solving the puzzle as soon as they were placed inside. Such a 'discovery' may at first seem mundane and hardly worth the name of science. What distinguished Thorndike's work was his painstaking, experimental approach to the study of the acquisition of new behaviour. He made a quantifiable science of learning.

In Thorndike's experiments learning was a direct consequence of reward. Unlike the toddler who seeks mastery for its own sake, the cat in the box learned the complicated action sequence because it was followed by access to food. Thorndike summarized his work: According to Thorndike's Law of Effect, a given stimulus calls forth a given response if the sequence has been regularly followed by a satisfying state of affairs.

In plain English, this means that being placed in the puzzle box (the stimulus) calls forth rope-pulling (the response) if such actions have been followed by food (pleasure). Thorndike experimented with a variety of 'puzzle' tasks, different animal species, and with the possibility of un-learning, that is, what happens when the reward is no longer forthcoming. On the basis of laboratory work, he concluded that the Law of Effect operated for all kinds of learning tasks and for many different species. Further, a process called **extinction** occurred when the reward was withheld. When this occurred, Thorndike thought that the learning originally 'stamped in' by the pleasurable experience became 'stamped out' by lack of satisfaction.

Although Thorndike pioneered study into the way that satisfaction prompts learning, it was B. F. Skinner who investigated the detailed operation of the Law of Effect. To do this, he invented an apparatus even simpler than Thorndike's. He placed the experimental animal in the box shown in Figure 8.2 with nothing inside save a lever and a food tray. After

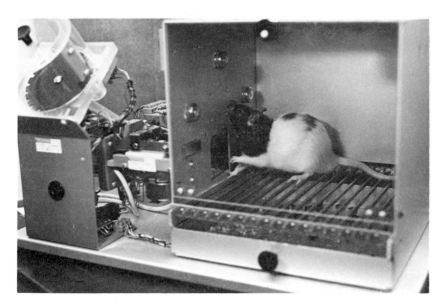

Figure 8.2 *A rat in a 'Skinner box', learning that pressing the lever produces a pellet of food*

pressing the lever, a pellet of food is automatically delivered to the food tray. In a sense, it's similar to employment; the 'worker' does a job and gets 'paid' for it. Typically, the first few food pellets have little effect on pressing of the bar-lever, but rats quickly learn the relationship between work and food. (See Figure 8.3.)

Using this apparatus, Skinner and his followers discovered a host of potential rewards, all of which bring about learning. These include ordinary ones such as food, and less obvious ones such as the opportunity to run in an exercise wheel or to look out of a window. As investigations continued, it became harder and harder to know in advance which experiences would be pleasurable and which not. Imagine an animal fed

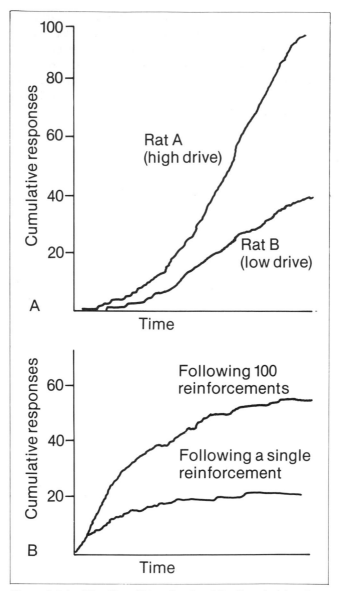

Figure 8.3 A. *The effect of drive: Rat A and Rat B are both learning to press the lever for food. Each step on the curve indicates one press. Rat A, though, has been without food for 30 hours, and learns more quickly than Rat B, who has been without for only 10*
B. *The effect of reinforcement: Two rats are 'unlearning' again now reinforcement has ended. The upper curve plots the presses of a rat who has had 100 reinforcing pellets. The bottom curve those of a rat who has had only one*

regularly on a luxurious diet. Delivering a small, dry pellet into the tray might not constitute a reward at all, and this would be verified by the fact that the delivery of pellets did not increase bar-pressing. On the other hand, an animal kept on a meagre diet might work like fury for the same dry pellets. Results such as these caused consternation among psychologists because it seemed impossible to draw up a comprehensive list of rewards. What was sauce for the goose might not be sauce for the gander.

Skinner resolved this thorny problem by avoiding terms such as 'pleasure' or 'satisfaction', using the word **reinforcer** instead. Literally anything can be a reinforcer as long as it increases the probability of the action preceding it. If turning on a light in a pigeon's cage makes his pecking at a disc more likely, then the light is a reinforcer. If bar-pressing increases in rats when it is followed by access to an exercise wheel, then access to the wheel is considered a reinforcer. Skinner defines reinforcers as those objects or events that increase the probability that responses they follow will occur again. For example, if a mother cuddles her baby after each smile, the cuddle is a reinforcer because it makes smiles more likely. Although it may seem similar to Thorndike's notion of 'satisfaction', reinforcers are defined by how they work; no assumptions are made about pleasure. A masochist might learn the names in the telephone directory for 20 lashes. In this unlikely case the lashes serve as reinforcers, demonstrating neatly that Skinner's definition allows one man's meat to be another man's poison.

Skinner also investigated punishment, which has an opposite effect to positive reinforcement. In these experiments, the rat receives an electric shock on the floor of his cage each time he presses the lever. Rats quickly learn not to press the lever, and so avoid future shocks. Punishment also conforms to the Law of Effect; an event or thing is called a punisher if it decreases the likelihood of the response immediately preceding it.

In further experiments, Skinner compared continuous reinforcement (reinforcing the animal every time he made a correct response) with intermittent reinforcement.

To do this, he plotted the amount of work performed by animals receiving reinforcers after each response, and compared it to the amount of work by animals whose reinforcers were delivered after some – but not all – responses. Much to everyone's surprise, intermittent reinforcement yielded the highest rates of responding and these responses were the most resistant to extinction. This is not as far-fetched as first it may sound. Imagine a child who searches for coins between the cushions of a chair. It is not surprising that he continues to look, despite the fact that he may be reinforced by finding coins only a few times. This child, like many a gambler, needs only occasional reward to keep the habit going strong.

At first glance, discussion of rats and pigeons may seem out of place in a book about children. Although Skinner conducted few investigations of children, his work contributes much to our understanding of their psychological development. Children learn to use spoons and to clean up their rooms because of parental reinforcers such as smiles, cuddles, and sweets. Similarly, they stop throwing food on the floor after mother delivers a light smack. The principles of learning inherent in these homely truths were known before Skinner established them in the lab. Skinner's genius was to insist on careful experiment rather than casual observation. He measured the learning and precisely defined the conditions that bring it about. Furthermore, he focused attention squarely on the important role of the environment in the process of learning. Family members and teachers often require actions that the child may not like. They control his behaviour by using the Law of Effect. Reinforcers and punishers are *instrumental* in bringing about learning in children as well as rats. For this reason, learning prompted by the outside environment is called '**instrumental learning**'.

Pavlovian learning, or *classical conditioning*

The essence of instrumental learning is reinforcement. A relatively neutral action on the part of man or beast is repeated or learned as a consequence of either positive reinforcement or punishment. A Russian investigator, Ivan Pavlov, investigated another kind of learning based on *association* rather than reward.

Pavlov was a physiologist working at the turn of the century on the digestive system. His experimental animals happened to be dogs and Pavlov noticed one day that they began to salivate as soon as their trainer entered the laboratory carrying bowls of food. Pavlov guessed that the dogs had come to associate the sight of the trainer with the presence of food in their mouths. Like his contemporary, Thorndike, Pavlov was not content with casual observation. Therefore, he performed a series of ingenious experiments showing how a person or thing (say, the trainer) or an event (say, the sound of a dinner bell) becomes associated with food and causes salivation.

The essence of this second type of learning, known as classical conditioning, is the association between two events. Repeated pairing of stimuli such as bell and food leads to the 'artificial' one taking on some of the consequences of the 'natural' one. Pavlov called the food the **unconditioned stimulus** and the bell the **conditioned stimulus**. The reason for these terms is quite simple; the conditioned stimulus is an object or event that does not originally call forth the response. Dogs all over the world salivate when food is put in their mouths but only Pavlov's dogs do so when a certain Russian trainer walks into the lab. Salivation prompted by something associated with food is called a conditioned response to distinguish it from the normal (or unconditioned) one. The terms used in the experiment are summarized neatly in Figure 8.4.

Although Pavlov experimented exclusively with animals his findings are also relevant to child development. Children may learn to associate

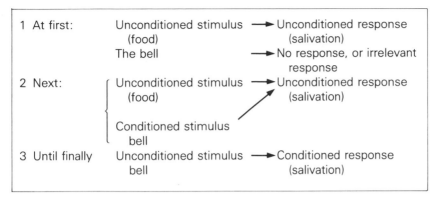

1 At first: Unconditioned stimulus ——▶ Unconditioned response
                (food)   (salivation)
                The bell   ——▶ No response, or irrelevant
                                              response
2 Next: ⎧ Unconditioned stimulus ——▶ Unconditioned response
             ⎪ (food)   (salivation)
             ⎨
             ⎪ Conditioned stimulus
             ⎩   bell
3 Until finally Unconditioned stimulus ——▶ Conditioned response
                bell   (salivation)

Figure 8.4 *Summary of Pavlovian conditioning*

the doctor with a painful jab and burst into tears when he walks into the room. In this case, the jab is the unconditioned stimulus and the doctor is the conditioned one. Something which did not originally call forth the 'natural' response begins to do so by being associated with it.

Extinction can occur in classical learning as well as in instrumental. Consider the examples above. If the doctor ceases to be paired with the jab, he will no longer bring forth screams when the child enters the surgery.

Similarities and differences between instrumental and Pavlovian learning

The essence of Pavlovian conditioning is the pairing of two stimuli such that the conditioned stimulus comes to elicit an involuntary response. In instrumental learning, the experimental subject performs a voluntary act such as pressing a lever or pecking a disc, and gets reward for it. In the former there is a pairing of two stimuli; in the latter, a pairing between response and reward.

Another difference between the two kinds of learning concerns extinction. In classical conditioning, extinction takes place when the two stimuli are no longer paired. In instrumental learning, extinction of the learned behaviour occurs when the positive reinforcer (or the punisher) no longer follows the learned response.

For many years psychologists tried to argue that the two kinds of learning were basically different. Skinner and his colleagues firmly believed that reinforcement stamped in a *response*. What the animal or the child learned was a specific action such as using a spoon or saying 'please'. Skinner thought he learned this because of parental rewards and punishment. Another way to look at this, however, is to claim that the child does not learn a specific response but rather some information about the relations between his own actions and adult's reward. Looked at this way, what is acquired in instrumental and Pavlovian learning is information about which things 'go together'. Learning occurs when the child or rat notices certain *associations* in the environment. Whether or not he performs an action is determined by reward and punishment. However, the learning itself is acquired when the animal notices that certain things regularly go together.

Observational learning

A third kind of learning has been studied in the laboratory and this kind appears the most effortless of all. The learner merely watches someone perform an act, then copies that person's (the model's) behaviour. Studies of observational learning have been conducted by Bandura and will be discussed in Chapter 13. What's interesting here is the fact that careful laboratory studies have demonstrated what laymen have known all along; people learn to do things by watching others. There is no need for reward, punishment, or Pavlovian conditioning.

Observational learning, often called modelling, is not hard to explain as long as one views *learning as the acquisition of information.* In the two kinds of learning discussed earlier in the chapter, learning occurred after pairing of objects or events. Here, learning requires no pairing, only a clearly performed action (say, hitting a cricket ball) in a clearly delineated context (say, during a one-day match). The learner merely watches; he need not perform. But as with other types of learning, the actual performance of a learned action at a given time and place will be influenced by the Law of Effect, although the initial learning may not be at all. And, of course, practice will make perfect . . .

What learning theories cannot explain

Recall the sophisticated studies of Piaget on the development of the child's understanding of objects. By the end of his first year the child knows that objects continue to exist when he cannot see them and that they exist in a space that's independent of his own actions on them. One day, the baby searches under the covers when a favourite toy disappears from sight, whereas the day before he lost interest as soon as it became invisible. How did he know that the toy was still there when it disappeared from his sight? Somehow, he began to search for hidden objects. If learning is the acquisition of new behaviour (and that's as good a definition as any) then we must conclude that the baby learned about **object permanence** without reward. He could not have performed his first-ever search for the missing object as a consequence of reinforcement because until that very moment, he had always lost interest. Nor had the baby been conditioned by Pavlovian procedures to find the toy because there's no natural (unconditioned) response of toy search. No, children *invent* novel actions. None of the material presented so far in this chapter can account for the baby's first search, because it all deals with the way that things in the child's surroundings (models or reinforcers) bring about learning. Piaget is concerned with a child's spontaneous learning.

Think also about the learning of language. A child may well imitate words he hears around him, saying 'milk' and 'bye bye', and get rewarded for being clever. But children do not take in learned sentences. They make up fresh ones as they need them. Some of them, perhaps, have never been said before – especially those with odd usages like 'buyed' or 'gooder'. Consider the following commonplace example. A young boy dashes into the kitchen, fresh from play in the garden, 'Mum. I runned outside'. Where did that sentence come from? He has not heard his parents use the word 'runned'. He invented it on the spot, and not surprisingly because one normally does add an *ed* to in the past tense.

There are more examples of children inventing or constructing new actions. Imagine the child sitting at Piaget's *papier maché* mountains. At six years, he does not appear to know that the mountains look different to someone sitting on the other side. Still, with no reinforcement and with no Pavlovian conditioning, one day he knows that the perspective of someone on the other side of the mountains is the opposite of his. How did this intellectual achievement come about? One might say that it was learned from experience, but one could not claim that it is learned according to the Law of Effect or the procedures of classical conditioning. Every day children invent and construct and imagine all manner of things which they have never seen before and for which they have been neither rewarded nor conditioned. It is these very constructions that intrigued Piaget. This does not deny the importance of reinforcement or conditioning. The principles of learning discussed in this chapter influence behaviour and parents and teachers use them daily (see Chapter 13). But much of the child's learning about the world, its regularities as well as its possibilities, happens quite spontaneously. Probably Piaget has come the closest to explaining how it happens. Intelligence unfolds spontaneously as the child grows older.

The contribution of learning theories to psychology

It has been argued that the theories discussed in this chapter (Law of Effect, Pavlovian conditioning, observational learning) cannot account for all of the complex and varied learning that occurs in childhood, nor indeed throughout the rest of life. So what's good about them?

(1) The learning theories discussed here bring into sharp focus the way that rewards and punishments can control behaviour. Although it was

argued earlier that learning can occur without reward or punishment, control over where and when a given action is performed is often determined by them. Although learning theories do not explain all new behaviour, they explain the forces at work in producing a given behaviour at a given time.

(2) The learning theories of Thorndike, Skinner, Pavlov and their followers are rigorously scientific. They are based on controlled laboratory experiment with a minimum of inference in interpreting the results. The work is consistently put to the test; hypotheses which are not supported by behavioural data are put aside and new ones worked out and tested. Further, various workers in this field build on one another's work, producing a unified body of investigation, sharing a common vocabulary.

However, emphasis on controlled laboratory experiment is at once a strength and weakness. Although it enables confidence in empirical results, work in the laboratory may miss out on important influences in the more natural environment. Because experimentalists look at the effect of one influence at a time (say smiling on the part of teachers), they may miss how a combination of rewards and punishments shapes behaviour in everyday life.

Some contemporary followers of Thorndike, Skinner, and Bandura leave the artificial world of the laboratory to study how reward and punishment affect children at home and school. When they do, they insist on careful definition of terms and formal hypothesis testing. However, the rigour achieved by the early theorists is often missing in the real world because every school is different, as are individual families. Still, the legacy of decades of laboratory work enables field studies of instrumental, classical and observational learning to be extremely rigorous. Learning theorists may be limited in that they miss the 'whole child', but the positive side of this limitation is a theory that lends itself to empirical test.

Thorndike and Pavlov insisted that the only way to develop the science of psychology was to study observable behaviour – not dreams, feelings or inner personality 'demons' such as the superego. The emphasis on observable behaviour of children advocated by those who call themselves 'Learning Theorists' has gone a long way towards making developmental psychology a science.

Chapter 9

Acquiring language

A girl of four was busy on the beach making 'sausage rolls' of damp sand. Her mother and a family friend sat nearby, contentedly watching. Suddenly the tide came in, drenching both child and rolls. 'Oh damn.' Her astonished mother turned to the friend in embarrassment. 'She copies her father. That's how they learn to talk, isn't it?'

The mother is only partly right. Certainly her daughter swears in English and not French because it's the language she hears at home. But the mother could hardly blame her husband if the daughter were to say 'I digged a hole', and children often invent sentences like this. Although the girl learned to swear from listening to others, imitation plays a minor role in the complex task of learning to talk. How do children understand and speak the language of their families?

Babbling and exchange games

Before babies begin to communicate, their parents have one-way conversations with them. Adults treat the burps and smiles of their young as if the child intended to tell them something and was using proper speech. Catherine Snow studied the one-sided conversations between mother and baby by visiting in the home and making audio recordings of normal family routines. Here is a sample record[1] from a baby in the first few months of life.

> MOTHER: Hello. Give me a smile (gently pokes infant in the ribs).
> BABY: (Yawns)
> MOTHER: Sleepy, are you? You woke up too early today.
> BABY: (opens fist)
> MOTHER: (touching infant's hand) What are you looking at? Can you see something.
> BABY: (grasps mother's finger)
> MOTHER: Oh, that's what you wanted. In a friendly mood, then. Come on, give us a smile.

By three or four months, the baby makes speech-like noises. Cooing and babbling reach their peak around nine or ten months when the baby

127

Figure 9.1 *Talking and discussion are essential human skills*

begins to string together sounds like 'ba-ba da go'. The sounds often have a rising and falling tone, a little like sentences, and they are produced when baby is both alone and with others. Has the baby learned to make speech-like sounds by imitating talk he hears around him?

Scientists believe that he has not. One reason for this view is that deaf babies babble despite the fact that they cannot hear adult language. Because of this many scientists think babbling is innate, an activity inherited as part of the 'pre-programmed' repertoire of the human species.

Further evidence supporting innate babbling comes from studies of children in other cultures. No matter what the parent language, babies babble in similar ways and according to a similar timetable. For example, all children begin with sounds approximating the English consonants *g* and *k* and the vowel *a*. It's not an accident that cartoonists picture babies with the sounds 'goo' and 'ga' coming from their mouths. When a little older, babies add the sounds *b*, *f* and *d* to their repertoire, whether or not these sounds feature in the language of their parents. (If children merely copied the sounds they heard, babbling would vary from culture to culture.) Further, if imitation led directly to babbled sounds, children would make all manner of noises instead of a restricted set.

Although early babbling is not language because it does not contain meaning, it can be a form of communication. Communication may be defined loosely here as a social exchange between speaker and hearer. Mothers and babies, for instance, communicate their pleasure in each other, the one talking during play and the other responding with babbles. Surely this is a deliberate communication on the part of both partners, although it's communication of feeling and not meaning.

Jerome Bruner has studied the play of mothers and babies by making video records of them in their homes.[2] He has found that communication can occur in object-games as well as in one-sided 'conversations'. Think of the simple game of give-and-take. Gradually babies as young as five months begin to take their turn in two-way games, exchanging bricks or toys instead of words. With every game of give-and-take, Bruner claims, babies acquire skill at taking turns in conversation. In less than a year they will slot words into places where action has been.

Figure 9.2 shows the history of one little boy, Richard, in the game give-and-take. At the age of 5 months 3 days he was the 'giver' less than 10 per cent of the time, and the taker quite a lot. By age 12 months 3 days, he and his mother shared the giving role about equally. Taken as a whole, Figure 9.2 shows that Richard began as a passive partner in the exchange, much like the baby in the conversation reported by Catherine Snow. Within six months, however, the little boy was an equal partner, able to give and receive objects with ease. Bruner says that the mother helps her baby learn language by doing most of the work in early exchanges. Adult assistance may be important in learning how to take conversational turns. Pure babbling, of course, appears in children with no special 'tutorial' from others. It seems that some communication skills are innate while others are learned.

Early words

With the beginning of recognizable speech, sometime around the age of one year, the baby moves to deliberate pronunciation of specific words. Now each word is expressed by a careful sequence of sounds, 'mama' and 'juice'. Instead of playing with sounds, the child controls his vocal apparatus with new precision. His vocabulary is limited to words whose pronunciation he can manage (babies never say 'thistle') and to objects and events familiar in their daily routine. Here is a conversation between a little girl, Alison and her mother.[3]

ACTION	MOTHER'S SPEECH	CHILD'S SPEECH
Alison drinks juice; takes another cup		'More'
Alison holds two cups together; putting them on floor		'More, more'
Alison reaches towards cups and can of juice. Mother pours juice in one cup	'Shall I help you? Shall I help you?' 'There.'	
Alison reaches for juice to be put in Mother's cup		'More Mama'
Mother pours juice into other cup	'OK. This is for . . .'	
Alison offers cup to Mother	'This is for Mommy?'	'Mama'
Alison taking cup from Mother	'No?'	'no'

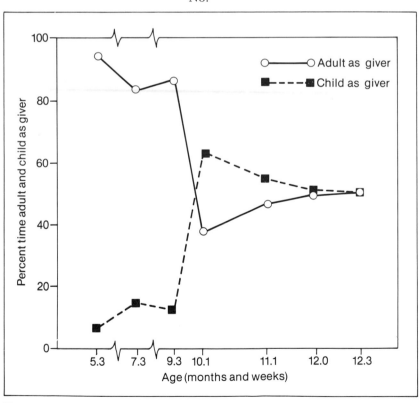

Figure 9.2 *How the game of 'give-and-take' develops over the first year. Up to the age of nine months, the adult plays the major part; by ten months or so there is a dramatic change*

Figure 9.3 *Even before babies talk, they communicate with sound and gesture*

ACTION	MOTHER'S SPEECH	CHILD'S SPEECH
Alison starting to drink juice		'da'
	'Alison gonna have it? Then Mommy'll have this, OK?'	
Alison drinks juice; Mother takes other cup.		

Alison and her mother engage in a proper conversation because the turns consist of words and not merely sounds.

Very young children acquire their first words slowly, and by the age of two they usually can say about 50 different ones. What must a child know to produce a word on his own, or to comprehend a word spoken to him by someone else? He must know the relationship between a series of spoken sounds ('bye-bye') and some real world event (such as leave-taking or disappearance). The relationship between a word and a real-world state of affairs is known as **reference** and children know something about reference well before they speak in sentences.

Piaget, and many others believe that children possess *concepts* of such things as apples, milk, hugging, jumping and possession before they utter a single word. These are part of normal sensory-motor schemas (see pages 95–7) in the first two years of life. With the beginning of language proper (i.e., meaning and not just sound play), the child learns that his sensory-motor schemas may have words attached to them. For example, at 10 months he knows much about milk and hugs, followed shortly with knowledge about the words which refer to these things.

The first 50 or so words in a child's vocabulary refer to commonplace things and events. They include important people such as 'mama' and 'daddy', favourite foods such as 'nana' (for banana), familiar animals such as 'doggie' or 'bow-wow', and action words such as 'kiss', 'hug' and 'fall'. They may also include words that describe routine events such as 'bath' or 'no' (for rejecting something).

How have we learned so much about early language? There are two methods for discovering what children know about words before they can put them together in sentences. One is to record their spontaneous speech by keeping a diary of what they have said each day. Early accounts like these were compiled by Leopold and Gregoire, as well as Piaget. Another way is to make tape or video recordings of children at selected times (say for two hours each fortnight). The diary method has the advantage of completeness because it can include every day in the child's life. If records are made at fortnightly intervals, a word present for a day or two might be missed entirely by the research. But diaries have their drawbacks too: they are often made at night or hurriedly during a busy day. For this reason, the diarist may forget important facts or be selective as to what to put into the notes. An added problem with diary accounts is the fact that there is no permanent record of how the word itself actually sounded. Recordings, on the other hand are available for countless viewings so that each detail of speech and behaviour can be scrutinized, leaving nothing to memory. However, recordings are technically difficult to make and time-consuming to analyse. Further, the machinery intrudes into family life, in some instances making the adults feel 'formal' or stilted in their activities with the child. It can be seen that there is no perfect method for studying language, although video tapes made in the child's home provide the best record of the development of words and sentences.

Once a record of child speech has been made the researcher is faced with the task of describing its meaning. This is not as easy as it appears, for children do not use words like adults do. Here is a list of children's early words, drawn from diary records of several different children, and including the referents that the child appeared to designate with each word.[4]

Word	First applied to	Later applied to
mooi	moon	cakes, round marks on windows, writing on windows and in books, round shapes in books, tooling on leather book covers, round postmarks, letter O.
buti	ball	toy, radish, stone spheres at entrance
ticktock	watch	all clocks and watches, gas meter, firehose wound on spool, bathscale with round dial
baw	ball	apples, grapes, eggs, squash, bell clapper, anything round
sch	sound of train	all moving machines
ass	toy goat with rough hide, on wheels	a few things that move (e.g. animals, sister, wagon), all things that move, all things with a rough surface
fly	fly	specks of dirt, dust, all small insects, child's own toes, crumbs of bread, a toad
bow-wow	dog	toy dog, fur piece with animal head, other fur pieces without heads

Table 9.1 *Small children's words, and what was meant by them*

Note that the words often refer to a larger group of things than an adult's would. Psychologists say that the child *over-extends* the meaning of many words. Why should he do that? One theory, proposed by E. Clark, is that the young child first associates a word with one or two particular features of an object. For instance, the child at first used 'mooi' to refer to the moon. Later, he extended it to marks on windows or in books, and even the letter O. Perhaps he had developed a rule that 'all things with round shape are known as mooi.' By using too few features to define a thing, the young child puts more objects into a word category than belong there according to the correct adult language.

Not all the over-extensions in the table are the result of the child's choosing one property for his definition; the word 'tick-tock' appears to be defined by two features: *round* and *machine-like*.

No matter how many features the child uses in his early definitions, there's no doubt that much of adult subtlety is left out. According to Clark, as the child grows older he is capable of using more and more features to define a word, till he defines them as adults do. For example, look at the word 'wristwatch'. Here, the object is defined by its time-keeping function, its size and shape, as well as its customary location on the body. This contrasts sharply with the word mooi, which is defined by only one feature.

There is other evidence concerning early word meaning and that comes from experiments on language instead of observations of spontaneous speech. Here, children are presented with miniature objects or drawings and asked to 'show me the doggie' or 'apple' or whatever. Because children respond by pointing, this is a test of word comprehension rather than word production. One study used this experimental method to discover that children knew more about word meaning than their spontaneous speech told us. For example, one child faced with several objects he himself had called 'apple' (some of which were *not* apples), pointed to the correct drawing and ignored the less appropriate objects. In cases like these, the child over-extended in production but not in comprehension.

The Clarks summarize their view:[4]

> 'These findings suggest that there may be two different steps in children's over-extensions. At the first step, they form a hypothesis about the meaning of a word – that doggie, for example, picks out mammal-shaped objects – and use that meaning both in production and comprehension. At the next step, they start gathering more information about the adult referents of doggie, aided by the non-linguistic clues adults provide as they talk to young children. For doggie, they might add that the animals are furry, bark, and so on, with the result that they learn gradually how to pick out appropriate referents for it. But since they do not yet have words for many of the objects that resemble dogs in appearance, they continue to over-extend doggie to point something out or to make a request. They stretch their meagre vocabulary to its limits in their attempts to communicate. Adults do much the same when learning a foreign language and when they come across objects they've never seen before. For example, on first seeing a zebra, one might well say it's a kind of horse.

Early sentences

Although the transition from *babbling* to *words* marks a triumph in linguistic development, there is another one ahead. With sentences, children can greatly increase the complexity of communication. The speaker who is restricted to isolated words is limited in the story he can tell and the facts he can describe. Imagine that you were witness to the following event: A boy carrying a shopping bag runs down the street. Another boy runs after him, finally managing to catch up. The second boy socks the first one on the nose, takes the bag, then ducks into a shop.

How on earth could you tell the whole story to a friend if you could not combine words into sentences. Well, you might say something like the following:

'Boy. Bag. Boy. Run. Hit. Shop.'

If you did, however, your listener would have little chance of understanding what you had seen. Who hit whom? Who did the running? What did the bag have to do with it all? And who on earth went shopping?

From this small example it can be seen that the rules for combining words into sentences enable language users to describe in precise detail things they have seen. In addition, sentences enable us to describe imaginary happenings, such as 'I saw two dancing unicorns in the garden last evening'. They also enable us to communicate our thoughts and feeling. 'I am afraid of failing.' 'Truth is stranger than fiction.' Try communicating those sentences by isolated words!

How do children learn the rules for making sentences? Most children of two years know the difference between 'the girl slapped the boy', and 'the boy slapped the girl'. Think how subtle is this difference: the words in the sentences are the same; all that varies is their order. In English sentences, the order of the words tells much of the story. Notice too in the example that the action took place in the past. Instead of 'the girl is slapping the boy' (action taking place in the present) we have the action completed in the past (e.g., past tense ending *ed*). In sum, the word order in sentences, as well as the endings on words, are part of the knowledge of mature language users. With it, they can communicate with precision, describe events not present, and even make up imaginary beings. By the age of two years, children have acquired the rudiments of sentence construction, although how they do it is still a mystery. For the next 10 years, they will increase these skills.

Studies of early sentences

One well-known scholar of children's language, Roger Brown, studied the language of three children as part of a research project lasting more than a decade.[5] Their names were Adam, Eve and Sarah. The first two were visited at home for two hours every fortnight, while Sarah was seen every week for an hour. Recording sessions were begun when children were just beginning to use more than two words together, and ended, at least in the case of Adam and Eve, when they were fluent producers of complicated English sentences.

The audio tapes collected by Brown and his colleagues were transcribed by typists and collated according to child's age. Thus, for each child a 'language corpus' was made consisting of his or her typical speech at various ages.

To begin, what do early sentences look like? Below is a small slice of a tape-recorded conversation between Adam and his mother.

ADAM	MOTHER
See truck, Mommy	
See truck.	
	Did you see the truck?
No I see truck.	
	No, you didn't see it?
	There goes one.
There go one.	
	Yes, there goes one.
See a truck.	
See truck, Mommy.	
See truck.	
Truck.	
Put truck, Mommy.	
	Put the truck where?
Put truck window.	
	I think that one's too large
	to go in the window.

Brown discovered similarities in the sentences produced by all three of the children. First, sentences were remarkably short. In fact, Brown described them as 'telegraphic'. Senders of telegrams are charged by the word, which encourages brevity, but the most penny-pinching sender cannot eliminate words on a random basis because some are more crucial to meaning than others. Suppose one wanted to convey the message 'I shall be arriving next Tuesday on the 8:05 train.' Which of the word groups below conveys its essence?

> 'arrive Tuesday 8:05 train'
> or
> 'shall next on the'

Although both sentences consist of four words, the first preserves the meaning of the original message whereas the latter does not. Brown hypothesized that children acted like senders of telegrams; they preserved the important words, the ones that conveyed most of the meaning, and eliminated the smaller 'functor' words (whose function was to modulate meaning).

Children not only know which are 'important' words and which ones they can leave out, they also know correct English word order. Some children's sentences are listed below, followed by their mothers 'expansion' of their children's speech into adult-style talk.[5]

CHILD	MOTHER
Baby highchair	Baby is in the highchair
Mommy eggnog	Mommy had her eggnog
Eve lunch	Eve is having lunch
Mommy sandwich	Mommy'll have a sandwich
Throw Daddy	Throw it to Daddy
Pick glove	Pick the glove up

Notice that children know enough of the rules of English grammar to put the subject of the sentences first (when the sentence has a subject) and the object of the verb last (when the verb takes an object). A **grammar** can be thought of as a system of rules for combining words into sentences. Anyone with a knowledge of English grammar will recognize that the following sentences are in accord with it:

All students study diligently
A ghost addressed me last evening

whereas these are not:

Study students diligently all
Evening last addressed ghost a

To summarize so far, children's first sentences are shorter than adults' because they eliminate the small 'functor' words (such as 'the', 'to' and 'am') as well as word endings (such as 'ing'). Their use of adult word order shows that they have a rudimentary knowledge of grammar. With it, they can invent sentences they have never heard before.

'Light bye bye' (when a candle flame goes out)
'Door cry' (when a creaky door squeaks)

With new-found knowledge about combining words into sentences, children can express the following meanings.[6]

---

1. They talk about actions, what happened to what and who does what:
   'Me fall.'
   'Bump table.'
   'Car go vroom!'
2. They are concerned, not to say obsessed, with the relationship of possession:
   'My teddy.'
   'Mommy hat.'
   'Daddy hair.'
3. Equally prevalent is the relationship of location:
   'Cup in box.'
   'Car garage.'
   'Mommy outside.'
4. Among other early meanings that find frequent expression at this stage are recurrence:
   'More milk.'
   'Tickle again.'
5. Nomination, or labelling:
   'That Teddy.'
   'This steamroller.'
6. And nonexistence:
   'Beads all gone.'
   'No more soup.'

Table 9.2 *Six different categories of early meaning*

Although the sentences of children two or three years old are short and lacking in functor words, they express a variety of meanings, including action statements, statements about possession and location, and even non-existence. What is even more interesting is that children learning different languages, including German, Hebrew and even Samoan, express the same kinds of meanings in their two and three word sentences. Brown argues that early sentences are much the same no matter which language the child speaks because they depend on, and are restricted to, the everyday schemas of sensory-motor intelligence.

Although we do not know for certain how children learn to combine words into sentences, studies such as those of Roger Brown provide some clues. Their learning task may be simplified because they don't express *all* kinds of adult meanings at first. By concentrating on the limited set of meanings listed above, the rules they must learn are reduced to a manageable number.

What are the meanings the young child cannot express? How is his language limited? Note that the sentences listed above had no instances of negation (I am *not* going), past tense (I walk*ed* home) plurals (here are the apple*s*) articles (I ate *an* apple) or questions (*Are you cross* with me?). No doubt children notice such things as number and past-present time, but they cannot yet express them in grammatical sentences. By the time children enter school, however, such complexities of grammar will be old hat.

Playing with language

Bruner argues that the baby's sound play and exchange games help him acquire turn-taking skills. But does the usefulness of play diminish once the child has learned to talk? Courtney Cazden believes that language play is as important to school children as it is to babies because it *focuses attention* on the sounds and meanings of language.[7] In the school years, rhyming games, nonsense songs, even riddles focus attention on the sounds and meanings of language and help children to spell, read and write. Think of the educational riches in the following riddle.

QUESTION: What goes BRM BRM under the water?
ANSWER:　Motor pike and side carp.

Part Two

Theory into practice

Who needs psychology? Psychologists study humans (and animals) systematically to find out 'what makes people tick' and what causes different kinds of behaviour. Developmental psychologists are particularly interested in children and in the process of both normal and abnormal development. Humans are complicated organisms, so there are many different aspects of children's development: emotional, physical, social, and intellectual are major areas. Part One has considered some major studies in developmental psychology which have led to theories of development. Psychological 'giants' such as Bowlby, Freud and Piaget have tried to explain how and why children develop the way they do. Others have asked questions such as 'How many basic abilities does a baby have at birth and how much does he have to learn?' Psychologists have been fascinated by how a baby learns skills such as talking, and later on other complex skills.

George Miller, a well-known American psychologist, asked a particularly important question in a speech entitled 'Psychology as a means of promoting human welfare'. It was, 'Why can't we give psychology away?' In other words, why are practitioners not using psychology? Although, as we shall see, there are increasingly areas in which workers in the field *are* using the research findings of psychology, a lot of new knowledge is simply neglected, and the reason why is an urgent issue facing future developmental psychologists.

Consider the idea of 'Psychology as a means of promoting human welfare'. Nurses, teachers, social workers, all those in the 'helping' and 'caring' professions, use their own explanation of human behaviour in their everyday work. Nurses use psychology when dealing with patients and indeed with doctors, teachers often show psychological insight in their handling of difficult (or not-difficult) pupils, while adults working in preschool groups reveal an often intuitive understanding of child development with their four-year-olds. So of course do parents. All these are using some form of psychological understanding or knowledge. We saw in Chapter 1 that psychologists try to go beyond commonsense to build a scientific theory of human behaviour. Yet theories presented in an introductory psychology textbook sometimes seem irrelevant to practice in the field.

Why is this? One reason is that psychologists doing research have tended to use experimental methods in the laboratory and these have forced them into artificial situations. In an attempt to construct scientific theories, they studied behaviour isolated from real life in carefully controlled conditions in the laboratory. Practitioners, on the other hand, worked to a large extent by trial and error in a situation where very few variables were ever constant. So although psychologists might have produced elegant theories, they offered little to the practitioners working in the busy classroom, the multiply-deprived family, or the noisy children's home. The artificiality of the laboratory situation caused many practitioners to doubt the representativeness of research findings and set them to look for theoretical backing from other subjects. Furthermore, the communication of the psychological findings has always been difficult since they are usually written up in learned journals and not readily accessible to practitioners.

We are all familiar with the fact that babies and children behave differently in different situations. In fact their parents do too. As will be discussed in Chapter 16, factors such as these have led to an increasing interest in research carried out in the child's own home or 'natural environment' where it is hoped that findings will give a more full picture of the child's 'whole' development and therefore have more practical relevance. Recently, developmental psychologists have been carrying out observational studies of mothers and babies at home, children in playgroup and nursery, as well as older children at school. These are areas in which psychological theory is increasingly informing practice or where applied psychologists have used psychological theory with clients or students. Research on mothering and observations of mother–baby interactions are now informing practice and policy in substitute care; observations of nurseries and playgroups do now help teachers and playleaders structure and plan the preschool environment and make the most of the time, materials and adults available. Learning theories do inform classroom practice, and theories of abnormal development form the foundation for therapeutic techniques.

Some of these areas will form the basis for Part Two of this book. Although the applications do not coincide directly with the theories in Part One, there are many close links. Much of Bowlby's work and later research has influenced policies on substitute care and working mothers. Freud's theories have had a wide influence both on the practice of therapy (psychoanalysis and play therapy) and also on our everyday explanations and understanding of some human behaviour. Piaget's work has informed education, and teachers, particularly in the USA, have tried out Piagetian curricula; many nursery and infant schools in the UK show the impact of the Piagetian concept of development.

Some applications are more well-developed than others. Applied psychologists, for instance in education, have developed sophisticated techniques of intelligence testing. Also, clinical psychologists have constructed different and sensitive therapies. On the other hand, the learning theories covered in Chapter 8, though very thoroughly researched by psychologists, have been slow to inform the practice of teachers or students, not surprisingly perhaps when much of the early research on learning was carried out on animals and in the laboratory. Nevertheless there are interesting applications from theories of learning, as will appear in Chapter 13. The area of the preschool, including aspects of mothering, caring, educating and social development, is one of the areas of most fruitful and prolific growth, both in research and in practice. Joint enterprise, between researchers and practitioners, is one of the most important ways in which psychology may contribute to practice, because researchers benefit from practical experience while practitioners profit from the discipline and perspective of science.

Part Two shows applications of psychology at different ages through childhood. This does not mean that each area of application is appropriate only to that particular age. Therapy and intelligence tests are discussed here in the context of older children, though of course they are useful with younger children too. Learning occurs throughout life, certainly not just during childhood. Preschool applications are by definition mainly restricted to the younger child, but much of the psychological theory behind them applies almost equally well to older children.

David Wood has said that 'the challenge facing the next generation of development psychologists is clearly not simply one of refining and revolutionizing their hypotheses about the nature of human growth. It is perhaps not too preposterous to say that their primary problem will be one of "giving psychology away".'

Figure 10.1 *The start of one little boy's day with a childminder*

Chapter 10

Early childhood: substitute mothers

There are today many children who are not cared for all the time by their own parents. Fathers bringing up children on their own and mothers who go out to work both need part-time help in caring for their children. Some mothers are under pressure and unable to care for their children, and these too need some form of alternative mothering. Also, children are born to parents who do not want them. There is a wide variety of provision for children whose parents are unable to provide complete care. It ranges from permanent adoption or temporary fostering to part-day childminding or nursery care. An increasing number of children are cared for in this way as economic and social pressures make it less possible for mothers to stay at home all day. What does psychological research contribute to practice in this area?

If we were to accept Bowlby's theory (Chapter 3) that continuous care by one mother (or full-time stand-in for mother) is as essential to a baby's emotional development as vitamins are to his health, then we would have to be fearful for the well-being of thousands of preschool children. Bowlby considered that there was a unique and irreversible bond between mother and child, and that if it were broken or absent, there would be abnormality in later years. Fortunately, recent research (see Chapter 4) has shown that babies are more flexible and resilient than Bowlby thought, and that the bond between mother and child, though important, is not exclusive, irreplaceable or irreversible. In fact babies are capable of forming attachments to several adults; they adapt to new situations, and they even recover from quite severe early deprivation. This does not mean that affectionate and continuing care is not important to children's emotional development, only that it does not have to come in the rigid form Bowlby supposed.

In this chapter we look at research studies of children who are cared for some or all of the time by adults other than their own parents. This should not only reveal how successful those forms of care are; it should help show which aspects of the mother–child relationships are important and should be incorporated in the care provided. This chapter will look at adoption, fostering, childminding and day nurseries, and also at the outcomes of these alternative forms of care. Substitute mothering is discussed here mainly as it relates to babies, though of course the findings apply also to older children.

Adoption and fostering

It has recently been shown that children do form an attachment to an adoptive mother even when adopted at quite a late age, and that there is not a critical point by which children must have formed their attachments, as Bowlby suggested. Most adopted children form successful relationships with their 'new' mothers and develop normally, though of course this is also affected by their emotional environments both before and after being adopted. A child who has had a succession of different caretakers before adoption, or one who is adopted into a home full of conflict, is likely to find it more difficult to settle and form attachments than another, luckier, child who is similar in other ways.

Foster children are often older when placed than adopted children. They also frequently stay in contact with their own families (which may be very problematic), and may have suffered severe and lengthy deprivation and conflict before they are fostered. Yet for them too attachments within a substitute family are possible and usually successful.

Follow-up studies

Most follow-up studies of adopted or fostered children now grown up suggest that the majority of children recover from early adverse circumstances and go on to live normal and healthy lives as adults. These studies are usually retrospective: they contact as adults people who were adopted when they were children. There are not many such studies, partly because they are difficult to carry out, but both British and American investigators have found evidence to show that the vast majority of fostered and adopted children do grow up able to cope. It looks as though children who are placed below the age of five years fare best of all (though it may be that children adopted young are exactly those who seem to have fewer problems in the first place). But overall the results suggest largely favourable outcomes of adoption, perhaps because adoptive parents are even more motivated and caring than the average natural parents.

The Triseliotis follow-up study

John Triseliotis reported a follow-up study of forty people born in 1956–57 who had spent between seven and 15 years each in a single foster home before the age of 16.[1] He interviewed both them and their foster parents when the children were 20–21 years old, and attempted to assess the success of the fostering relationship. Again what appeared to be important was the quality and continuity of the care and the relationship; he found that if this was adequate the effects of earlier disruptions and suffering faded and were eventually reversed so as to allow the children to develop normally. He found that 60 per cent of the former foster children were coping very well and concluded that people who grow up in long-term foster homes where they are wanted and integrated as part of the family generally do well in later life.

The Tizard study of adopted children

Barbara Tizard and her colleagues Judith Rees and Jill Hodges studied a sample of 65 children who had been placed in residential nurseries before the age of four months, and who when they were three were either adopted, returned to their mothers or left in the nursery.[2,3] This study is a LONGITUDINAL STUDY which followed the development of these children over a period of time in order to look closely at their progress.

> LONGITUDINAL STUDY
> In a longitudinal study the investigator studies one group of subjects at regular intervals over a long period of time, for example once a year for ten years. This method clearly takes a long time to produce results, in contrast to A CROSS SECTIONAL STUDY, which samples several groups at different ages.
>   Barbara Tizard carried out a longitudinal study when she followed a group of institutionalized children to see how staying in the institution, being adopted, or returning to their parents affected them.

The nurseries provided plenty of stimulation and toys and nurses but the nurses rarely stayed with the nursery long, and so were actively discouraged from forming close relationships with the children, since these would inevitably be broken off. In fact, it was found that on average 25 different nurses had worked with each child for at least a week by the time he was two years old. Thus, up to the age of about three-and-a-half, none of the children had had the opportunity to form an attachment to a particular mother figure, and the emotional atmosphere of the nurseries was cool. Compared with children living in families, these nursery children were more clinging, and less willing to approach strange adults, but also shallowly attached to a large number of nurses. In other respects, their behaviour was little different from any other children.

Four groups of children were compared: a group who remained in the institution, an adopted group, a group who were restored to their mothers, and a CONTROL group who were with their families all along. The children were followed up at two years of age, four-and-a-half and eight. At two, when all the children (except the controls) were still in the institution, none had formed an attachment to a mother or mother substitute, but by four-and-a-half more than half had. Twenty of the 25 adoptive parents were deeply attached to 'their' children and believed those children were deeply attached in return. However, though the adoptive parents were highly motivated and spent much time and energy giving their children the adult attention and affection they craved, at four-and-a-half years, those adopted children were still more attention-seeking and overfriendly than the controls. So clearly there was some residual effect of the early institutional upbringing.

At eight, the adopted children were compared again. By now the adoptive parents all believed the children had formed deep attachments to them, but many of them still said they believed the nursery experience had affected the children unfavourably, since they had grown difficult to manage and were still unnaturally over-affectionate. At school too the adopted children (and the children restored to their parents also) tended to be more restless, fidgety, irritable and quarrelsome, and to have problems in making friendships with other children. All this suggests that though children from institutions do become attached to their new 'parents', and though they do grow up to lead quite normal lives, nonetheless some aspects of their behaviour may take a lot of time and effort to alter. This takes great patience and maturity, and strong motivation – which people prepared to go to the trouble of adoption usually have. In fact, in the Tizard study, the children restored to their own parents fared less well than those who were adopted.

Though it is clearly better to adopt sooner rather than later, children can be successfully adopted when they are far from babies. In the Tizard study, six children who were still in the nursery at the age of four-and-a-half were subsequently adopted. In the United States, Alfred Kadushin made a follow-up study of 91 children adopted between five and 12 years of age and found that the great majority were perfectly successful. Tizard concludes that 'compared with the alternative placements available to these children, that is, continued institutionalization, long-term fostering, or restoration to their natural families, adoption seems clearly the best solution to the children's needs'.

These studies have shown that children are capable of forming close attachments to 'new' mothers even at a late age (up to 12). Clearly there are enormous differences in the earlier life experiences of the children placed for adoption and in the ways in which these children respond and adapt to their circumstances. Yet the vast majority of them show a resilience in the face of deprivation and an ability to respond to a warm and continuous adult relationship even after a severely disrupted early childhood. The qualities which seem to be important in a foster mother or adoptive mother are naturally those that matter in a natural mother (except that they are needed in larger measure): they are warmth, consistency and the stimulation and attention which makes a child feel he belongs. It has been suggested that the crucial characteristic of the parental role is its partiality for the individual child; the child needs to know that to someone he matters more than other children, and that someone will go to *unreasonable* lengths, not just reasonable ones, for his sake. For most adopted children, this is indeed the case, for they are usually fulfilling the adoptive parents' long-felt desire for a child.

Early experience

Research evidence leaves no room for doubt that the first five years of life are important for emotional, intellectual and social development. This is a time when a child is developing most rapidly, and is learning more than at any other time in his life. Indeed Freud wrote 'neuroses are only acquired during early childhood (up to the age of six), even though their symptoms may not make their appearance until much later . . . the events of the first years are of paramount importance for . . . a child's whole subsequent life . . .'.

However, psychologists have more recently reached the conclusion that it is not *just* the first five years that matter so much. Later years matter also. Enduring influences make an enduring impression, whereas children usually recover from transient disturbances or disruptions. Ann and Alan Clarke, who were among the first to take this view, pointed out that in real life it is rare for problems before the age of five *not* to be followed by problems later, so one cannot claim that only those before five were important. Family breakdown at four, for instance, might be followed by lower standards of care, lower living standards, behaviour problems at school, all leading to further trouble and disturbance. One couldn't say that only the family breakdown would have affected a child's future behaviour: events following the breakdown were just as responsible. In fact, without the continuing disruption the child would recover and behave quite normally again. Children are more resilient and adaptable than previously thought, and development is a continuous interaction between a child's genetic makeup and his constantly changing environment. And the child of course plays an active part in determining what the environment will be. His behaviour affects the way people treat him, which in turn affects his behaviour.

Caring outside the home

In a society in which increasingly mothers are going out to work when their children are still quite young, part-time care is needed more and more. Bowlby's original claim that the young child needed the continuous

149

and uninterrupted presence of the mother in order to grow up normally, and his statement 'if you don't do your five years' hard labour when the child is young, you do it later', had a profound effect on mothers in the 1950s. Pressures on mothers today are often conflicting. Economic and other factors demand that they go out to work to supplement the family income, while baby books offer different advice on the advantages and disadvantages to both mother and child of her working outside the home. Some recommend her to stay at home at least for the first few years, while others point out the benefits both to mother and to baby of some time off in their life together. For many mothers there is no choice but to go out to work. And there are many single mothers and single fathers. What are the implications of the 'shared care' when the parent goes out to work and the child is cared for by somebody else?

Surprisingly little research has been done on this question, but what has been done suggests that shared care need not alter the way a child becomes attached. Children do form attachments to several adults (see Chapter 4) and the strength of their attachment seems to depend not on continued presence as much as on the quality of the time together. A child is more likely to develop a strong attachment to an adult who plays, talks and responds attentively for two hours a day than to one who is at hand all day but engaged in washing-up or other tasks which do not involve the child.

Who looks after the child when mother (or father) is away at work? There is a variety of provision available: childminders or day nurseries for full-time care: schools and playgroups (as well as other local groups) for part-time. Childminders are usually women who look after young children in their own homes. Day nurseries are run by Social Service Departments, and children between the age of one month and five years are admitted if they are thought to need care on social or medical grounds. Nursery schools on the other hand are run by education authorities and they are more interested in early learning than in physical care. There are also some combined centres which aim to integrate the two forms of nursery provision. In the remainder of this chapter, we will discuss childminding and day nurseries. Nursery schools and classes are covered on pages 173–82.

How successful is preschool care in contributing to the children's well-being? What aspects of the mother–child relationship are transferrable to care outside the home? What sort of a relationship does the childminder have with a child? Do children thrive in a day nursery? What can a mother do to help a child to feel easy with a new caretaker, away from his own home?

Childminders

Childminders are usually married women with their own families who earn some money by looking after other people's children for part of every day; they are required by law to be registered with the local authority and are the responsibility of Social Service Departments. They usually take between one and four children into their own homes and care for them alongside their own children. From what we know about children becoming attached to many adults, childminding ought to be the ideal form of care. Also, according to Lady Plowden, 'Childminders . . . can give a young child that continuity of relationship in a homelike atmosphere within the community that is so important to his development if his own mother cannot care for him during the day.' Ideally the childminder would offer the child a chance to form another strong attachment and increase his experience of the world outside home while letting him keep his main attachment – to his mother. But what are the realities?

Two studies of childminding

Betty Mayall and Pat Patrie used INTERVIEW and NATURALISTIC OB-SERVATION methods to study 39 registered childminders living in London: they interviewed the minders and the mothers and observed the children with both.[4] They found bad news: 'The children' they said, 'spent a low-level, under-stimulated day in unchanging, often cramped surroundings. Many did not get the love and attention they needed.' But that study was set in a tough, deprived, inner-city area, with all kinds of problems. Perhaps this wasn't a fair sample of childminding (though it tells us a lot about life in inner cities).

SURVEY METHOD

A survey is a collection of information about people or events. The investigators may use INTERVIEWS to collect the information, or they may use official records or questionnaires instead. Some surveys use large numbers of subjects – for instance the National Opinion Poll. The Census surveys the entire population.

The other study, carried out by Bridget Bryant, Miriam Harris and Dee Newton, looked at minding in Oxfordshire.[5] They found no bad housing, no overcrowding – none of the problems of depressed inner London. The minders were warm, affectionate and conscientious. Yet still there were problems.

This study was a SURVEY. The researchers interviewed mothers and minders. (The interviews were based on a questionnaire so they would follow a similar pattern and could be compared with one another.) They also made an interview recording of the minders' and mothers' diaries of 'yesterday', and 20-minute observations of each child at home and at the

Figure 10.2 *At the childminders. This minder knows the value of play*

minders. They set out to look both at the quality of care and at whether the children were thriving. What they found is of great interest.

On the care side:

1. Fewer than one in four of the minders thought the mothers should stay and settle their children in for the first few days. More than half preferred them to leave the children at the door and go straight off. Yet the psychological research into attachment tells us that this is bound to lead to distress.

2. The minders led busy lives, and had little time to give individual attention to the children in their care.

3. They also felt their job was to look after, not to stimulate or educate. Yet research shows that a loving relationship requires plenty of play and chat – interaction and stimulation for both adult and child. We also know that understimulation results in poor intellectual, emotional and language development.

So how did the children thrive?

1. One in four seemed to thrive quite well.

2. Of the rest, about half were unnaturally quiet, passive, detached and 'good' at the minders, but quite happy at home. And half were too quiet and good at both places.

3. Some children, about one in four of the total, were clearly

disturbed or in distress, or had impoverished speech. They needed help.

Bryant, Harris and Newton suggested that, since the childminders of the unhappy children were not detectably different from those of the happy ones, it might be that some children were just not suited to minding. Those would be the ones who were already insecure at home, worried whether their parents wanted them. They would be 'good' and withdrawn at home and would tend to behave in the same way in another home too. The minder, after trying and failing to 'get through' might become a bit distant herself. That would confirm the child's worries about being rejected – he would have another 'bad' relationship.

But Bryant and her colleagues showed that minding *can* work. They blame the fact that it often doesn't partly on the fact that mothers and minders hardly talk to each other – not about what matters anyway. Their relationship is rather ambiguous. The minder doesn't set out to replace the mother, yet she is one herself and the child is in her home on her terms. If he doesn't seem happy, his mother is reluctant to say so – that would be criticizing another mother. And the minder may feel – often rightly – that the mother doesn't want to accept that her child is unhappy. If she *has* to go to work for instance, she may not be able to do much about it except worry.

New relationships require careful preparation and handling if they are to be good for a child. First, great care should be taken to help each child to get to know his minder, and to settle him in when he starts. Mother and minder should care for the child together for a while before the minder takes over. And they should constantly compare notes on how the child is behaving and developing. Is he showing some abnormal or unusual behaviour while he is at the minder's? Minders also need to spend less time on their own chores and more time actively stimulating and playing with the child. Also, children should be encouraged and able to bring their own toys to the minder's so that they feel a sense of identity and continuity which enables them to settle and thrive. Finally, minders should be on the watch for children who are excessively passive, quiet and well-behaved; they may have problems.

Day nurseries

The other form of full-time care is the day nursery, usually run by Social Services Departments for children deemed to be 'in need' on social or medical grounds. The reasons for admission to day nurseries are usually poor housing, the disability of the child or his parents, or the need to provide relief for a single parent under severe stress. Children who attend these nurseries are therefore often very needy – physically, emotionally, and socially.

Figure 10.3 *The day nursery is home between the hours of nine and five*

A typical day nursery provides for between 20 and 65 children of a wide age range (one month to five years). In theory, nurseries have four main objectives, though in practice emphasis varies between nurseries: (i) physical care and comfort, including feeding; (ii) emotional development and a sense of security and confidence; (iii) help in handling relationships with other children and adults; (iv) basic language and educational skills in preparation for formal schooling. In contrast with nursery schools and classes, most (not all) day nurseries tend to emphasize physical care and training, particularly since so many of the children are in such desperate need of basic physical provision and comfort.

Observational study of nurseries

Caroline Garland and Stephanie White made a NATURALISTIC OBSERVATION

Figure 10.4 *Children play with one another while their parents work*

study of a small sample of children in day nurseries (although their study also included private nurseries and playgroups).[6] They found a clear distinction between nurseries who felt their main task was to help deprived children with *intellectual* difficulties (for instance learning to talk) and those who felt their chief tasks were physical *care* and emotional support. ((i) to (iii) in the paragraph above). Commitment to both together seemed impossible. Garland and White found that the distinction in what the nurseries thought they were for coincided exactly with another distinction. The care-oriented nurseries tended to be rather child-centred places (or child-and-parent-centred places) where the nurses believed the children should decide what they wanted and needed, and that their views should where possible be respected. The education-oriented nurseries tended to be much more rigid places, where nurses felt they were the experts who knew what was best, and that if they relaxed their grip chaos might break out.

Day nurseries differ widely in how far they believe that 'care is education and education is care', but since they do cater for small children in need – and also for their parents, who may also be in need, depressed or inadequate, Garland and White suggest that it is the *care* orientation that is the right one, and that children will in any case not advance much intellectually while they feel insecure. There must of course be stimulation too, but not at the expense of emotional warmth.

Do substitute mothers work out?

Looking at adoption and fostering, the answer appears to be yes, on the whole. Adoptive and foster mothers are capable of taking over the essential aspects of the maternal role, do form strong attachments with 'their' children, and do bring them back towards healthy development even after severe deprivation. In many ways it seems easier to be a full-time substitute mother than a part-time one.

Looking at childminding and day nurseries, the answer is less clear. According to current attachment theory, shared caretaking should work well. Mothers should be able to go out to work having formed the primary attachment with their children, provided that they spend time actively and attentively involved with their children some time each day. Those children should be able to form a 'secondary' attachment to other adults, including childminders or nursery nurses. Young children usually form attachments to several adults – a hierarchy of attachments, with one or two primary attachment adults and possibly several others to whom they have formed less strong attachments. An outside caretaker, whether minder or nursery nurse, is not a substitute mother, but part of a caretaking continuum on which different levels of attachment coexist to ensure emotional security for a young child. Looked at this way, childminding and day nurseries should 'work'. The fact that they often do not can be explained by lack of communication and lack of knowledge. This is an area where psychological research really does have a lot to offer.

Chapter 11

Early childhood: play

When a mother says to her young child 'Go and play', she might mean throw a ball, pretend to be a doctor, mould a plasticine model, paint a picture, shake a rattle, chase another child, play a game of marbles, or any one of a wide variety of activities. It may be difficult to see what these different activities have in common but it is clear that they are all spontaneous, active and pleasurable for their own sakes.

Most people would agree that play is a 'good thing'. Young children get enormous pleasure from painting, pretending and make-believe, stories, making things, and other play activities. No-one would doubt the pure enjoyment value of play. But what is the significance of it? Is it sufficient to leave a child in a room with toys or objects? Will he play spontaneously? Which activities do children enjoy at different ages? Is there a purpose to play other than enjoyment? How can adults best join in? These are some of the questions to which psychologists have been turning, realizing as they do that the child's first five years, during which he may spend a considerable amount of time at play, matter particularly. How does play contribute to overall preschool development? Is it important? It would be useful to have the answers to some of these questions so that preschool children both at home and at playgroup could get the most out of their play. Nursery teachers and playgroup leaders could be more confident that they were providing the best possible opportunity for each child.

Throughout childhood each new skill that is learned means a new game to be played. The one-and-a-half-year-old is usually quite happy playing on his own, discovering and repeating different actions, practising skills he has mastered and exploring their variations, apparently enjoying the movements for their own sake. Then, by the age of three, children are happy playing together in small groups and learning about life through pretend and make-believe; the most simple cardboard box may become a fire engine and Teddy an endangered child. Such make-believe clearly serves an important function and will be considered later. After a child enters school at the age of 5, his play tends increasingly to be dominated by complicated situations and rules, showing the increasing complexity of his understanding and thought.

In this chapter we will be considering how the different kinds of play are

Figure 11.1 *Play*

closely linked to a child's development. Jean Piaget (see Chapter 7) carefully studied the different kinds of play of children of different ages including his own. He then constructed a theory which explained how play fits in with overall development and the important function which play serves in the development of intelligence.

Piaget's theory

Piaget considered that the development of play was closely linked with the development of intelligence and moreover that one clue to the stage of a child's development might be found by observing his play. For Piaget play has an important role in the development of intelligence of which the opportunity to master and practise skills at different stages of development is an example.

Chapter 7 introduced Piaget's theory of the development of intelligence and its stages: sensory-motor, pre-operational, operational. These stages are mirrored in the different types of play (mastery play, symbolic or make-believe play, and play with rules) which characterize children of different ages, although children absorb and incorporate play from earlier stages into the play appropriate to their current age.

For instance, this is Piaget's daughter Jacqueline at about one year:[1]

> J. was sitting on her cot and I hung her celluloid duck above her. She pulled a string hanging from the top of the cot and in this way shook the duck for a moment, laughing. Her involuntary movements left an impression on her eiderdown: she then forgot the duck, pulled the eiderdown towards her and moved the whole of it with her feet and arms. As the top of the cot was also being shaken, she looked at it, stretched up then fell back heavily, shaking the whole cot. After doing this some 10 times, J. again noticed her duck: she then grasped a doll also hanging from the top of the cot and went on shaking it, which made the duck swing. Then noticing the movement of her hands she let everything go, so as to clasp and shake them (continuing the preceding movement). Then she pulled her pillow from under her head, and having shaken it, struck it hard and struck the sides of the cot and the doll with it. As she was folding the pillow, she noticed the fringe, which she began to suck. This action, which reminded her of what she did every day before going to sleep, caused her to lie down on her side, in the position for sleep, holding a corner of the fringe and sucking her thumb. This, however, did not last for half a minute and J. resumed her earlier activity.
>
> This sequence of behaviours makes plain the difference between play and strictly intelligent activity. In the case of the schemas successively tried out with new objects J. merely sought to assimilate the objects, and, as it were, to 'define them by use'. Since there was adaptation of the schemas to an external reality which constituted a problem, there was intelligence properly so called. In the present case, on the contrary, although the process is the same, the schemas follow one after the other without any external aim. The objects to which they are applied are no longer a problem, but merely serve as an opportunity for activity. This activity is no longer an effort to learn, it is only a happy display of known actions.

Piaget called this mastery play, or practice play, and it corresponded to his sensory-motor stage of development (0 to 2 years). Just as during the sensory-motor period, the baby enjoys movements for their own sake and learns to master and coordinate motor skills, so in play he begins to practise and control his movements and to explore the world of touch, sight and sound, and the effects he can have on them. This sort of play consists mainly of repetitive movements and exploration. Piaget distinguishes between play and 'strictly intelligent activity', and wrote 'after learning to grasp, swing, throw etc., which involve both an effort of accommodation to new situations, and an effort of repetition . . . the child sooner or later (often even during the learning period) grasps for the pleasure of grasping, swings for the sake of swinging, etc. In a word, he repeats his behaviour not in any further effort to learn or to investigate, but for the mere joy of mastering it and of showing off to himself his own power of subduing reality'.

Symbolic or make-believe play

At about the age of two, Piaget observed his daughter Jacqueline play a new and very different kind of game.[1]

> At 2;1(9) J. put her doll's head through the balcony railings with its face turned towards the street, and began to tell it what she saw: 'You see the lake and the trees. You see a carriage, a horse,' etc. The same day she seated her doll on a sofa and told it what she herself had seen in the garden.
>
> At 2;1(13) she fed it, talking to it for a long time in the way used to encourage her to eat her own meals: 'A little drop more. To please Jacqueline. Just eat this little bit.' At 2;3(25) she set it astride a gate and pulled its hair back from its ears to make it listen to a musical box. At 2;7(15) she explained her own games to it: 'You see, I'm throwing the ball,' etc.
>
> At 2;5(25) she prepared a bath for L. A blade of grass represented the thermometer, the bath was a big box and she merely stated that the water was there. J. then plunged the thermometer into the bath and found the water too hot. She waited a moment and then put the grass in again: 'That's all right, thank goodness.' She then went up to L. (she actually did so) and pretended to take off her apron, her dress, her vest, making the movements but not touching the clothes. At 2;8(0) she played the same game.
>
> At 2;6(22) she walked to and fro pretending to be holding a baby in her arms. She carefully put it down on an imaginary bed, made it go to sleep, 'Go to sleep, baby,' then woke it and picked it up. The same day she pretended to be carrying her mother: 'Mummy's very heavy,' then imitated the farmer's wife feeding her hens, with her apron turned up (but without anything in it). Already the detail of all these scenes was quite well developed, but there was no symbolic object; the words were only accompanied by gestures. The game with the imaginary baby recurred at 2;7(1) with new details, but J. stopped talking when anyone came near. From a distance she was heard saying: 'Now we're going for a walk,' etc. The same day she was carrying in her arms a young lady she had recently seen. At 2;7(1) she added a new subject, the postman, and reading a letter.

This symbolic or make-believe play coincided with the pre-operational

Figure 11.2 *Six-year-old boys transform themselves into firemen in make-believe play, while two girls become 'ladies' chatting over the telephone*

period (approximately 2 to 7 years). This is the age at which the child uses symbols in play, learns language and how to pretend by making something stand for something else. The essence of pretend play is that the child transforms himself or an object into something else. Jacqueline made the grass stand for the thermometer and herself stand for the mother. At this stage symbolic play becomes the predominant form of play, since the child is rapidly learning language and trying out his use of words and symbols.

For Piaget, this ability to symbolize or make something stand for something else is important in helping the child transform sensory-motor schemas into concepts. The child of two years who understands how to make a blade of grass stand for a thermometer, for example, is also learning how to make a word stand for a thing.

An American psychologist, Catherine Garvey, admirably showed how language is the vehicle for make-believe play when she carried out a NATURALISTIC OBSERVATION study of pairs of children playing behind a one-way viewing window in a nursery school.[2] The children were observed in a playroom and each 15-minute session was videotaped. In this way she was able to make a detailed analysis of children's spontaneous play in a social situation and found that although young children take time in learning to interact with other children, three-year-old children were capable of sustaining a make-believe conversation together, particularly if left alone by adults. Here is one of Catherine Garvey's recordings which illustrates some of the components of pretending and conversation.

At the beginning of the extract the girl is holding a baby doll and the boy is watching her put it to bed. At (3) she herself assumes the role of the baby and shows it by speaking in a higher-than-normal pitch, with a whining tone. The asterisks indicate her out-of-baby-role (i.e. she is being herself and giving directions to the boy, whose parental role she is prompting). These prompts are produced in her normal speaking voice. At (26) she resumes her own identity and asks a literal question, thus ending the episode of make-believe.

Girl (3 years 3 months)	Boy (2 years 9 months)
*(1) Say 'Go to sleep now.'	
	(2) Go to sleep now
(3) Why? (Whining)	
	(4) Baby . . .
(5) Why?	
	(6) Because
*(7) No, say 'Because!' (emphatically)	
	(8) Because! (emphatically)
(9) Why? Because why?	
	(10) Not good. You bad.

(11) Why?

        (12) 'Cause you spill your milk.'

*(13) No 'Cause I bit somebody.'

        (14) Yes, you did.

*(15) Say 'Go to sleep. Put your
      head down.' (sternly)

        (16) Put your head down. (sternly)

(17) No.

        (18) Yes.

(19) No.

        (20) Yes, okay, I will spank you.
            Bad boy. (spanks her)

(21) My head's up (giggles)
(22) I want my teddy bear
      (petulant voice)

        (23) No, your teddy bear go away
            (sternly)

(24) Why?

        (25) Cause he does (walks off with
            teddy bear)

*(26) Are you going to pack your
      teddy bear?

This make-believe dialogue shows the child using special voice effects to signal pretence. These children are exploring aspects of their own lives and routine by playing at roles which they observe and are not yet assuming in their own lives.

Play with rules

Finally, Piaget observed *play with rules* which characterizes the child in the operational period (approximately 7 years onwards).[1]

> The game with the seat became general in the class, by imitation. The players jumped two by two on to a seat, one at each end, and ran along it towards one another, the collision when they met causing one to fall off and leave the way free for the victor. But while the little ones (who began the game) played almost without rules, the older children of seven or eight very soon began to observe certain norms. They started at the same moment from each end, sometimes standing at the same distance from the seat; moreover, the girls and boys played separately, but this may have been from choice, without previous decision.
>
> Three five-year-old boys, playing at jumping one, two, three, or more steps of the school stairs reached a stage which was a beginning of rules. They had to jump as far as they could: anyone who fell lost,

and the turn only counted if a boy jumped from the same step as the others. Obviously there is nothing very complex in these rules, but they are a beginning which is capable of extension.

As the child's thinking becomes more logical, so his games and activities come to incorporate rules. At first children prefer to make up their own rules and are unable to follow 'the rules of the game'; it is only later in their development that they are able to follow standard rules laid down for everyone. This coincides with the development of thinking.

Piaget's theory is complicated and he uses difficult words to describe very complex and abstract ideas. Recall that intellectual adaptation is characterized by two processes, **assimilation** and **acccommodation**. Through assimilation the child takes in information about the outside world and modifies it to fit in with his own understanding and experience, whereas by accommodation he changes and develops his own understanding thus fitting in with objects and events in the external world. In play, assimilation is more important than accommodation, since in play the child acts on the world and changes it to fit in with his own experiences and understanding.

Although he made no claims to give practical advice, Piaget's ideas have had a wide impact on the practice of early childhood education. When children reach two or three years they may attend playgroup for all or part of the day. Here they learn to play with other children, to share and co-operate and to develop the skills of social life. What have more recent researchers found when they have looked at play in the nursery school or playgroup?

Sylva's Oxfordshire study

When Kathy Sylva and her colleagues went into Oxfordshire playgroups, they found mastery play and symbolic play, for they were observing children between the ages of three and five years, who were at the pre-operational stage and had incorporated mastery play into their present play activities.[3] There was no play with rules, for this develops at about the time a child starts school. The main question of this NATURALISTIC OBSERVATION study was how factors in the environment of the preschool hinder or nurture play. Given that play is an integral part of a child's preschool development (intellectual, social and emotional), what factors in the preschool environment offer the child the best opportunity for development? Which aspects encourage conversation and concentration and which appear to be merely 'occupying'? Sylva made an observational study of 120 children aged three to five years, taking two 20-minute observations of each 'target child' and recording:

> The child's task, be it art, or story listening, or watching others
> With whom was he doing it
> What he was saying and what was said to him

What materials he used
What 'programme' was in force at the time of observation; for example, was it free play or group story
Whether there were signs of commitment or challenge, such as pursed lips or intent gaze

They looked at many different activities and tried to evaluate which factors were more conducive to the children's development during play. Four kinds of information were recorded: activity (what was the child doing?) language (did the target child talk to another child or adult or was he spoken to?) social setting (was the child alone or in a group?) and play themes (was there a coherent theme to a period of activity?). Here is an extract from a 20-minute recorded and coded observation.

Minute	Activity	Language*	Social setting	Play theme
1	Puts hat on. Makes 'fire engine' noises	TC → CS (about hats) TC + CS: 'Dor dor dor dor.' TC → C: 'What's here?'	Small group	Pretend
1·5	TC with 2 CS on steps.	C → TC: 'Here's mine.' (showing a toy)	Small group	
2	Talking and moving with the 2 CS, playing on steps.	T → CS: 'What have you there?' TC → T: 'fire engine'	Small group	
2·5	Places large cardboard box beside steps, throws hat off. Steps carefully from top of steps onto cardboard box. _hollow | box_	TC → C: 'Steps on it.' C → TC: 'I want to come down.'	Small group	Gross motor play
3	Goes up steps and climbs down onto cardboard box again Crawls in hollow area under steps with C.	TC → C: 'Can I come in?' C → TC: 'Yes.'	Small group	
3·5	Then gets out and allows other C to go in hollow. C pushes box away.	TC → C: 'Shall I do it for you?' TC → C: 'Don't do it.' C → TC: 'It wasn't me, it was Simon.' TC → C: 'Stop it.'	Small group	
4	Leans over edge from top of steps. CS below push box away, then back. TC climbs carefully and gingerly from top of steps onto box.	TC → C: 'Stop it Simon.' TC → C: 'If you do it . . . I'm going down – don't push will you.' C → TC: 'No.'	Small group	
4·5	Fetches large egg-box carton. Places it below steps. Goes up stairs and climbs down into carton.	TC → C: 'I'm going up stairs.' TC → C: 'I'm going up stairs.'	Small group	

* TC = target child, C = other child, S = staff member

Minute	Activity	Language	Social setting	Play theme
	c gets in carton. TC pushes him in, then watches	TC → c: 'Shall I do it for you?'	Small group	
5	Takes another box from other 2 cs Watches 3 cs with boxes	c → TC: 'Get another box.' TC → cs: 'We need that box.'	Small group	
5·5	Leaves, goes to nearby playplax on table (2 cs). Places one ring on another, then examines other pieces of construction material and tries to fit them together		Small group	Small-scale construction (playplax)
6	Works with construction kit. (1 other c)		Child pair	
6·5	Runs down room to fetch woodwork (which he made earlier – he has seen s setting up woodwork bench).		Solitary	Small-scale construction (woodwork)
7	Holds his woodwork (complicated – several pieces nailed together). cs bring big cartons near woodwork bench.	TC → cs (about boxes)	Small group	
7·5	Picks up and holds saw Tentatively starts to saw cardboard box – stops. (s and 3 cs fixing up bench.)		Small group	
8	Holds wood over vice. Unscrews vice, wood slides in, then tightens vice.		Small group	
8·5	Saws top of block, which wobbles badly. c watches him and wobbling wood	TC → c: 'Falls off.' (about woodwork)	Child pair	
9	Holds onto vice and stretches arm to reach something (without letting go of vice) c tries to get vice.	TC → c: 'No!' s → TC + c 'Only two at a time on the bench.'	Child pair	

Complete instructions for making a child observation study of this kind appear in *Childwatching at Playgroup and Nursery School.*[3]

This record shows in detail part of the day of one child in a playgroup; it is an important record because not only does it show the various different activities, but it also leads on to some kind of evaluation of each activity. For Sylva and her colleagues were particularly interested in materials, events and social interactions that would encourage concentration and complex activity. They drew the distinction between complex play and simple play: 'There are two levels of play. One merely keeps children occupied, the other contributes to their educational development.'[5] The play activities recorded were coded either 'challenging' or 'ordinary' and an attempt was made to discover those activities or aspects of activities which could be called 'educational' and which challenged the children and might indeed stimulate development. Look at some examples of 'challenging' and 'ordinary play'.

CONSTRUCTION PLAY

High level of challenge

A child is at the lego table. He roots in the box of lego bricks and selects a base plate. He carefully fits bricks onto the base, choosing them from the box. He continues this careful building, looking in the box to find the 'right' bricks, not just using any brick. Although his construction doesn't look like a representation of a real-life object to the adult observer, the child is systematically and purposefully following some plan of his own design.

Ordinary play

The child at the lego table takes apart some bricks and scatters them on the table. He builds a 'tower', taking bricks from the table as they come to hand. He stacks bricks one above the other with ease, then takes them apart, builds another tower in the same way. He is engrossed and systematic in his actions, but the activity is routine, repetitive; he doesn't add any new elements or combine ideas, and he is rather 'slapdash'.

VEHICLE RIDING

High level of challenge

A child is riding his tricycle around the playground when suddenly the trike stops moving although he is still pedalling. He pedals for a moment, looking down at the wheels. He dismounts and squats down, examining them. He turns the pedals, touches other parts, looks at them. He sees that the chain has come off and carefully tries to fit it back in place. He is solving a problem; his activity is complex, combining ideas, goal-directed, purposeful, systematic.

Ordinary play

A child grabs a tricycle and pedals round and round the playground. He is clearly adept at cycling, it requires little or no mental effort from him (only physical effort), and he isn't trying to steer the trike around a particular course of obstacles; rather he appears to be simply 'letting off steam'. His activity is routine, repetitive, familiar, and not cognitively complex.

Pretend

TC and C have constructed a train with large boxes, etc., as in the above example. C climbs onto the front announcing he's the driver. TC climbs on behind and says, 'I bought a ticket. Let's go to the

Figure 11.3 *For the five-year-olds in the top photograph, football consists only of kicking the ball. They are not old enough yet to understand the rules of play. Formal games with rules require operational schemas*

seaside – I've got my spade and we can make a sandcastle and go in the sea.' c calls out 'All aboard. We're going to the sea.' TC pretends to sound the whistle, pulling an imaginary rope. 'Toot, toot!' c drives the train, assisted by TC. Another c bangs into the train with a large cart. TC shouts, 'The train's crashed – get an ambulance!'

TC is with two other cs in the playground. One says, 'I'm the Bionic Man' and pretends to hit another with a 'karate chop'. All play-fight, pretending to hit each other and shoot with 'space guns' while shouting the names of the character each is playing – Batman, Incredible Hulk, etc. Their play doesn't develop beyond announcing the role and pretend fighting of a stereotyped nature.

The Oxfordshire study produced some important findings. Jerome Bruner has already questioned the educational value of too much time spent on activity such as rough-and-tumble play and too many unstructured materials such as water, sand, and dough. Too often, children are left to play with the sand and water with no plan or structure, and, while this is enjoyable and may provide opportunities for emotional expression, it is not challenging. The Sylva study found that structured activities with definite goals *were* challenging, while unstructured materials and 'leaving the children to do their own thing' were less so. Sylva writes: 'In most of the activities in which there is a great proportion of complex behaviour, the child builds, creates or completes something tangible. He has an objective in mind and can judge whether what he is doing will further that objective or not. Of course, he may not have an image in his head of the exact form a painting should take, but he often knows whether he is pleased with the result of adding a strong colour or an additional form. The realization that something has 'come off' implies a standard in the mind, whether conscious or not'.

Bruner also emphasizes play as a source of novelty. In play the child can try out many novel combinations and create different situations and objects by exploring materials and opportunities offered to him. Discovering new ways of making or combining objects or symbols gives the child the chance to be creative and to experience flexibility; this would seem to be a particular benefit from preschool education and play opportunities. Through creating new objects, paintings, models, shapes, a child takes his first steps towards creativity. The more expressive materials like sand and dough may also enhance creativity if care is taken over the presentation of the materials and objects are included with them.

The Sylva study showed the benefits to the children of a healthy balance between free and structured times of day and the importance of some structured activities in every playgroup session. They make some practical recommendations as to how the playgroup or nursery school may encourage play to its maximum benefits.

Firstly, children learn most from objects and activities with a clear goal. Activities which encourage concentration and therefore probably intellec-

Figure 11.4 *Structural engineering problems had to be solved to build the tall tower – an example of challenging play. Painting also requires concentration, and the boy on the right is not easily distracted*

tual development are art, small scale construction for instance with lego, pretend play and puzzles. Some appropriate materials might be paints and paper, clay and plasticine, construction materials and dressing up clothes. Of course there should be many other things too – small children wouldn't want to concentrate all the time.

Secondly, children work well in pairs, and this has been shown to improve the intellectual level of their play. The preschool years are important for the child's communication and language and children learn much from each other. Creative activities, construction, and make-believe are obvious kinds of play which provide the opportunity for conversations between children; though sometimes guidance is needed to stimulate wider and more flexible use of language.

Finally, extra adults to chat to children are invaluable in any nursery or playgroup (and a rota of parents would do excellently for this purpose). Adults who are actively engrossed in tasks with the children provide a unique opportunity to stimulate language and to help some activities.

Is play important?

Consider the fact that children play in different ways as they grow older and develop. Each stage of development is accompanied by a different kind of play. The very young child learns and explores routine movements and skills by mastery play. He takes in information about the world around him by touching objects, realizing the cause and effect of different movements, and observing the regularities which he can cause simply by repeating a pattern of actions. As the child enters a more social world,

Figure 11.5 *A two-year-old practising motor skill at play*

gradually interacting with more adults and other children he develops make-believe play and learns about symbols and then language. Again, he is taking in information about his world and the cause and effect of interaction with others. Finally the child develops the capacity for logical thought and tries this out through games with rules.

As children grow and develop, they play in different ways reflecting their own levels of competence. It is therefore possible to watch children at play and to infer something about their stage of development and possible delays and problems in development (this theme is picked up in Chapter 14 when the focus is on play therapy).

This chapter has concentrated mainly on cognitive aspects of play and in particular on Piaget's theory. There are of course many other ways of studying play and its importance and psychologists do not yet know all the answers to the questions asked at the beginning of the chapter. Play *does* seem to be important to several aspects of development. Children do need many different kinds of play experiences in order to develop normally. Play becomes increasingly complex as a child gets older because his intellect is developing and his social and emotional experience broadens as he interacts with many other adults and children. Children learn much of the language and customs of their own society by observing others around them, then practising in play. It is important that children be stimulated to play, and given lots of opportunity to play at their own level of development. Is play important? It is the work of the preschool child and is one of the activities most significant to his overall development.

171

Figure 12.1 *A nursery school playground – the source of all kinds of skills*

Chapter 12

Early childhood: socialization in the preschool

The three-year-old who ventures from his home out into school or playgroup is faced with a new social world of adults and other children. This may be his first contact with others of his age, who now begin to play an important role in his life. This may also be the first time he has regular contact with an adult, other than his parents, who is important to him. The preceding chapter explored the intellectual benefits of children's play in the nursery school, this chapter now looks at the importance of the **socialization** that goes on there as well.

In this chapter we will focus on the socialization and social development of children in nursery school. Between the ages of three and five, children develop from an egocentric curiosity the capacity to get on with their peers and to benefit from group activities in both nursery and infant school. How is this achieved? Socialization, according to Dennis Child, is 'the whole process by which an individual, born with behavioural potentialities of an enormously wide range, is led to develop actual behaviour which is confined to a much narrower range – the range of what is customary and acceptable for him according to the standards of his group'. Much of what goes on in nursery school is socialization. But before going deeply into the concept of socialization, a word about various kinds of preschools.

Nursery schools and classes are usually run by local education authorities, and they start from the conviction that a three- or four-year-old child benefits from the social experiences and educational stimulation of a nursery and is therefore better prepared for the start of his school life at five years. By contrast with day nurseries and childminding, nursery schools and classes have a specifically stated educational purpose (rather than a caring one). The staff:child ratio is high (usually about 1:13), staff are professionally trained, and equipment is generally excellent. Out of the 1,221,495 children who attended some kind of preschool provision in England and Wales in 1977, (29.8 per cent of all children under five) 6.7 per cent attended nursery schools and classes. About five times as many children attended playgroups (see Figure 12.2).

Playgroups are in many respects like nursery schools and classes, except

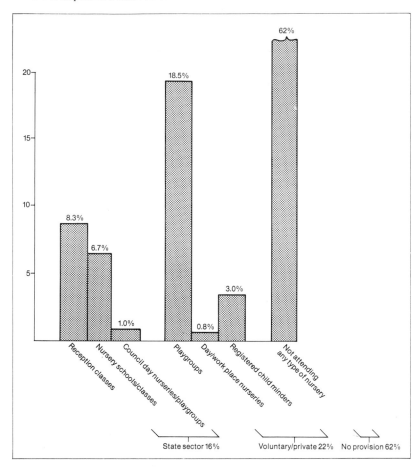

Figure 12.2 *Percentage of children under five attending different kinds of preschool provision (England and Wales, 1977)*

that they are private (not State organized) and the staff are not professionally trained (though most receive training through the Pre-school Playgroups Association). They are usually organized by parents who will use, for instance, a church hall on several mornings each week. The parents choose a playgroup leader who is chiefly responsible for the day-to-day arrangements, and they usually take turns to help out. The essence of a playgroup is parent involvement.

Playgroups usually closely resemble nursery schools and classes in the activities which are encouraged, though more elaborate equipment is usually available in the nursery school. Since the objectives (to stimulate and enhance children's intellectual and social development) and the methods are often similar, in this chapter the reference to nursery school includes playgroup.

174

Socialization

The process of socialization begins early on at home, but for the three-year-old child the nursery increases its scope. The nursery provides the opportunity to mix with other children and develop social competence, and it also puts the child in a position where he has to take into consideration the wishes, needs and demands of other children and adults. At home, he may have begun to learn 'manners' (for example, saying please, or eating with knife and fork), and he will have learned that it is not always possible to get his own way. Some responses learned at home will be further reinforced in nursery school and therefore acquire greater strength as habits, while others lose strength when they are not rewarded by other children (the 'peer group') or by teachers. (Recall that Chapter 8 showed that reinforcement is a powerful factor in learning.) Parents (first and most important in socialization) begin to shape a child's behaviour by rewarding the good behaviour they wish to encourage and punishing the bad behaviour they wish to get rid of. Teachers continue this pattern of reward and punishment (using as reward, smiles, attention, stars and even sweets) in their attempts to change children's behaviour and help them become social beings. To a certain extent, too, the child's peers provide strong reinforcement for certain kinds of behaviour, as for example the show-off child whose outrageously cheeky behaviour is maintained by the approval and laughter of his peers. In the nursery, peers play an increasingly important role in a young child's life, both as reinforcers (consciously and unconsciously) and increasingly as models. The idea of learning from a model (often called observational learning or learning by imitation) is particularly important to an understanding of the process of socialization.

Observational learning

Observational learning has been extensively studied by Albert Bandura[1] and various colleagues. They carried out various experiments to find out how far models influence aggressive behaviour in children. In one experiment, nursery school children were placed on their own in a room with an adult; each child played with a toy on one side of the room while the adult, the 'model' played on the other side of the room. In one experimental condition, the 'aggressive model' condition, the child observed the adult behaving in a bizarre and aggressive way toward a large inflatable doll (a Bobo doll), punching it, kicking it, throwing things at it and shouting at it; in the second experimental condition, the child observed the same adult behaving in a subdued, unaggressive manner to the same Bobo doll. For comparison purposes there was a control condition where the adult played quietly with various toys. After this session, all the children were taken to another room (with the Bobo doll) where they were mildly frustrated by having the toys taken away, and their responses to this frustration were observed. Bandura found that those children who had observed the aggressive model showed agressive behaviour towards the doll, often exactly imitating the bizarre actions of the aggressive adult model. On the other hand those children who had been exposed to the unaggressive adult model showed less aggressive behaviour even than the control group. In later experiments, Bandura carried out the same study but used adult models on film; the results were the same and the filmed models proved to be as effective models for observational learning as the models there in the flesh.

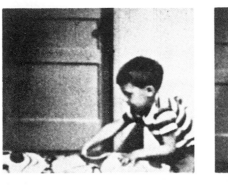

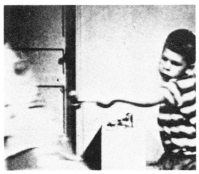

Figure 12.3 *Bandura's Bobo doll experiment. Children who had just seen an adult behaving aggressively towards the doll then behaved the same way themselves. The poor quality of the illustrations is due to the fact that they are taken from a video recording*

These experiments have shown the power of learning by **imitation**. At home, parents act as powerful models for their young children. For example, an aggressive father may be successfully modelling similarly aggressive behaviour in his child. We saw in the last chapter how young children act out adult roles in their make-believe play, skilfully imitating the exact gestures and movements of adults. Likewise in the nursery school, the teacher becomes a significant model for observational learning during play. As well as rewarding and encouraging appropriate behaviour and characteristics, and punishing or ignoring others, the nursery school teacher becomes a readily available, powerful, and usually attractive

176

model – often exerting as strong an influence as the child's first socializers – his parents. For example, if either parents or teachers use physical or verbal violence to punish unwanted behaviour, the result may well be that the child imitates and learns the aggressive punishment behaviour rather than stops his undesirable behaviour. Often, but not always, the nursery teacher works alongside the parents in encouraging (rewarding) *and* modelling the same behaviour and discouraging (punishing) other; clearly, where this happens it will result in more efficient learning; problems may occur where the child experiences one set of reinforcements and kind of modelling at home and quite another in the nursery school.

In the nursery school the role of the peer group is equally important for reinforcement and as a model for imitation. Indeed children acquire social skills at least as much from each other as from adults; they discover through trial and error the subtleties of interaction and social communication. At play or tasks involving cooperation, children in the nursery begin to learn something of the give-and-take necessary in real life. Nursery groups are usually organized so that there is considerable opportunity for free play; this enables the children to discover for themselves the 'rules' of friendship and social contact – how to approach others, to control aggressive impulses and to express affection.

Some of the most striking changes in behaviour at this age are linked to the child's growing sense of his own identity and increasing independence. He delights in the mastering of new skills and enjoys exploring the world outside his home. Understanding his parents' affection and feeling the security of the home attachment, he is able to interact happily with other adults.

Independence

The psychoanalytic writer Erik Erikson emphasizes this age for the development of 'autonomy' or independence. The child gradually learns to choose and to decide, and to accept the consequences of choice. He gradually realizes that individuals are valued differently depending on what they can do and learns to form relationships outside the home and to trust other adults and children. A nursery expert, Dowling, writes:

> Opportunities for developing independence must be predominant in every area of the nursery; self-service milk arrangements will allow the individual the chance to pour for himself and to decide what quantity he can drink, convenient toilets mean that the child can go to the lavatory as and when he wishes, the choice to play inside or out with a variety of materials, to attend a story session or not, and to select one's playmates are all the beginnings of decision making for life. A child who is capable of making decisions and acting on his own initiative will grow rapidly in self-confidence.

What do we find when we look at what is happening in the nursery school? Lesley Webb used an 'informal INTERVIEW technique' to ask mothers: 'What do you think has been the greatest benefit (to your child) of nursery school':[2]

> The main thing I've noticed is her independence. In everything. Well, compared with her little friends – well, there isn't a comparison. She's streets ahead!

> They don't come round you all the time when they've been to nursery. Seems as if they learn to do without a bit – well, not all the time, but – well, he does things by himself and then he says, 'Come and look, Mummy'. I don't have to baby him, if you know what I mean.

and

> They learn them to be independent. You can't do it all at home. Not the same.

Clearly many parents found attendance at nursery class a help in developing a child's independence.

Learning social skills

Several researchers have made observational studies of nursery children, with the aim of describing what typically takes place in a nursery group.

Peter Smith and Kevin Connolly in Sheffield looked at the social interaction of groups of nursery children ranging in age from two years nine months to four years nine months.[3] They observed the children during free play sessions and recorded their various activities, particularly in relation to the length of time the children had attended the nursery. They found that sociability in play, rough-and-tumble play, laughing and smiling, were all correlated even more highly with length of nursery experience than they were with age. So it appears that nursery children do learn how to play with other children, how to approach and initiate friendship, and how to appreciate and handle the subtleties of interaction with others.

Learning sex-appropriate activities

Sex-role learning is an important part of social development and nursery school activities are important where young children are experimenting with different roles particularly through make believe play. This aspect of **socialization** begins early in the home, with parents reinforcing feminine behaviour (and toys and colours) in girls, and masculine behaviour in boys. Already by the age of three or four, most children have learned that

Figure 12.4 *Learning to get along with one another is an important part of socialization*

society expects different kinds of behaviour from boys and girls, men and women. The fact is that what they learn is not always to the advantage of girls. They learn for example, that 'mummy' looks after the home and children (though she may also go out to work) and 'daddy' goes out to do 'real' work. They know also that girls are encouraged to play in the home corner with dolls and with books, while boys are allowed to play more aggressively and with trucks and tricycles, large building bricks and constructive toys such as lego. In addition, children's television, films and books encourage sex-role stereotypes; for example, a survey in the United States of America in 1972 looked at 2,750 stories from 134 children's books and found a very strong tendency to sex stereotyping: 'Boys make things. They rely on their wits to solve problems. They are curious, clever and adventurous. They achieve; they make money. Girls and women are incompetent and fearful. They ask other people to solve their problems for them . . . in story after story, girls are the onlookers, the cheerleaders . . . even accepting humiliation and ridicule. In 67 stories, one sex demeans the other – and 65 of these involve hostility of males against females.' How is this maintained in the nursery class?

We have seen how young children learn both by reinforcement and by imitation. They are rewarded by parents and teachers (both consciously and unconsciously) for sex-appropriate behaviour. We have seen also that peers in the nursery class act as powerful socialization agents in both of these ways; they reinforce behaviour in each other and they serve as models for imitation and identification. Psychologists have found that boys tend to play in groups, 'packs' or on their own, while girls tend to

179

Figure 12.5 *Friends become important as well as parents*

play more in smaller groups of two or three. In this way boys are more susceptible to pressure from their peers (and this develops increasingly till they reach 'gang behaviour' of adolescent youths). Boys are more anxious to identify with the masculinity and male characteristics of their peers. Corinne Hutt[4] has shown that young children show a particularly strong tendency to imitate the behaviour of their same-sex peers and, as anyone who has spent time in a nursery class will have seen, even at this age, there

Figure 12.6 *Children learn by observing each other*

is often a strongly masculine 'leader' whom other boys are eager to imitate and identify with. That is less true among the girls.

Children learn sex differences at an early age. Asking children of two-and-a-half the question 'are you a girl or a boy?' resulted in many wrong answers. But as they grow, young children observe the differences between men (police, soldiers, fathers, robbers) and women (mothers, teachers, nurses). Another way in which they learn is by identification with father or mother, and so by taking on the masculine or feminine role or behaviour of the same-sex parent.

Identification

Observational learning and imitation explain why a young child does many things, but don't help us when we ask why the child chooses to imitate one person rather than another. The concept of **identification** (see Chapter 5) may help us to understand this. It is the concept proposed by Freud to explain how young children resolve the conflicts presented by strong feelings toward the opposite sex parent; the young boy identifies with his father and seeks masculine activities outside the family, while the young girl identifies with the mother and pursues more feminine activities and interests. Identification is the name given to the rather subtle way in which a young child absorbs or 'assimilates' the characteristics of another person, without any direct teaching or learning; the characteristics of another person (initially parent, later teacher and peer) are felt by the young child as belonging to him. Paul Mussen writes: 'Responses acquired by identification seem to be emitted spontaneously, without any specific training or direct rewards for imitation, and they are generally relatively stable and enduring rather than transient.' Within the nursery class, it is possible to see the results of children's early identification with their parents, then their shift of focus to the nursery teacher, and finally as they grow older the way they identify more and more with their peer group and the leader figures within that group. Much of this is achieved through make-believe play and fantasy. The processes of socialization do not stop after nursery school of course – they also continue in the home and in the neighbourhood and also in later life.

We began the chapter by considering the notion of socialization. 'The English nursery schools have always viewed their task as being in some part a socializing one.' This process seems to have included two quite different types of behaviour – the 'low-order' skills, (such as habits of cleanliness), and 'high order' behaviour (like forming relationships).

What are the benefits of nursery school and playgroup?

It is difficult to evaluate the benefits of nursery or playgroup attendance, since one can never find exactly similar children to compare. It is never possible to say that, for example, 'Darren's adaptability or sociability was caused by his attending a nursery class from the age of three', or that 'Mary's anti-social behaviour on entering the infants' school was due to her not attending a nursery school.'

One cannot find other children to compare because it is not possible to know whether the children who are sent to nursery before the age of five are typical of the whole population. There may be so many reasons for sending a particular child to nursery school, such as the mother having to or wanting to go out to work, family under stress, the recommendation of the health visitor in cases of mild handicap, or parents being motivated to send their child to a nursery either for their own or for the child's good. It is therefore impossible to separate the effects of nursery education from the effects of life in a particular family. At best, it is possible to carry out comparisons using broad measures of sociability or adjustment. But what do these tell us? They seem to tell us that, although five-year-olds who have been to nursery or playgroup *are* more sociable than five-year-olds who have not, these differences tend to disappear with time.

Yet there is a wide range of benefits and opportunities provided by nursery schools and playgroups. Children of this age enjoy playing with each other and learning the rules of friendship and the skills of coopera-tion and give and take.

A variety of different activities and materials, and separate 'corners' and 'tables' ensure that children work and play in manageable groups and are given the opportunity to interact with each other. Children need to learn to listen and to take turns and help even very shy children to make a contribution to the day. Although socialization begins in the family, where the child is faced with his first social relationships, his first models and identification figures, it is in the nursery that he encounters the wider world. Nurseries provide both intellectual and social stimulation, lots of different activities and play and lots of children to do them with.

It seems that when the staff who run nurseries and playgroups are clear about their goals and when there are several adults to talk to children and help them in their play, nurseries offer great opportunities to the under-fives for both social and intellectual development. This does not mean that children who do not attend nurseries and playgroups are at a disadvantage when they begin school, though they may be less used to working and playing in groups and may take longer to settle in to infants' school.

Chapter 13

The school years: learning

When a child starts school, formal learning becomes of prime importance, and how to facilitate learning becomes a major concern of the teacher. Many ask the question: 'How do children learn?' or alternatively: 'Why do children not learn?' or: 'How can we improve children's learning?' Schools might have fewer problems if the answers to these questions were known for certain.

In ordinary language, learning is a process by which people acquire specific new knowledge or skills. There are many psychologists who study learning in this sense, and many (like Piaget for example) who are interested in the gradual changes in children's *general* thinking about the world.

There is a smaller group of psychologists who are particularly interested in the effects of reward and punishment on learning, and – by some historical accident – these are known as learning theorists, though they aren't the only theorists of learning. They are Thorndike, Skinner and Bandura (among others) and their work is discussed in Chapter 8.

This chapter will look at the work of Skinner (and his focus on reward or **reinforcement**) and at the very different approach of Piaget. Both of these have influenced what goes on in the classroom, but in very different ways.

Piaget's ideas have been more widely taken up at primary school level, while Skinner's have been used with older children, but both psychologists have influenced general educational ideas and practice. This chapter considers Piaget's ideas about discovery learning contrasted with Skinner's work on programmed learning.

Piaget

Although Piaget made no specific recommendations about educational practice, he served for many years on a UNESCO committee devoted to how theory should be extended to educational practice, and a whole approach has arisen out of his theory of intellectual development. Piaget observed his own three children, and later many other children, finding out about the world around them without being taught, and he noted

Figure 13.1 *At five, children begin more formal schooling. Ten years later, the process continues . . .*

carefully how the children progressed from one achievement to another. He saw children motivated by their own curiosity and desire to find out; and intellectual development appeared to occur spontaneously. Piaget's ideas have given rise to a general approach to education called discovery learning.

Recall (Chapter 7) that Piaget believed thinking to be an active process.

Children are not creatures who passively take in information, but rather they actively organize experience and, by doing so, modify the **schemas** they already have. Piaget drew a distinction between development and learning. By development he meant general changes in thinking – modification of the schemas – according to an unchanging order of stages. Learning on the other hand, for Piaget, implied the acquisition of specific behaviour for handling a particular task in a particular context.

Piaget held that a child's world and understanding are completely different from those of an adult, since the child goes through stages that are characterized by different kinds of understanding – **sensory-motor**, **pre-operational**, **operational**. Piaget's stages unfold and develop in invariant order, each one dependent on the one before and gradually evolving into the next. It is this spontaneous and gradual unfolding which is central to Piaget's idea of development.

There have been many Piagetian curricula applied particularly to junior education, and Piagetian ideas have permeated much of nursery and infant education too.

Discovery learning

A young girl dressing her dolls and moving them about in the dolls' house, perhaps in imitation of real life, is learning by discovery. She actively manipulates the different dolls, picks them up, changes their clothes, moves them from one room to another, and so learns about the properties of objects. She has no teacher and no programme, yet she is learning. A seven-year-old kneeling outside the school carefully collecting and observing snails, drawing spirals and looking up in a nature book is learning by discovery some of the properties of nature, of shapes and of mathematics.

Perhaps the key concept in discovery learning is the *act* of discovery itself. For Piaget emphasizes activity in intellectual development, and states that the child must act on things to understand them. Almost from birth the young child touches objects, feels them and picks them up, shakes them, looks at them and gradually through active manipulation learns about their various properties. At this early sensory-motor stage, the young child discovers for himself about the world about him; and this process of active exploration continues through the rest of intellectual development. The child is intrinsically motivated, he is naturally curious, eager to learn and to explore the world about him. Give him the opportunity to learn and he will do so – without being taught. Discovery learning is really opposed to the idea of teaching if by teaching is meant the traditional process of imparting information, or modifying behaviour, or even 'filling up an empty vessel with knowledge'. The idea is rather to provide the materials and the environment for the child to explore and let him then do the rest almost by himself, motivated to learn by his own curiosity.

So what happens in the Piagetian classroom? The Piagetian teacher aims to bring the activities of the classroom and the school 'into harmony with processes of development'. The lessons and materials given to children should be determined by knowledge of the stages of development. This is known as a 'readiness' approach and assumes that intellectual growth takes its own time and should not be accelerated. The sensory-motor child needs materials and time to practise activities and to develop his understanding at that level. Ask the pre-operational child to solve a logical problem and he will make mistakes, since for him the problem will have a different meaning; but he will learn from his mistakes. The child is naturally curious and at different stages is 'ready' for different materials and activities. Some children are 'ready' (have mastered the basic skills, such as shape recognition) to learn to read at three years, while others not until five or six years. The Piagetian teacher does not speed up the process but rather waits for development to unfold.

What is the role of the teacher in a discovery learning approach? Apparently the child learns for himself without teaching. Is the teacher therefore necessary? The teacher is important in two major respects. First, she must know what stage the child has reached, which activities he has mastered, and where he still lacks competence. Knowing this, she can provide him with materials, events and activities which will offer him the opportunity to practise those skills and to exercise his intellect on tasks relevant to life in his society. The teacher can guide and facilitate the child's natural and spontaneous growth by her choice of what is provided in the classroom. Secondly, she can help in the process of 'stage shift', that is the child's development from one stage to the next. She does this by providing and showing the child's obvious conflicts and discrepancies, so that he modifies existing schemes and ways of understanding and learns new ones. For example (see page 104) the pre-operational child aged about five years does not understand that the quantity of water remains the same amount even when poured into differently shaped glasses. The 'stage shift' occurs as the child begins to perceive the conflict (in pouring water back and forth and never adding or taking any away), and then realizes that the amounts must remain the same. The teacher may help in this process by showing up the conflicts, pouring the liquid and discussing with the child the various possibilities. The teacher's role is demanding, sensitive and very busy.

And the child? In the Piagetian classroom the child is actively engaged in exploring the environment and learning about the world and society around him. He is motivated by his own curiosity. The young child is pre-logical and therefore develops different schemas from the older child – and avails himself of different materials and activities. The way he perceives and understands depends on the stage he has reached, so however often something is explained or demonstrated, he can only assimilate it to his own level of understanding and his own picture of the world. Moreover he learns by active exploration and by involving himself

Figure 13.2 *Six-year-olds 'discover' several ways of measuring*

Figure 13.3 *Absorbed in discovery about time*

in the processes of development. He therefore develops by handling, manipulating, counting, and experiencing materials rather than by sitting at a desk taking in information. He is involved in an active construction and reconstruction of his world view and his understanding of what goes on around him.

The task of the teacher is to select materials, and at times indirectly to suggest activities, so that the child will of his own accord do things that contribute to his overall growth and development. This is a 'readiness approach' and teaching must reflect the path of spontaneous cognitive development.

The discovery learning and readiness approach has spread widely through nursery and infant schools. It fits well with ideas of individual learning and social development of young children. However, when a child leaves junior school, the pressure of examination curricula often comes to determine the nature of his learning experience. Teachers are pressed to convey a certain body of knowledge, pupils are pushed towards mastering particular examination curricula. Although some secondary schools have developed 'discovery' learning approaches, particularly in integrated subjects in the first two years, the emphasis in secondary school is increasingly on formal learning and teaching.

We move on to describe a highly formalized and systematic form of learning which has developed from the ideas of the American psychologist B. F. Skinner.

Skinner

Skinner showed that using his theory of instrumental learning (see page 122) it was possible, by appropriate reinforcement, even to teach a pigeon to play ping-pong.

Figure 13.4 *Each pigeon receives reinforcement if it knocks the ball into the trough on its opponent's side*

Recall that for Skinner reinforcement is that process whereby a reward increases the probability of a response, and learning, by his theory is the change in behaviour which occurs as a result of reinforcement. A reinforcer (see Chapter 8) is defined functionally as an event which increases the likelihood or frequency of responding; for example, giving a rat a food pellet increases the likelihood of its pressing a lever, giving a child a cuddle may increase the frequency of his smiling, or paying a child any form of attention may increaase any form of attention-seeking behaviour. In fact, many different events may act as reinforcers, and in real life situations these are rarely planned and usually simply occur. The idea of reinforcement is crucial to Skinner's theory and to its applications to practice.

By rewarding approximations to the desired behaviour (here ping-pong) Skinner was able to teach the pigeon by a process he called **shaping of behaviour**. Each small step in the right direction was reinforced until the pigeon had mastered the complete movement; first the pigeon would be rewarded for standing in the right position until this behaviour was reliably established, then he would be reinforced for standing there *and* pointing his beak in the direction of the ball, then he would receive reinforcement for standing and pointing his beak *and* approaching the ball, and so on until he performed the desired action in complete form. This procedure requires very careful planning, so that the successive steps are gradual, consistent and followed immediately by reward. Important points are:

(i)   a particular action or goal is specified and then broken down into a sequence of smaller steps
(ii) any movement in the right direction is immediately and consistently rewarded, but gradually more and more is demanded of the pigeon in order to gain the reward
(iii) reinforcement is immediate

Shaping has also been used successfully with humans, in many different settings, and particularly with children. Rather like a pigeon, the child is at first rewarded for any small step in the right direction, and is then gradually required to do more and more to be rewarded until finally he is doing exactly what is required. This procedure has been particularly effective with mentally handicapped children learning to eat with knives and forks, or dress themselves, since these are actions which are readily definable and broken down into a series of component steps each of which may be reinforced in a process of successive approximation.

Human responsiveness to reinforcement makes it possible to plan a programme to maintain, change or **extinguish** (get rid of) particular behaviour. This can happen in schools or in other institutions and can be concerned with academic learning or with modifying undesirable be-haviour. In the case of undesirable behaviour, the teacher has to identify those events within the school or classroom that are acting (probably unrecognized) as reinforcers, and rearrange things so that they do not. This is discussed further in Chapter 14 (on behaviour modification). But one of the most widespread and most powerful applications derived from Skinnerian principles is the idea of programmed learning in class. This became popular in the 1950's and the 1960's and is still used today in educational institutions.

Programmed learning

Programmed learning is literally a programme of learning. It may consist of a carefully planned textbook or series of worksheets, or a small box with a series of slides, or a tape recorder plus slides, or a small computer. The underlying idea is the same and is derived from the same procedures which Skinner used when he shaped the behaviour of his pigeons:

(i) a particular goal is specified and then broken down into smaller steps
(ii) any movement or progress in the right direction is immediately and consistently rewarded
(iii) reinforcements are immediate and carefully scheduled.

Thus small items or steps of the subject matter to be learned are presented in a logical sequence at such a pace as to guarantee success, and immediate feedback ('right' or 'wrong') is given before the next item of information is presented. Immediate feedback is an excellent reinforcer. It will readily be seen that there are, at first glance anyway, several advantages. The 'lesson' is *carefully planned* and the goals and objectives *specified*. The pupil takes an *active* part in his learning, receives *immediate feedback*, and can proceed at his own pace. The teacher can also monitor the *individual* progress of a large number of pupils at the same time. Language laboratories or remedial reading laboratories are good examples of this. Each student sits in his own booth with his own individual programme of work and then proceeds at his own pace under the overall care of the teacher. The material to be learned is carefully specified and

Figure 13.5 *Programmed learning*

then broken down into suitably small units in a logical sequence, so as to guarantee success most of the time. If the pupil makes a mistake, he is informed immediately and the information is re-presented, sometimes in a different form and with further explanation.

There are many different forms of programme which have been derived from Skinner's ideas. Two forms will be described here: the *linear* and the *intrinsic* programme. In a *linear programme* (see Figure 13.6), a limited amount of information is presented and a question asked; the pupil is required to write an answer or fill in a missing word. The next step provides the correct answer (immediate feed-back) and then the next piece of information. The programmes are constructed in such a way as to ensure maximum success, by proceeding with a slow and detailed presentation of information such that the pupil rarely if ever makes an error.

In the *intrinsic programme*, information is also presented with a question, but a number of possible answers are given for the pupil to choose from. If the answer is correct, the programme moves onto the next step, whereas if it is incorrect, the programme moves into another step, or series of steps, which give further explanation and show the pupil how he was wrong or how he misunderstood. This system more closely imitates the function of the good teacher, who diagnoses weaknesses and explains areas which are not fully understood by the pupils. This is clearly rather more difficult for one human teacher to achieve for each of 30 pupils. This system claims to take more account of individual differences and to point out to each student why he is right and why he is wrong – that is, to enable him to learn from his mistakes.

Programmed learning requires that the information is presented in a finely graded series of small steps (just as in Skinner's shaping process). At each step the student is required to answer specific questions and is thus actively participating in the learning. The correct answer appears after each step and provides immediate reinforcement. The steps are usually arranged in such a way that the student makes very few if any errors. Programmed learning has been used particularly successfully in teaching languages, mathematics and remedial reading where it is possible to arrange information in a logical series of small sequential steps. It is less good at teaching students to write original essays on Shakespeare.

The two theories

Look into any family home or classroom and you will see that every parent and teacher has his or her own personal learning theory. How does the mother discipline her child? Does she hit him, or will she give him sweets? Does she show him by example or allow him to find out for himself? Is the teacher using question-and-answer techniques, rewards, project work or rote learning? Of course, no one theory has all the answers.

1 Learning should be fun. However, in the early stages of learning a subject, students often make many errors. Most people (do/do not) like to make errors.	
do not	
2 When a student makes many errors in learning, he often decides that he does not like the subject. He would be more correct to decide that he does not like to make _____.	
errors	
3 For a long time, educators, psychologists, and people in general thought it was impossible to learn without making a large numbers of <u>errors</u>. In fact, they even had a name for this kind of learning. They called it 'trial-and-_____'' learning.	
error	
4 Recent developments in the psychology of learning have cast serious doubts as to the necessity of 'trial-and-error' learning. If the learning material is carefully prepared, or PROGRAMMED, in a special way, the student can master the subject while making very few errors. The material you are reading right now has been prepared, or _____ in this special way.	
programmed	
5 The basic idea of programmed learning is that the most efficient, pleasant, and permanent learning takes place when the student proceeds through a course by a large number of small, easy-to-take steps. If each step the student takes is small, he (is/is not) likely to make errors.	
is not	

Figure 13.6 *A linear programme, with the correct answer marked bottom left of each item*

There is a whole range of ways one can think of the child learning and the views of Skinner and Piaget are the two extremes of that range. According to one the child learns as a result of events in his environment, while according to the other the child learns spontaneously when he is ready. In practice, although there are elements of both in every learning situation, there is a tendency for infant educators to follow a more Piagetian approach – providing the material and the opportunity for the infant to learn when he is ready by discovery. At a more formal stage in secondary school more use is made of programmed learning. This

6	A <u>programme</u>, then, is made up of a large number of small, easy-to-take steps. A student can proceed from knowing very little about a subject to mastery of the subject by going through a _____. If the programme is carefully prepared, he should make (many/few) errors along the way.
programme few	

7	Programmed learning has many features which are different from conventional methods of learning. You have already learned one of these principles. This principle is that a student learns best if he proceeds by small _____.
steps	

8	The features of programmed learning are applications of <u>learning principles</u> discovered in psychological laboratories. You have learned the first of these principles. You can guess that we call it the Principle of Small _____.
Steps	

9	The principles on which programmed learning are based are discovered in (psychological/astrological) laboratories. The first of these principles is the Principle of Small Steps.
psychological	

10	The first principle of programmed learning is The Principle of _____.
Small Steps	

11	What is the first Principle of Programmed Learning?
____ ____ ____ ____ ____	

distinction does not reflect what Piaget and Skinner intended with their theories, and indeed Piaget's concept of intellectual development extended well into adolescence and beyond, while Skinner's ideas have been used successfully with very young babies.

Those teachers who favour a discovery learning approach will encourage children to participate actively in learning by asking questions, making models and carrying out well-planned project work. On the other hand, the more formal programmed learning approach enables a body of knowledge or information to be taught systematically and tested immediately. Classroom practice to a certain extent reflects individual teachers' images of children. Are they empty vessels to be filled with knowledge? Are they eager and ready, merely needing stimulation, time and opportunity to learn? Do they respond to reinforcement or are they motivated by their own curiosity?

Different theorists reply differently to these questions. The two theories discussed in this chapter are summarized below:

	Role of adult	Mode	Motivation	Timing	Nature of learning
Programmed Learning (based on Skinner's work in learning theory)	Write the programme	Formal	Reinforcement	Programme determines pace and timing	Fact centred
Discovery Learning (based on Piaget's work on the development of intelligence)	Provide a suitable environment	Informal	Child's own curiosity	Child's readiness determines pace and timing	Child centred

Table 13.1 *Two approaches to learning summarized*

Chapter 14

Childhood: problems

For most children, growth from infancy through childhood progresses relatively smoothly, and although almost all experience minor problems with sleeping, eating, temper tantrums, or withdrawn behaviour, these usually disappear with the passage of time. A small number of children, however, do experience delays or distortions in their otherwise healthy development, so that they cause problems or difficulties for themselves, or for others (such as parents and teachers) who are trying to help. Although some of these delays are inherited, others are caused by adverse events or circumstances. This chapter concentrates on this latter group – delays caused by difficult events or experiences.

Problems may be due to a particularly traumatic event, to unsatisfactory home circumstances, to an awkward personality or perhaps a combination of all three. Problem children, as they are often called, can make lives (including their own) increasingly difficult at home, school, both, or even outside on the streets. They can do this in a wide variety of ways. Examples range from excessive aggression or timidity, difficulties in getting on with adults or other children, tantrums, thumb-sucking or bed-wetting (beyond the age for these), or antisocial and delinquent behaviour. If these problems are sufficiently severe or persistent, adults concerned with such a child may seek help or therapy for him.

Most help or therapy assumes that the problem lies within the child and aims to 'cure' it. But a growing number of professionals feel that problems within an individual are merely a reflection of difficulties within a family or school, or even more broadly, a reflection of the problems or evils of society itself. This wider view which defines the problem as not in the individual but in the society in which he lives, would of course attempt to remedy it at that level. Philosophical points like that, though, are beyond the scope of this book. We shall stick to theories and techniques of therapy, and how they seem to help.

Different psychological theories have given rise to different therapies. Of the many that exist, two will be considered here. Skinner and other learning theorists provided the impetus for *behavioural therapy* (or behaviour modification as it is also called), while Freud and other psychoanalysts produced the ideas behind *play therapy*. These two kinds of therapy (and many others), have been used successfully to facilitate

Figure 14.1 *A problem?*

healthier development for children. This chapter looks at behaviour modification, and play therapy, and at the psychological theory behind them.

Studying behaviour

At the beginning of this century, Thorndike was working on the Law of Effect and the American J. B. Watson was redefining psychology as the science of behaviour: 'Mind, consciousness, souls, and ghosts were all one to Watson', write Brown and Herrnstein, 'and none of them had any place in a natural science. Even if the mind exists, said Watson, it cannot be studied since it is, by definition, open only to private inspection.'[1] Watson rebelled against all methods of psychological investigation that used talk or thought as their source:[2]

> Behaviourism . . . [holds] that the subject matter of human psychology is the behaviour of the human being. Behaviourism claims that consciousness is neither a definable nor a usable concept. The interest of the behaviourist in man's doings is more than the interest of the spectator – he wants to control man's reactions as physical scientists want to control and manipulate other natural phenomena. It is the business of behaviouristic psychology to be able to predict and to control human activity. I should like to go a step further now, and say, 'Give me a dozen healthy infants, well-formed, and my own specified world to bring them up in and I'll guarantee to take any one at random and train him to become any type of specialist I might select – doctor, lawyer, artist, merchant-chief and yes, even beggar-man and thief, regardless of his talents, penchants, tendencies, abilities, vocations, and race of his ancestors.'

Watson (and subsequent learning theorists) adopted an extreme environmentalist and determinist standpoint. They did not believe that abilities, personalities, or any behaviour had much to do with inheritance or instinct. Such things were, they thought, completely determined by learning and experience, and the mechanism for this was the formation of the **S-R (stimulus-response)** associations described in Chapter 8. People are, they claimed, entirely the products of their environment and its pattern of stimulus-response reinforcements. Furthermore, Watson's goal was to describe, predict and *control* behaviour, and later learning theorists, notably B. F. Skinner, have applied his principles to the control and change of both human and animal behaviour. These concepts have been used to control human behaviour in programmed learning (and in behaviour modification).

One way that applied psychologists look at human behaviour is in terms of what reinforces it; they regard present behaviour as a result of previous reinforcement. According to the principles of learning theory, learned behaviour may be extinguished by removing the reinforcement that is maintaining it, and then new and more appropriate behaviour can be reinforced in its place. If all human behaviour is viewed in this way it becomes easy to see how it could be modified and controlled.

Since, according to this view, all human behaviour is the product of an individual's learning history, it is possible to analyse the reinforcements, change them appropriately and thus modify an individual's behaviour in any direction. Part of the behavioural therapist's skill lies in identifying what it is that is doing the reinforcing. For instance, for a child whose parents tend to ignore him, even their anger may be rewarding – it is at least better than nothing! He may then be reinforced for behaviour that makes parents angry. Behaviour modification has in fact been used with a high degree of success both in classrooms and in hospitals.

Learning theory has had a strong influence on psychology and current psychological theories and methods owe much to Watson's redefinition of psychology as the study of behaviour. But it is in its applications that learning theory has had widest impact, particularly in the modification of behaviour by programmed learning and behaviour modification.

Behaviour therapy or modification

Behaviour therapy focuses not on any underlying cause but on *symptoms*. It assumes that the cause is in part (faulty) learning, but concentrates on the present. Behaviour therapists ignore the unconscious (see Chapter 5 and later in this chapter) and regard neuroses (personality disorders) as just a collection of bad habits. Since all habits (good and bad) are learned, they can also be unlearned, and this applies also to emotional habits (for instance little Hans's fear of horses). Behaviour therapists do not look for underlying causes of problem behaviour. In this they are completely different from medical doctors who seek and try to cure the underlying cause or disease in order that the symptoms will disappear and all be well.

Using techniques derived from learning theory, behaviour therapists set out to substitute new and more appropriate behaviour patterns for the *maladaptive* ones. Whether the 'inappropriate behaviour' (about which someone is complaining) be a spider phobia, tantrums, bed-wetting, a nervous tic, excessive anxiety, or antisocial behaviour, behaviour therapists abide by the following principles:

 (i) Most behaviour, good or bad, appropriate or inappropriate, is learned (or conditioned).
 (ii) If behaviour is reinforced when it occurs, it will tend to be repeated (this is learning by reinforcement).
 (iii) If behaviour is not rewarded, or is punished, when it occurs, it will tend to decrease in frequency.
 (iv) Behaviour may be changed in strength and frequency by its consequences (reinforcement: reward or punishment) or by the time relationship between response and reinforcement.
 (v) The timing of reinforcement is important for its effectiveness and immediate reinforcement is usually more effective, particularly with children.
 (vi) Observational learning or imitation of a model is a powerful source of learning.
 (vii) Behaviour modification is the systematic programming of situations and reinforcements so as to change an individual's response to aspects of the environment and to encourage (or discourage) particular forms of behaviour.

There are several different forms of behaviour modification using different programmes of reinforcement. Some examples: *Extinction therapy* consists of finding and eliminating the positive reinforcement for the undesired behaviour. *Systematic desensitization* involves training the patient (by reward) to relax in the presence of a situation that previously caused fear or anxiety. The two responses, relaxation and anxiety, are incompatible and the therapist ensures that the relaxation response is stronger than the fear response (this therapy was based on the principles of classical conditioning – see Chapter 8). *Aversion therapy* uses an unpleasant event such as a small electric shock to get rid of habits such as smoking, and *modelling* has been used successfully to change habits and patterns of behaviour.

The general procedure usually includes:

(i) Identification of the problem.
(ii) A decision on what kinds of behaviour are to be decreased and what increased.
(iii) A precise definition of problem behaviour. What does the individual actually *do*? How often does he do it? How often does he perform the desirable ('target') behaviour which is to be substituted?

For example:

Behaviour to be decreased	Behaviour to be increased
Fighting	Getting on with other children
Swearing	Using acceptable language
Wetting the bed	Waking with a dry bed
Withdrawing from social events	Participating in social events
Screaming at sight of a spider	Sitting still at sight of a spider
Explosive behaviour	Standing still even if frustrated
Moving about the classroom	Staying in place longer
Throwing food on the floor	Eating with a knife and fork

Table 14.1

From this varied list of activities (from home, school or hospital) it will immediately be seen that the desirable behaviour is incompatible with the undesirable. Therefore if the one can be established, the other is *automatically* excluded.

(iv) Establishment of a baseline against which change may be measured (a table which shows how often the undesirable behaviour occurs over a period of time; for example, say a child moves from his seat on average 17 times in a 30-minute period).
(v) Identification of what aspects of the individual's environment could be changed. What reinforces him for behaving in a particular way? From this, identification of appropriate rewards (praise, smiles, attention, tokens or Smarties) or punishments (being ignored or put

out of the room, or being deprived of relaxation or treat) and a plan for a systematic and rigorous programme of reinforcement. It is important that the reward be immediate and continuous (at least in the early stages) in order to get rid of old inappropriate habits and build up new habits.

(vi) Measurement and evaluation of the behaviour change.

Two case studies follow of behaviour modification in action.

The case of Jean[3]

A family known to us at the clinic asked for our assistance in managing their three-year-old daughter, Jean. Jean had been suffering from gastroenteritis and had just returned home from hospital where she had spent one week. The mother complained that Jean was having frequent tantrums, continually following her around the house and demanding that the mother carry her. At night time, Jean refused to go to bed and screamed until lifted – this usually happened after 20 minutes' screaming. There were other problems in the household but these are not dealt with here.

Observation. This was carried out in the home setting and specimen recordings were taken by the therapist. During observation time father was at work and the older sibling at school. Mother was asked to continue with her usual chores. Observations taken over a period of one and a half hours revealed the following sequence. Each time mother attempted to leave her seat, Jean followed and demanded to be lifted. If mother refused to pick her up, Jean screamed until she complied, usually after about two or three minutes. While Jean was being carried by mother, or was following her, mother constantly reprimanded her. At the beginning of the observation period, Jean's toys were strewn about the floor. On each occasion that mother picked up any of these toys, Jean screamed and mother dropped the toy within two or three seconds. Jean also screamed when mother turned on the radio or attempted to read the newspaper. This screaming stopped when the radio was turned off or the newspaper laid down.

Plans. Following this observation we decided to proceed directly to a management plan. The following strategies were adopted:

(1) Mother was asked to ignore Jean's demands to be carried (instructed to pretend she was not there).

(2) Mother was also asked to ignore Jean's screaming behaviour and to continue with the chores. To facilitate this, mother and therapist drew up a list of tasks which she could do in the next few hours: tidy upstairs, go to the toilet (this had been a problem as Jean was insisting on accompanying the mother), wash the dishes, tidy Jean's toys, read the newspaper, or listen to the radio.

(3) When Jean stopped screaming, mother was instructed to approach her, talk to her, cuddle or play with her. If the screaming recommenced mother was instructed to again ignore the child.

Intervention. The plans were put into immediate effect and therapist observations recommenced. When mother went upstairs, Jean followed her demanding to be carried. Later, when mother came downstairs, Jean remained on the landing and screamed for 15 minutes. Mother began to tidy the toys and Jean came into the same room where she screamed for a further 10 minutes. Immediately Jean was quiet, mother was cued to pick her up and cuddle her. However, mother could not continue to give Jean undivided attention so she left her after five minutes and went into the kitchen to wash the dishes. Jean started to scream again. As instructed, mother ignored this behaviour but again cuddled Jean when she stopped screaming. The procedure was continued over a two-hour period during which the screaming was reduced to occasional episodes lasting for a few minutes. At the end of this session, father returned from work and the day's programme was reviewed and discussed with him.

A plan was evolved for coping with Jean's bedtime behaviour. The parents were instructed to put Jean to bed after playing with her for a short time and to ignore the subsequent screaming. If Jean came downstairs she was to be returned to bed without any interaction. It was explained to the parents that they could check on Jean at night if her prolonged screaming caused them concern. However, they were instructed to confine interaction to the minimum and not to engage in argument or discussion. Therapist observations taken the next day revealed that daytime behaviours were improved. The mother's event records showed only two tantrums on that morning. Further, mother had generalised the principles. Jean had demanded an early lunch, which mother found inconvenient, so mother stated that she would have lunch at the normal time. She ignored the subsequent tantrum and Jean took her lunch one hour later. Visits were made on the subsequent two days and observation showed that the daytime behaviours had maintained their improvement. Night-time crying was now lasting only five to ten minutes. Over the next two months, parent records revealed continued and maintained improvement. This case, which was regarded as fairly straightforward, required about five hours' therapist time.

The case of George

George, a seven-year-old child, was referred to us with a wide range of behaviour problems. His parents were unable to cope with his disobedience, verbally abusive behaviour, messy eating habits, physical aggression and hyperactivity. The family's social life was curtailed as both parents felt unable to take George out visiting or to entertain their friends. George had even coerced his parents into bringing his breakfast to bed each morning.

George had two older siblings – a girl aged 13 and a boy aged nine – neither of whom had ever presented behavioural problems. The parents' marital relationship appeared to be satisfactory. The case history indicated that George's behaviour problem had begun shortly after he was two years old and had gradually worsened since then. There was no history of brain injury or physical illness and he had not presented any problems at school.

Observation. In the 10 days following the initial interview, four observation sessions, each lasting one and a half hours, were conducted in the home. During these sessions both parents and siblings were present. The observations substantiated most of the above-mentioned complaints about George's behaviour. Both parents were inconsistent in dealing with George and they exhibited high frequencies of commands (on some occasions 30–40 commands per hour) which they failed to follow up. They rarely carried out threats, often omitted to label or praise socially appropriate behaviour and any social approval which was employed was used in an attempt to reduce disruptive behaviours, for example, 'That's a good boy, George; sure you wouldn't hit Daddy with the poker'. Over these observation periods, approximately 90–95 per cent parent – children attention was directed towards George; his two siblings only receiving five per cent.

Plans. As the problems were multiple it was decided initially to modify only one behaviour. As non-compliance was the major problem we decided to focus on it with an intensive programme. Intervention was to be carried out in the home under several hours' direct therapist supervision over a period of four days. In order to make maximum use of this time the parents were asked to stay off work and George was kept from school. The parents were instructed in, and practised, the sequence for time-out. They were asked in the early stages to overact their commanding and rewarding styles. In selecting rewards we decided initially to use material rewards in addition to attention and praise, as we assessed that George was relatively unresponsive to social approval. At first the parents were to use three social rewards for every material one. The following is a list of the rewards used: social approval, sweets, crisps, fruit, trip to shop with mother, ride in car with father and trip to harbour with father. The latter three rewards were known to be valued activities. The punishment to be used was five minutes' time-out in the kitchen corner. Physical force, to remove the child to time-out, was to be employed if necessary. Duration in time-out was only to begin when George was sitting quietly on his own.

Intervention. At the beginning of the first day of intervention the parents explained the rules to George. Following these instructions he was immediately non-compliant (he refused to stop jumping over the furniture) and his mother took him to time-out. George screamed and kicked and required physical restraint for 20 minutes before he quietened and duration could be timed. There were two further time-outs that afternoon which lasted 45 and 35 minutes, respectively. No occasions for reward were observed. It was during this first day that the therapist's presence was most critical as the parents needed continual encouragement during the implementation of time-out. In view of the long punishment times we suggested that the parents use George's brother as a confederate to model time-out. On succeeding days the length of time-out reduced dramatically, varying between five and 15 minutes. George also began to exhibit many instances of compliance for which he was rewarded.

During these four days it became evident that the mother was more successful than the father in managing the contingencies. We frequently had to cue the father to keep to the instructions. In order to facilitate further improvement in the father's style we drew up the following contract. The parents agreed to monitor each other's behaviour towards George. When one partner's behaviour deviated from the programme rules (for example, by giving a third command, failing to implement time-out or failing to praise) the other partner was to levy a fine of five cigarettes. This contract was operational for two weeks. Initially, the father was losing 25 to 30 cigarettes per day, while the mother lost only five or ten per day. Over three or four days the father's style improved considerably.

After a period of four days' intensive intervention, George's compliance increased dramatically. Visits were then carried out once a week, with daily telephone calls made in the intervening days, during which time any problems which arose were discussed. In the succeeding days the parents began to generalize the programme instructions. For example, at meal times they removed George from the table when he was disruptive (and if he persisted with this behaviour he was put into time-out); if he messed the bathroom he was asked to clean it and on refusal to do so was sent to time-out – this cycle was repeated until he complied. Disruptive behaviour in the evening resulted in George being sent early to bed. The parents also noted that the older siblings' behaviour had improved and they believed that this resulted from their own increased consistency in handling. One month later the improvement was sustained, but George remained hyperactive and showed a very short attention span. He was rarely able to remain still and concentrate on one activity for longer than 30 seconds at a time. As behavioural methods are not usually very successful in managing hyperactivity we prescribed a drug (methyl phenidate) which ameliorated this problem considerably. At one year follow-up the behaviour improvement was sustained.

Play therapy

Chapter 5 showed how Freud used the 'talking cure' to help adults with their problems. (Little Hans was the only *child* treated by Freud.) Using techniques of free association, slips of the tongue, hypnosis and dreams,

Freud aimed to reconstruct the past life of his patients and to find the traumatic event or events that had caused development to go wrong. Freud also believed it was necessary, using these techniques, to get in touch with his patients' unconscious wishes, needs and desires, for it was here that problems were rooted. In the course of development, according to Freud, people were forced to repress desires (like their sexual or aggressive instincts), or to regress (go back) to an earlier developmental stage. Or they might be fixated (stuck) at a particular stage. In these cases it was the task of therapy to uncover the vast mass of the iceberg (the unconscious) only the tip of which was apparent in everyday life.

While play therapy is the term used to describe the psychoanalytic technique of using play as a means of getting in touch with a child's unconscious and thereby helping him, there are almost as many different forms of play therapy as there are play therapists.

Freud's daughter, Anna Freud, was one of the earliest to use play therapy. She regarded it as a form of 'analysis': that is, a way of uncovering and changing ways in which a child's development had been distorted. Her techniques aimed to make the child aware of his conflicts and problems, to redirect 'fixated libido' more appropriately. She saw play as the 'window' to the child's unconscious. Another psychoanalyst put it like this.

> The therapist hopes that the child will learn enough about himself to recognize his feelings and his defenses and deal with them directly. In the process of achieving this, one tries to make the unconscious conscious to the child . . . Child psychoanalysts work above all on the past, thereby providing a cleared and improved ground for future development.

The child is given a playroom full of toys and other materials and is allowed considerable freedom as to what he does or how he plays. The therapist is friendly and interested but makes no direct suggestions. The aim is to accept the child for what he is, thereby giving him the confidence and the 'permission' to be himself. Gradually he finds himself through play and by expressing his hitherto hidden and unknown feelings and fantasies he is able to come to terms with them and himself.

All forms of play therapy assume that play provides a window into the child's unconscious and that the child expresses, through play, his deepest wishes and desires, fears and fantasies which may be the root of his present difficulties. Past events and unconscious feelings are considered to be the key to the understanding and cure of present problems.

The case of Dibs

Virginia Axline, an American play therapist, has written a vivid account of her therapy in *Dibs: In Search of Self*.[4]

Figure 14.2 *Children in therapy can reveal and express their feelings by the nature of their play in the sand*

It was lunch time, going home time, and the children were milling around in their usual noisy, dawdling way, getting into their coats and hats. But not Dibs. He had backed into a corner of the room and crouched there, head down, arms folded tightly across his chest, ignoring the fact that it was time to go home . . . He always behaved this way when it was time to go home. [his teacher] reached down and patted his shoulder . . . like a small fury Dibs was at her, his small fists striking out at her, scratching, trying to bite, screaming 'No go home.' . . . The teachers had tried their best to establish a relationship with him, to get a response from him. But it had been touch and go. Dibs seemed determined to keep all people at bay. . . .

There was something about Dibs' behaviour that defied the teachers to categorize him . . . His behaviour was so uneven. At one time, he seemed to be extremely retarded mentally. Another time he would quickly and quietly do something that indicated he might have superior intelligence. If he thought anyone was watching him, he quickly withdrew into his shell . . . He was a lone child in what must have seemed to him to be a cold, unfriendly world . . . he was only five years old.

Virginia Axline describes the therapy sessions, explaining some of the ideas and principles underlying her work.

I didn't want to rush him. Give him time to look around and explore. Every child needs time to explore his world in his own way . . . I attempted to keep my comments in line with his activity, trying not to say anything that would indicate any desire on my part that he do any particular thing, but rather to communicate understandingly and simply, recognition in line with his frame of reference. I wanted to let him lead the way. I would follow. I wanted to let him know from the beginning that he would set the pace in that room and that I would recognize his efforts at two-way communication with some concrete reality basis of a shared experience between the two of us. I didn't want to go overboard and exclaim about his ability to do all these things. Obviously he could do these things. When the initiative is left up to the individual he will select the ground upon which he feels his greatest security. Any exclamation of surprise or praise might be interpreted by him as the direction he must take. It might close off any other areas of exploration that might be far more important for him. All people proceed with a caution that will protect the integrity of their personality. We were getting acquainted. These *things* Dibs mentioned, objects in this room that were not involved with any serious **affect** [that is, emotional significance], were the only shared ingredients at this point for communication between us. To Dibs these were safe concepts. Occasionally he would glance at me, but when our eyes met, he would immediately look away . . . He needed to develop strength to cope with his world, but that strength had to come from within him and he had to experience personally his ability to cope with his world as it was. Any meaningful changes for Dibs would have to come from within him. We could not hope to make over his external world . . .

I wanted him to feel and experience his total self in our relationship – and not to confine it to any one kind of behaviour. I wanted him to learn that he was a person of many parts, with his ups and downs, his loves and hates, his fears and courage, his infantile desires and his more mature interests. I wanted him to learn by experience the responsibility of assuming the initiative to use his capacities in his relationships with people. I did not want to direct it into any single channel by praise, suggestion, questions. I might miss completely the essence of this child's total personality if I jumped to any premature conclusions. I waited while Dibs stood there thinking. A very slight and fleeting smile crossed his face.

'I will finger paint, play in the sand, and have a tea party,' he said.

'You are planning what you want to do during the rest of our hour?' I said.

'That's right.' he replied. He smiled more openly now . . .

'That's right,' he said, 'People are mean so I don't talk to them. But I speak to the truck. I say goodbye to the truck.'

'A truck can't say anything to hurt your feelings, can it'? I said.

'The truck is nice,' Dibs said.

He walked over to the sandbox, sat down on the ledge and raked his fingers through the sand. He pulled out a toy soldier, held it in his hands, and looked at it for a long time. Then he turned towards the sand, dug a hole with his hands and buried the soldier. On top of the mound of sand he placed a toy truck. Without a word, he made this graphic statement to dramatize his feelings . . .

. . . He went over to the doll house and took the dolls out. He re-arranged the furniture.

'The mother is going for a walk in the park,' he said, 'She wants to be alone and so she goes walking in the park where she can see the trees and the flowers and birds. She even goes over to the lake and watches the water.' He moved the mother doll away through his imagined park. 'She finds a bench and sits down to feel the sun because she likes the sun.' He placed the mother doll on a block and returned to the house. He picked up the sister doll 'The sister is going away to school. They have packed the bags and sent her away from home and she goes far away all by herself.' He moved the sister doll to a far corner of the playroom. Then he returned to the doll house and picked up the father doll.

'He is in the house alone. He is reading and studying . . . He does not want to be bothered . . . Then he goes over and unlocks the little boy's room.' He quickly put down the father doll and picked up the little boy doll. 'The boy opens the door and runs out of the house because he doesn't like the locked doors.' He moved the boy doll, but not too far from the house . . . he wept bitter tears. 'I weep because I feel again the hurt of the doors closed and locked against me . . . They used to lock me in my room.' . . . It had been a rough hour for Dibs. His feelings had torn through him without mercy. The locked doors in Dibs' young life had brought him intense suffering. Not the locked door of his room at home, but all the doors of acceptance that had been closed and locked against him, depriving him of the love, respect and understanding he needed so desperately. Dibs picked up the nursing bottle and drank from it briefly. Then he put it down and looked steadily at me. 'I'm not a baby any more,' he said, 'I'm a big boy now. I don't need the baby bottle' . . . Dibs grinned. 'Unless sometimes I want to be a baby again,' he said, 'However I feel, I will be.' He was relaxed and happy now. When he left the playroom he seemed to leave behind him the sorrowful feelings he had uprooted there.

'Today I am six years old.' The teachers were pleased with Dibs. So was I . . . I felt confident that the ability Dibs used in the playroom and at home would spill out into his other experiences. His intellectual abilities had been used to test him. They had become a barrier and a refuge from a world he feared. It had been defensive, self-protective behaviour. It had been his isolation . . . 'It's a wonderful playroom,' he said, 'It's a happy room.' It had been at times a happy room for Dibs, but there had been some sorrowful moments for him, too, as he dug around among his feelings, reliving past experiences that had hurt him deeply. As Dibs stood before me now his head was up. He had a feeling of security deep inside himself. He was building a sense of responsibility for his feelings. His feelings of hate and revenge had been tempered with mercy. Dibs was building a concept of self as he groped through the tangled brambles of his mixed-up feelings . . . Through this increasing self-knowledge, he would be free to use his capacities and emotions more constructively . . .

Dibs had come to terms with himself. In his symbolic play he had poured out his hurt, bruised feelings, and had emerged with feelings of strength and security . . . The feelings of hostility and revenge that he expressed towards his father, mother and sister still flared up briefly, but they did not burn with hatred or fear. He had exchanged the little, immature, frightened Dibs for a self-concept strengthened by feelings of adequacy, security and courage. He had learned to understand his feelings. He had learned how to cope with them and to control them. Dibs was no longer submerged under his feelings of fear and anger and hatred and guilt. He had become a person in his own right. He had found a sense of dignity and self-respect. With this confidence and security, he could learn to accept and respect other people in his world. He was no longer afraid to be himself.'

In her therapy, Virginia Axline allowed Dibs to direct the play activities and to set the pace and progress of the sessions. She assumed that his unconscious fears and wishes, as well as his earlier suffering, would come out in the play sessions, and by expressing them in the safe and protected playroom at the clinic, he would be better able to come to terms with them. Axline never directed Dibs, or suggested activities to him, rarely questioned him or interpreted his play to him, and always accepted him for what he was (however he was). She allowed him to use the playroom as he chose and made it 'safe' for him to express any feelings he might have without judging him. Dibs had exactly one hour a week in which he could do anything, feel anything, say anything without fear of approval or disapproval and the play therapist assumed that this would enable him to come to terms with and cope with the difficulties he was experiencing in the rest of his life.

Axline's play therapy aimed to recognize the feelings which Dibs was expressing and to communicate those feelings back to him in such a manner that he could gain insight into why he behaved as he did. A variety of materials in the playroom, such as sand, water, and a nursing bottle, allowed Dibs to '**regress**' to an earlier developmental stage (see Chapter 5); dolls and dolls' house permitted him to 'act out' and express his feelings, fears, and wishes; and paints, water and clay helped him to express himself. Play became a vehicle for the expression of feelings, the playroom was used as a secure place in which he could be completely himself, and Virginia Axline became the warm and permissive adult with whom Dibs could express his feelings and communicate without disapproval, judgement, interruption or control.

The theory of play therapy

Following Freud's psychoanalytic tradition and theory, play therapists take for granted the benefits of exploring the past and bringing to the fore a child's inner feelings and fantasies, enabling him to grow fully by coming to terms with his 'unconscious' past and present. In one sense also, they consider present problems and difficulties to be 'symptoms' of underlying 'causes' (for example, earlier emotional problems, unresolved conflicts at home, innate drives of aggression, some early trauma), and they believe that these 'causes' need to be uncovered and 'treated' in order for the child to overcome his present problems. Play is the medium through which the child best communicates and expresses himself; the therapist uses this communication to help him resolve his conflicts and come to terms with himself. The psychoanalytic background to play therapy may be summarized like this:

(i) Play is the child's natural medium of self-expression.
(ii) What a child does in free play may symbolize 'unconscious' wishes, fears or preoccupations that he is not aware of. (Some play therapists make interpretations to the child to increase his awareness.)
(iii) A child may 'play out' unconscious feelings and thus bring them out into the open or into his 'conscious' mind. By becoming aware of his feelings and expressing them he may learn to understand and deal with them, control them or otherwise come to terms with them.
(iv) The relationship between child and therapist is important. This relationship facilitates the child's spontaneous play and expression; it may also give him the opportunity to 'project' feelings (which he may have for his mother and father) onto an adult, thus expressing them 'safely'.
(v) Play therapy (like all psychoanalytic techniques) aims to uncover the past history and causes of a child's present difficulties. It is as though, by reliving and facing past feelings and conflicts, the child will better resolve them and come to terms with them and this will facilitate healthy development.

Like psychoanalytic theory, play therapy has been criticized for being unscientific and impossible to evaluate. As Chapter 5 made clear, most psychoanalytic hypotheses and assumptions are not readily testable or measurable. What *is* therapy and how is it measured or evaluated? It is possible to see the kind of activity and process in Virginia Axline's account of her work with Dibs, and this case appeared 'successful' if by 'success' is meant Dibs' resultant own happiness and ability to get on with his parents and friends. But what caused the success? The therapeutic technique? The toys? Virginia Axline's warm personality? The fact that an adult sat with Dibs once a week? There is no way of knowing or evaluating the outcome, and Dibs' 'cure' was probably related as much to the relationship he had with the therapist as to the technique or process of play therapy.

It is always difficult to evaluate play therapy, since the individual relationship is as unique as the individual's problems. It is difficult to find a CONTROL sample and thus to check what would have happened to a particular child if the same amount of time had passed *without* therapy.

The two therapies

Consider the case of Dibs. His behaviour changed and his problems were solved as a result of play therapy, as a result of his expressing feelings, conflicts, aggression, hostility and coming to terms with his feeling within the safety and structure of the play situation. It was assumed that Dibs' early childhood and emotional experiences were directly related to his present behaviour, and furthermore that his healthy development was hindered by unresolved emotions at an unconscious level. He was considered emotionally 'ill' and the causes of his disease were looked for in his early childhood experience; the therapist attacked the present problem by tackling its assumed causes.

By contrast both Jean and George were 'treated' only for their problem behaviour. No one sought the reasons or causes for it. The children's habits were changed by identifying aspects of their environments which could support or change the behaviour and applying a systematic programme of reinforcement.

Both therapies have been successful in solving children's problems, though they start from very different assumptions and hypotheses about human behaviour. Clearly, neither viewpoint necessarily provides a *complete* explanation of human behaviour, though both are sufficiently useful to continue in service, with their own successes, problems, variations and devotees.

	Focus of sessions	Role of therapist	Role of parents or other friends	Possibility of formal evaluation?
Play therapy (based on Freud's work)	Play, talk with therapist	Non-directive (usually)	Very little	No
Behaviour modification (based on learning theorists)	Making programme	Design programme. Reward/ punish	Offer systematic reward	Yes

Table 14.2 *The two therapies summarized*

Chapter 15

The school years: intelligence

What does it mean to say 'Jane is more intelligent than John?'. Teachers, parents, even children themselves, make this kind of statement frequently and confidently. Everyone has some idea of what they mean by 'intelligent', though an intelligent gypsy or musician may have somewhat different qualities from an intelligent sailor or mathematician.

Although children differ in the things they enjoy doing and are good at, one child showing particular talent for music, another for sport, yet another for arithmetical calculations and another for creative writing, teachers (and parents) rarely hesitate in picking out the brightest or most intelligent children in a class or group and conversely, the least intelligent.

What is intelligence?

So what qualities in a child enable one to say 'Jane is more intelligent than John?' If ten people were asked to define 'intelligent' they would probably come up with ten slightly different definitions. This is partly because intelligence is not a 'thing' of which people have greater or lesser amounts, like height or weight. Yet psychologists have been trying to measure intelligence since the beginning of the century and it has been said that 'intelligence testing is psychology's major practical contribution to society at large.'[1] However, psychologists do not usually define intelligence as separate from IQ (intelligence quotient) and generally assume for practical purposes that intelligence is simply what intelligence tests measure. The IQ is simply the score gained from an intelligence test. Because intelligence is so difficult to define, psychologists have devised tests by which a person's verbal, problem-solving, arithmetical and other abilities are all tested and together labelled as 'intelligent behaviour'.

Intelligence testing

Intelligence testing has always been necessitated and justified by the education system. The first intelligence test was devised by the Frenchman Alfred Binet, who was asked to develop a more systematic technique

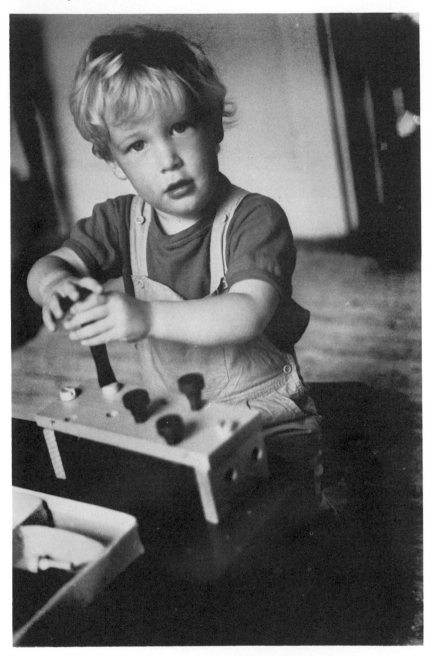

Figure 15.1 *Is intelligence a score on a standardized test, or an ability to solve problems in the real world?*

Figure 15.2 *Intelligence is revealed in many activities not connected with school. Successful poker requires plenty*

for identifying mentally retarded children in elementary schools. If there were no schools, there would be no intelligence tests. Consequently, intelligence testing has always been to a greater or lesser extent related to school functioning and school-type attainments.

At five, a child enters primary school and a world where his progress is being continually assessed and compared both with his own previous progress and that of the others in the class. An increasingly formal curriculum demands continued assessment of children's attainment (how much have they learned?) and of their potential (how much could they learn?) Is Jane doing as well as she could? How much progress has John made this year? How does John compare with Jane? Teachers have their own methods for answering these questions and devise their own tests to see how much of a particular body of knowledge has been learned. However, psychologists have devised more general and, they hope, 'objective' tests which claim to give a measure of a child's intelligence (in comparison with all other children of his age) and to predict his future performance. One of these was the old 11 plus examination, which used to be used to select children who would benefit from grammar school education. However, because of its unreliability, and the implications of this unreliability, the 11 plus examination was abandoned and the present system of comprehensive secondary education set up.

What is an intelligence test?

An intelligence test is a test which aims to measure intelligence – and intelligence is what intelligence tests measure. It is possible to break this unhelpful circle by looking at the development of intelligence tests (or IQ tests) to see what psychologists meant by intelligent behaviour. In 1933, the British psychologist Cyril Burt wrote:[2]

> By intelligence, the psychologist understands inborn, all round intellectual ability. It is inherited, or at least innate, not due to teaching or training; it is intellectual, not emotional or moral, and remains uninfluenced by industry or zeal; it is general, not specific, i.e. it is not limited to any particular kind of work, but enters into all we do or say or think. Of all our mental qualities, it is the most far-reaching; fortunately, it can be measured with accuracy and ease.

The first IQ tester, Alfred Binet

At the beginning of this century, Binet was asked by the French Government to find a way of identifying those children who were so backward that they were not likely to benefit from going to school; the French State schools were overcrowded and 'slow' children were supposed to hinder 'brighter' children from making progress. So Binet devised the first intelligence test (in 1905 with his co-worker Simon) which is still used in revised form today and sometimes for the same purpose. Intelligence testing originated as a way of selecting children for different types of education and has been used mainly for that purpose; it is therefore closely related to school attainments and abilities which are useful for academic success in a Western world.

How did Binet devise the test? He watched children solving different kinds of problems and built up a set of questions or items which were typical of the performance of children of different ages, and which discriminated between the bright and the dull ones (See Table 15.1). At each age level he had items which could be answered by about two thirds of the children of that age, such that individual children could be compared with 'average' children of the same age. If a child could answer the questions for age levels six, seven, eight, nine, ten that meant that he was as intelligent as the average ten-year-old. Thus his mental age (MA) would be 10, regardless of his actual age (chronological age – CA).

Binet worked out the standards for his test by giving it to very large groups of children at different ages and working out the averages (norms) for each age group. This enabled him to place individuals in relation to their peer group – average, above average and below average. (The Stanford-Binet (1917) was an adaptation made by an American, Lewis Terman. This was again revised in 1937 and is still sometimes used today.)

Age Level
Two   Build a four-block tower
Three   Copy a circle
Four   Name objects (shown in pictures) from memory
Five   Copy a square
Six   A table is made of wood, a window of ------
Seven   In what way are wood and coal alike?
Eight   What should you do if you found on the streets of a city a
        three-year-old baby that was lost from its parents?
Nine   What is foolish about 'Bill Jones feet are so big that he has to
        pull his trousers on over his head?'
Ten   How many words can you say in one minute?
Eleven In what way are a knife blade, penny and a piece of wire
        alike?
Twelve Repeat these seven digits backwards: 5, 9, 6, 7, 3, 8, 1

Table 15.1 *Typical questions from the Stanford-Binet test*

Three important issues emerge from this early view of intelligence testing: (i) the concept of IQ itself, (ii) the distribution of intelligence in the population and (iii) intelligence as an innate and stable capacity which can predict future performance.

The concept of IQ

By contrast with Piaget (see Chapter 7) Binet assumed that intellectual growth (or intelligence) was rather like physical growth; children grew mentally with age as they did physically, so that the older the child the more items on the intelligence test he could do. A dull child was like a normal child but retarded in growth. So the 'average' eight-year-old (CA = eight) would have a mental age of eight (MA = eight). A brighter eight year old might have a MA of ten because he could answer questions up to the ten-year level and a much duller eight year old might have a MA of six because he could only answer questions to a six-year level.

A German, Wilhelm Stern, pointed out that the mental age scores from Binet's test could be expressed MA/CA × 100 to give an IQ score. This enabled comparison between different age groups, whereas the MA score gave no indication of the age of the child. For instance, a child of six, eight and ten could all gain a MA of 10 yet be of relatively very different 'intelligence'. The bright eight-year-old with an MA of 10 has an IQ of 10/8 × 100 = 125, and a dull eight-year-old with an MA of 6 has an IQ of 6/8 × 100 = 75. An IQ of 100 is the average by definition.

In practice an IQ score derived from the Stanford-Binet test may be used by practising psychologists to place children in different schools (for example, if a child has an IQ below 70 he may go to a special school,

IQ	Description	Percentage of the population in each group
Above 139	Very superior	1
120–139	Superior	11
110–119	High average	18
90–109	Average	46
80–89	Low Average	15
70–79	Borderline	6
Below 70	Mentally retarded	3
		100

Table 15.2 *Percentage of individuals with high, average and low IQs*

though there are many other factors which are taken into account in a recommendation for such a school).

The normal distribution

The normal distribution is a method of representing the way in which many human characteristics are spread amongst the population. Most people are average and therefore account for the central 'bulk' of the bell-shaped curve (see Figure 15.3) while a small minority have very unusual

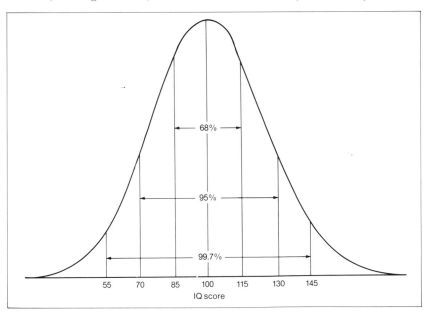

Figure 15.3 *The normal distribution or bell-shaped curve, here showing the relative frequency of IQ scores (though height, weight, and many other things follow a similar curve). Sixty-eight per cent of scores fall between 85 and 115, 95 per cent fall between 70 and 130, 99.7 per cent fall between 55 and 145, and only 0.3 per cent beyond these extremes at either end*

characteristics, for example, they may be very tiny or very tall and account for the outer edges of the curve.

Figure 15.4 is a GRAPH showing what percentage of the children from a large sample scored within which IQ ranges. It will be seen that most children scored around 100, while very few scored below 50 or above 150. This graph is an example of the 'normal distribution' (see Figure 15.4).

Francis Galton discovered in 1870 that, if one measured a large enough sample of people, many of their characteristics (weight, height, head size, foot size – and by extension, mental capacity) would roughly follow this statistical pattern. A perfect normal distribution, is actually defined as one where a given proportion of all scores should fall within a particular distance of the average.

When Binet designed his intelligence test, he made the assumption that intelligence also followed the normal distribution. He in fact used this

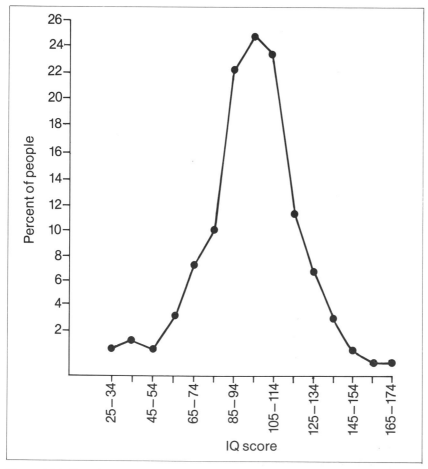

Figure 15.4 *Distribution of IQs for 2904 children aged two to 18; this is the group used for the standardization of the revised Stanford-Binet test*

HISTOGRAM
It is often useful to represent scores graphically, in order to
see how they are distributed, or spread. The set of scores is
divided up into suitable intervals (i.e. 6' – 6' 6", or 100 –
125), and the number of scores falling in each interval is
totalled. The height of each column represents the number
of scores within the interval it represents. In the example
below, the IQ scores of a class of children are represented in
intervals of 10 IQ points. It will be seen that a large number
of children had scores between 90 and 100, and between
100 and 110, and that there were decreasing numbers of
scores towards the two extremes.

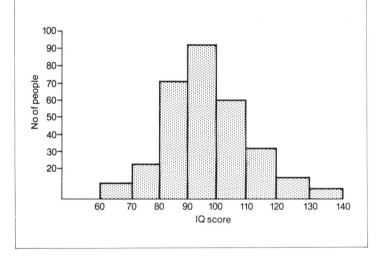

assumption as an additional check – eliminating questions that didn't
produce results in accordance with what a perfect normal distribution
would predict.

Intelligence as an innate and stable capacity

Early intelligence testers and psychologists thought of intelligence as a
quality that was largely inherited and that was fixed and stable at birth.
Therefore, they believed that with suitable measuring instruments and
techniques, it was possible to measure intelligence, in much the same way
as it was possible to measure height or weight. Furthermore, since
intelligence was supposed to be a stable characteristic, IQ scores were

GRAPH
Another way of representing a set of scores is to draw a graph. The horizontal axis represents the actual scores, and the vertical represents the number of people obtaining that score. The example below represents the same set of scores as the histogram opposite. The graph is a more detailed presentation than the histogram, since each score is plotted rather than each total of scores within a particular interval.

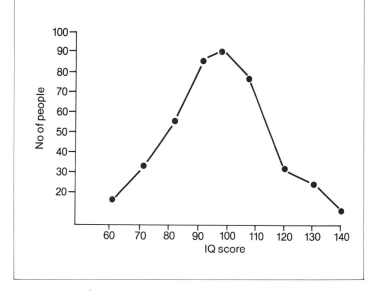

taken early on in life and were supposed to be able to predict future performance. Yet this could be a considerable problem; children who believe themselves to be dull, and are taught as if dull are not likely to become brighter suddenly. More happily, bright young children are likely to benefit from the predictions made about them.

Intelligence 'factors'

After Binet had devised the first intelligence test, other psychologists who believed in the principle of testing nonetheless became dissatisfied with the notion of intelligence as *one* quality which could be measured by one test. Realizing that there were many different kinds of intelligence, or many abilities that contributed to overall intelligence, these psychologists devised ways of defining intelligence by reference to its components. The British psychologist Spearman suggested a general factor 'g' (later equated with some idea of general intelligence) with various different specific factors. In the USA Thurstone suggested seven or eight 'primary abilities' (verbal comprehension, word fluency, number, space, memory, perceptual speed, reasoning) which contribute to overall intelligence.

Piaget's approach

Piaget's approach to the idea of intelligence contrasts strongly with the 'psychometric' approach above. Piaget thought of intelligence as the *process* of thinking (see Chapter 7). These adaptations change *qualitatively* as the child develops (not quantitatively, year on year, as Binet claimed). For Piaget intelligence is 'essentially a system of living and acting operations; i.e. a state of balance, or equilibrium achieved by the person when he is able to deal adequately with the data before him. But it is not a static state, it is dynamic in that it continually adapts itself to new environmental stimuli.' Since intelligence is a constantly changing level of adaptation it cannot be measured (according to Piaget) though progress may be charted by a series of tasks which show the qualitative stage a child has reached.

More recent intelligence tests

The education system demands that children be assessed and at times selected for suitable educational provision. The whole notion of testing assumes that it is possible to make a meaningful measurement of abilities which contribute to overall intelligence, and more recent tests have taken into account the fact that the several abilities may be measured separately within one test. The most commonly used intelligence test (though the Stanford-Binet is still used) is now one devised by an American, David Wechsler, whose tests the WAIS (Wechsler Adult Intelligence Scale) and the WISC (Wechsler Intelligence Scale for Children) and the WPPSI (Wechsler Preschool and Primary Scale of Intelligence) give two scores – a verbal IQ and a performance IQ – and a profile of scores over the ten different subtests (see Figure 15.5)

The test includes ten subtests which are supposed to tap ten different kinds of ability. The kind of questions asked in the WISC are questions of general knowledge and comprehension, arithmetic, vocabulary, reasoning (for the overall verbal scale), and non-verbal items such as puzzles, arranging a picture sequence in logical order, pointing out missing parts of pictures, making designs with different coloured bricks from a copy and coding (for the non-verbal performance scale). This test has the advantage that two separate scores are obtained for verbal and non-verbal tests and therefore children with problems or difficulties of language are able to show a 'non-verbal intelligence' score. The profile makes it possible to see

WISC profile

Clinicians who wish to draw a profile should first transfer the child's scaled scores to the row of boxes below. Then mark an X on the dot corresponding to the scaled score for each test, and draw a line connecting the X's.

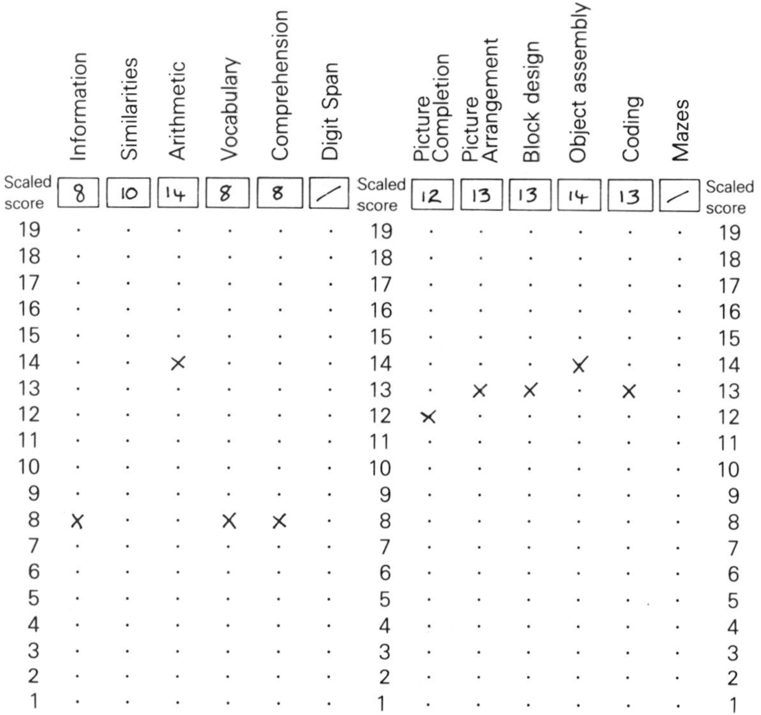

	Year	Month	Day
Date tested	80	9	29
Date of birth	71	12	25
Age	8	9	4

	Raw score	Scaled score
Verbal tests		
Information	10	8
Similarities	10	10
Arithmetic	13	14
Vocabulary	21	8
Comprehension	11	8
(Digit span)	(___)	
Verbal score		48
Performance tests		
Picture completion	18	12
Picture arrangement	30	13
Block design	30	13
Object assembly	24	14
Coding	41	13
(Mazes)	(___)	
Performance score		65

	score	Scaled IQ
Verbal score	48	97
Performance score	65	121
Full Scale score	113	109

Verbal tests — scaled scores: Information 8, Similarities 10, Arithmetic 4, Vocabulary 8, Comprehension 8, Digit Span /

Performance tests — scaled scores: Picture Completion 12, Picture Arrangement 13, Block design 13, Object assembly 14, Coding 13, Mazes /

Figure 15.5 *Profile and subtest scores for one child who took the Wechsler Intelligence Scale for Children (WISC)*

how a child scores in all the different areas and to relate these areas to programmes at school.

The Wechsler tests enable a psychologist to give separate scores to the different abilities. The child gains a 'raw score' which is the total number of questions he got right on a particular subtest and this is converted to a 'scaled score' by reference to the child's age and then to standardized tables. This means that the child's actual score is compared with the standards of children that age, and he is given a scaled score in relation to that standard. The subtest scores are then added up to give a verbal total score and a performance total, and these are converted to IQ by reference to another standardized table.

The many-pronged Wechsler tests can be related to areas of progress at school and in fact they do correlate highly with school performance (see page 38 for correlation). This may indicate no more though than that the children who are good at IQ tests are also good at school. This is not quite the same thing as indicating who is or is not intelligent.

Figure 15.6 *A fourteen-year-old attempts the block design subtest of the WISC*

Other factors that affect testing

Returning to the original statement at the beginning of the chapter: 'Jane is more intelligent than John.' This may mean that Jane has a higher IQ score than John or that Jane is brighter at school, better at maths, more articulate or better at problem solving. But there are several other factors that should be taken into consideration, such as home environment. It has been found that children from 'deprived' backgrounds often do poorly on intelligence tests, as do many children from minority ethnic groups. Although some psychologists believe this to be due to inherited differences, it may be that intelligence tests are usually constructed by middle-class white people using middle-class language, experiences and concepts and therefore biased in favour of this group. They are certainly biased towards and linked with formal education. Further, children from different backgrounds have very different early experiences and the major intelligence tests are biased in favour of white urban American or English children who have had more experience of the kind of information sampled by the tests.

The main recent criticism of intelligence testing is that the tests *are* socially or culturally biased in this way and therefore invalid and unfair. It's not only that tests may not be measuring intelligence, but also that they may be producing results that systematically flatter white middle class people. And after all, what is intelligence? Intelligent behaviour or language in one social or cultural group may be very different from that of another; the concepts and experiences familiar to some children may be completely different from and inappropriate to the life experiences of other children. According to this, we should not say 'more or less' intelligent behaviour, but many different kinds of intelligent behaviour. Yet intelligence tests sample the kinds of activities and abilities which are traditionally useful within the school curriculum that is, academically oriented skills.

Jane may be well-behaved, well motivated and always successful in class tests; on the other hand John may be disruptive, poorly motivated and never interested in tests or school work. So Jane comes to be labelled 'clever' and John 'stupid', and the teacher may have quite different expectations of the two children; she may, indeed, treat them differently. These differences will show up on an intelligence test and Jane may well gain a higher IQ score than John, even though outside school John is an enthusiastic and knowledgeable animal lover and Jane is completely bored and unimaginative at home.

So what do intelligence tests tell us? The IQ score is useful because it gives an indication or estimate of a child's present level of functioning (on the particular test and the particular date of the test). It is *not* a magical number which stays with the person all his life, fixed and unchanging. One of the dangers of IQ scores is that they may be misinterpreted or misused and the child labelled. However, when appropriately used, taking into account the limitations, the IQ score may provide a useful indication of a child's mental ability and may then enable a teacher with the help of a psychologist, to recognize underachievement and take steps to remedy it. Recently some psychologists are moving away from traditional IQ tests and making more detailed curriculum-referenced assessments.

Alternatives to IQ testing

The psychologist Bill Gillham has said that in any case 'mental testing is currently in a state of recession – or revolution, depending upon your perspective'.[3] There is a trend towards using intelligence tests and IQ scores to describe a child's *present* intellectual 'behaviour' (in school) or 'as systematic attainment samples which approximately describe the present intellectual status of a child but neither explain his condition nor determine his subsequent performance'. Psychologists are increasingly making more broadly-based and practical assessments which aim to describe the present level of a child's intellectual behaviour and understanding and to find out what he can do and what he cannot do *at a particular time*. This is quite different from labelling a child permanently with an IQ score. It is also more helpful, as it can identify ways in which a child can be helped to progress in those areas where he has difficulties.

IQ tests sample different abilities and compare how one child functions with the average functioning of children in similar situations. However, as mentioned earlier, they present a particular selection of questions at one particular time and are not necessarily related directly to the classroom situation in which the child finds himself.

Educational psychologists use IQ tests to help them and teachers to find out why a particular child is failing to make expected progress at school. Recently some psychologists have preferred to develop different forms of assessment that are directly related to remedial activities. These have been described by Bill Gillham:

(i)   Accurate identification of those children whose level of attainment is a problem
(ii) An expanded and detailed assessment to find out exactly what a child can and cannot do, i.e. what a child needs to be taught and what he already knows
(iii) An understanding of how the child understands the learning tasks and of how teaching has been organized for the particular child
(iv) A more-or-less detailed specification of remedial procedures relating to the detailed assessment and referring to the curriculum on offer to the child
(v)   Determining criteria and methods for evaluating progress

These methods are more concerned with developing the child's 'effective intelligence' and this implies a different approach to the concept of intelligence.

According to this approach, intelligence would be seen more as Piaget's 'adaptation', that is the ability to adapt to and to cope with the environment which presents itself. If the environment is an inner-city classroom, different strategies or different 'intelligence' may be required to achieve success from that required in a rural setting or in a different cultural context. Defining intelligence within a particular context and with reference to a particular purpose restores meaning to the concept of intelligence and relevance to the process of intellectual assessment.

Part Three
Method

Figure 16.1 *Observation and recording – two essential features of experimental method*

Chapter 16

Methods used in psychology

We all have notions about the world and about ourselves. They are formed from our own experience and from what we hear from our parents, teachers, other adults and children. From what we hear and read we construct a rough and ready 'common sense' psychology of our own, much of it shared by philosophers, writers and artists, all of whom also study human beings. The 'man in the street' has a perfectly workable understanding of what people are likely to do in certain situations, and why.

So what contribution does scientific psychology make? Its major task is to go beyond common sense and hearsay and to look at what actually happens in as objective a way as possible. Does a particular statement fit the facts? Is a theory an adequate explanation? And so on.

Like many others, psychologists are interested in human *behaviour* (some are also interested in animal behaviour). However, unlike others, they are involved in *scientific* study and are continually observing what people or animals do, producing theories of why they do it, and collecting evidence to support or refute them. Of course, they are also interested in 'mental' processes such as thoughts, perceptions, dreams, emotions, memories, feelings, but these can only be studied indirectly, through observing what the person (or animal) actually does. We can only observe what we see, though from this we may be able to infer something else.

All psychology is really about *observation*. It is concerned with observing behaviour, recording or measuring events and trying sometimes to draw conclusions. But it starts from observation, and may be defined as the scientific study (or observation) of behaviour.

Behaviour

A word more about behaviour. Although psychologists are interested in what makes people do what they do and be the way they are, it is not possible to study or observe these directly. Seeing, feeling, dreaming, thinking, remembering are all processes assumed to be going on from some behaviour which may be directly observed. How can I tell that you feel sad? Because I observe that you are crying. How do I know you are hungry? Because I can see you ogling the food and licking your lips. However, psychologists use the word behaviour to mean any activity which they can observe; thus speech, sleep, the beating of the heart, are all behaviour in the psychologists sense. So is a person's report about his own ideas or feelings. Behaviour really means observable activity and psychology is the study of it.

How do psychologists study behaviour? The word scientific may conjure up a picture of a laboratory where white-coated scientists make occasional adjustments to immensely complicated arrays of gadgets probably controlled by a computer. Much psychological theory has indeed been derived from studies carried out in the laboratory (though not usually by scientists in white coats). Experimentation is certainly a very important research method. Common to all psychological investigation are the basic principles of scientific enquiry: observe objectively and carefully, form a hypothesis, test it by further investigation.

The psychologist might want to test the commonly held belief, for example, that watching television at night is bad for children. But what does this mean? Is all television anytime after dark 'bad' for all children? What about educational programmes in the early evening for teenagers? What does 'bad' mean and how can this be measured? In order to investigate his hunch, the psychologist needs to be more specific and think out a working definition of his terms; he has to narrow down and define his area of interest and investigation sufficiently to be able to collect some results and test out his ideas and predictions. Perhaps he means that watching any television after 9 p.m. causes children below the age of nine years to be tired next morning. Now he has a hypothesis from which he may make predictions and which he can test. In order to find out whether his hypothesis holds true or fits the facts, he makes observations within or outside the laboratory which will substantiate or disprove it.

The aim of early psychologists was to build a science of behaviour that like biology or physics seeks laws and relationships of cause and effect in the natural world. However, human behaviour is complex. Further, it is investigated by humans, who may not achieve the same objectivity about themselves as they can about rocks or gases. Also, some flexibility is needed in studying complex behaviour which can't be reproduced on demand in the laboratory – except in the most stilted fashion. Experimental methods have not always proved to be the most effective, and a number of others have also had to be developed.

Experiments in the laboratory do have the advantage though that the environment can be controlled, so that the psychologist can single out factors he is interested in and change and manipulate those (while keeping the rest constant). For example, if he wants to find out the effects of lack of sleep on ten-year-olds' learning, he might bring a group of ten-year-olds into the laboratory and try to hold their environment and activities constant except for the amount of sleep. He then might compare one group who slept an ordinary night of ten hours and one group who only

Figure 16.2 *Sophisticated technological apparatus enables the experimenter to monitor the learning curves of a rat in a Skinner-type experiment over a long period of time*

slept three hours. He would make sure, for instance, that they all heard the same amount of noise, and that some didn't get hold of some coffee. In the controlled environment, any differences between the two groups of ten-year-olds could be more confidently assumed to be due to the lack of sleep.

On the other hand, laboratory methods are frequently criticized for creating an artificial situation. People in the laboratory behave so differently from real life that any conclusions drawn from the laboratory must be applied with caution elsewhere. It is impossible to manipulate humans in the way that it is possible to manipulate for instance the volume of gas or the temperature of a liquid, so generalizations from the laboratory to human life are dangerous. Psychologists do need to be aware of the difficulties of generalizing from the laboratory to real life, but some particularly interesting and important discoveries have been made there.

The rest of this chapter will cover techniques both in and out of the laboratory.

Carrying out an investigation

Hypothesis

Having decided on the idea which he wants to investigate, a psychologist formulates a hypothesis, that is a testable statement which he then aims to verify or to refute. The original idea may start as a hunch derived from something he has read or heard and whose truth he wishes to verify. In order to be clear about what he is investigating, he needs to define his terms precisely and to make a statement of what he thinks may happen. He makes the statement in the form of a prediction, and this formal statement of prediction is the hypothesis.

For example, returning to the idea that watching television makes children tired next morning, this could be stated in the form of a hypothesis. '(I hypothesise that) children under nine who watch television after 9 p.m. will be found to be more tired next morning than equivalent children who do not.'

Subjects: humans and animals

Having formulated a hypothesis, a psychologist has to decide on his *subjects* – those individuals who will be studied. Clearly the nature of the study determines to a great extent the kind of subjects chosen, whether they are adults, males or females, six-year-olds, teenagers or new-born babies. However, there are also ethical or other considerations which prevent some investigations being carried out on human subjects; in some of these situations animals are used and it is assumed that the findings will be relevant to, or at least suggestive about, human beings.

In developmental psychology, animals have frequently been used in studies where time or ethics prevents the use of human subjects. Using animals as subjects enables psychologists to carry out manipulations impossible with humans. Harlow's choice of rhesus monkeys (Chapter 2) enabled him to manipulate a variable (the mother's presence) which he could not have studied so systematically otherwise. This study shed important light on the 'surrogate mother' issue for humans as well as monkeys. Development proceeds more quickly in animals and it is therefore possible to follow growth from infancy to adulthood or indeed over several generations. The use of animals assumes that humans have developed from the animal world by evolution and that there is sufficient continuity to justify cautious generalization.

Having selected the kind of subject, the psychologist must select a group or sample from the population of those subjects. The population of British six-year-olds is all the six-year-olds in Britain. When a psychologist gathers results from subjects in a study, he does not want the results and conclusions to be applicable only to those particular subjects; but nor, on the other hand, is it practicable to carry out a study on the whole population. There must be a sample from the population which will be representative and unbiased, and which will enable results and conclusions to be generalized to that population as a whole.

Sample

It is of no scientific value in testing hypotheses about normal children if the sample is uncharacteristic, e.g. particularly docile or aggressive or intelligent. Results drawn from these subjects could not be generalized. The sample also needs to be sufficiently large. Suppose one wanted to test whether, for example, redheads were impulsive. If 80 per cent of a sample of 2,000 were, that would tell us something significant. If 80 per cent of a sample of five were, that could just be coincidence.

Psychologists sometimes attempt to obtain a random sample, that is a collection of individuals drawn by lot. This might be done by drawing names out of a hat, or by taking the first 50 names from an electoral register (though this would provide a random sample only of those qualified to vote). Alternatively it would be possible to take the first 50 people born in one year, or the first 50 people from a busy London shopping street, though both of these methods would introduce a slight bias into the sample (the shopping street sample for instance would be short of full-time workers and of people who avoid leaving home).

In practice, however, psychologists often have to carry out experiments on the sample of people available to them, such as psychology students, housewives, children from a particular school or adults of a certain professional group. In order that the experiment may be repeatable by other experimenters, the type of subjects is always mentioned when the experimenter describes his study.

Having selected a sample of subjects, the psychologist decides on an appropriate method of investigation.

Longitudinal or cross-sectional studies.

When a psychologist wants to look at change over time, or the effects of some factor on later development, he must choose between longitudinal and cross-sectional studies. Both these methods enable him to look at development at different ages. In a longitudinal study, the same group of children is studied repeatedly over an extended period, while in a cross-sectional study the investigator selects groups of children of different ages and studies them at that time. For example, an investigator using the longitudinal method might follow up a group of children at yearly intervals between the ages of five and ten to study the development of logic; the same study could be made using the cross-sectional method and studying six different groups of children aged five, six, seven, eight, nine and ten years. Clearly the longitudinal method is expensive and time-consuming, and can be difficult to carry out since subjects move house or lose interest. On the other hand, it eliminates individual differences between subjects – there's no danger that what looks like development may be a difference between some very bright eight-year-olds, for instance, and some very uncooperative seven-year-olds. An example of a longitudinal study which is still in progress is the National Child Development Study, carried out by the National Children's Bureau. That followed and still follows the progress of all the people in Great Britain born during the week of 3–9 March, 1958. The sample of about 16,000 have now been followed up four times (at 7, 11, 16, and 23 years) and their progress on a number of different measures has been recorded.

Hypothesis, subjects and temporal nature of study decided, the psychologist next has to choose between using experimental method or one of a variety of non-experimental methods.

Experimental method

The essential feature of experimental method is the manipulation of variables. The experimenter has an idea or hunch which he formulates as a research hypothesis, and he manipulates or changes one variable in order to see what effect this has on another. The variable which he manipulates (say, amount of television watched) is called the *independent variable* and the one on which he measures the effect or change is the *dependent variable* (tiredness next morning). In order to be sure that the change observed in the dependent variable is due to the independent variable and not to other factors in the subject or the environment, he carries out the experiment in carefully controlled conditions, like a laboratory, where everything can be held constant except for that one factor he is manipulating. There are clearly all sorts of factors which influence human behaviour, some of them unknown to the experimenter or the subject himself, but the experimenter does his best to get rid of as many as possible so that he may find out the effect of the one factor in which he is interested.

By manipulating one variable while controlling all others, a psychologist can draw conclusions about cause and effect with a degree of confidence not possible with non-experimental methods. Probably the commonest way to design an experiment in psychology is to divide a group of subjects randomly into an experimental group and a control group, then introduce a change for the experimental group and no change for the control. Here the experimental manipulation is the presence or absence of the independent variable and the effect of the independent variable on the dependent variable is clear from the differences between the two groups.

For example, the hypothesis: 'Watching violent television programmes has an effect on aggressive behaviour' has been investigated by experiment several times (and actually not always with the same result, which shows how important it is to describe experiments exactly. Otherwise results can't be compared).

In 1971 an experiment was actually carried out by Feshbach and Singer, over a period of six weeks, in residential schools, which acted as the 'laboratory' or controlled environment in this case, since there the experimenters had control over the activities and television viewing of the subjects (all boys). All the boys watched a minimum of six hours television a week; those who were assigned to the experimental group had to select their programmes from a list of particularly violent films and programmes, while those who were assigned to the control group had to select their television viewing from a list of non-violent programmes. Their aggressive behaviour was measured by personality tests taken at the beginning and end of the six weeks and by behaviour-ratings made by the teachers or house-parents. These particular experimenters found that, in general, viewing violent television programmes over the six-week period did not produce any increase in aggressive behaviour.

What were the variables in this study?

Variables

Variables are simply things that vary (or change) or are caused to vary (or change). In an ideal experiment, the experimenter manipulates the *independent variable* (IV), holds all other variables constant while he observes and measures changes in the *dependent variable* (DV). In this experiment, the violent or non-violent television programmes (manipulated by the experimenter) were the independent variable and the boys' aggressive behaviour the dependent variable. The variables to be held constant range from environmental variables such as noise, temperature, space, or distractions, to subject variables such as the difference in sex, age, intelligence, background or previous experience of the variables being studied by the experiment. In the television experiment the experimenters controlled as many variables as they could by having the boys in a constant environment, the residential school.

Controls

This word has cropped up several times already and is one of the concepts most important to experimental method. Apart from its usual meaning (as in 'controlling the environment') it has a particular meaning. A control group is a group for whom the experimenter does *not* alter the independent variable. This group is needed for comparison. For instance, if a scientist is testing a new drug, he will give half his subjects the drug and half a pill or injection containing no drug at all, (and of course he will not say which subject is getting which). Then when he compares the two groups he can see the effect of the drug without worrying about whether his subjects are simply suggestible and have convinced themselves that the drug works. Of course, it is very important that the control group is similar to the experimental group in all relevant respects (for example, age, sex, IQ, home background and previous experience) and that they undergo exactly the same procedure except for the experimental or independent variable.

The experimental and control groups may be *matched* on important characteristics. Another way of making a suitable control group is to allocate the subjects randomly either to the experimental group (in this case that viewing violent television programmes) or to the control group (viewing non-violent television programmes). This makes it reasonably likely that odd factors that could affect results will be spread more or less equally over both groups.

In addition to using control groups there are ways of arranging the experiment which control for variables such as tiredness and practice; these are to do with the order in which the subjects carry out the conditions of the experiment. In the television experiment there are two conditions, condition A (experimental) and condition B (control). If all the boys went through both conditions (i.e. watched violent programmes for a six-week period and watched non-violent programmes for a six-week period) this would be called a *repeated measures* design. If the boys were randomly allocated to the two conditions, this would be an *independent subjects design*. If the subjects were matched in pairs (e.g. twins) and one of each pair allocated to one condition, the other of the pair allocated to the other condition, this would be a *matched pairs* design.

The way subjects are allocated may affect the results, since subjects may become tired, bored or practised if they do both conditions, yet if they only do one there is more possibility that differences in result might be due to differences in subject allocation.

Controls in psychology help to ensure that observations are as 'pure' as possible, repeatable and generalizable. They provide an important means of making the study of behaviour 'scientific'.

Non-experimental methods_

Experimental method is only one of many ways in which psychologists study behaviour. It is not always possible or desirable to study behaviour in the laboratory. A young baby, for instance, might behave very differently in a strange laboratory from how he does at home with familiar people and toys around him.

So, moving outside the laboratory, there are many different ways of collecting information, some formal and rigorous, others less formal. A psychologist might be found sitting in the corner of a nursery recording observations of a particular child playing (this is *naturalistic observation*) or he might make detailed notes and a reconstruction of a subject's past history (*a case study*); he might go out into the High Street and interview a sample of people for their views on children (*survey*) or he might collect facts from a large health centre seeking a possible link between smoking and lung cancer (*correlational study*).

Naturalistic observation

Naturalistic observation involves careful and detailed observations of behaviour in a natural setting. The method was originated by ethologists who aimed to record and classify animal behaviour patterns.

Figure 16.3 *The observer records but does not intrude on the children's natural play*

Konrad Lorenz (see Chapter 3) was carrying out an ethological study when he observed the greylag goslings who followed him immediately after they were hatched. Although ethologists originally studied animals in their natural setting (i.e. usually the wild), there is growing interest in child ethology, in which children are studied in *their* 'natural' environments (playground, home, or park).

Here is an example of a careful animal observation:

> My technique of habituating the gorillas [i.e. getting them used to me] was simple but essential, for I could only obtain unbiased data on their behaviour if they remained relatively unaffected by my presence. I usually attempted to approach the group undetected to within about 150 feet before climbing slowly and in full view of the animals onto a stump or the low branch of a tree where I settled myself as comfortably as possible without paying obvious attention to them. By choosing a prominent observation post not only was I able to see the gorillas over the screen of herbs, but, reciprocally, they could inspect me clearly, which was the most important single factor in habituating the animals. Under such circumstances they usually remained in the vicinity to watch me, and even approached me to within five feet. I found it remarkably easy to establish rapport with the gorillas. This process was greatly facilitated by the placid temperament of the animals, and by certain conditions which I imposed on myself: (a) I carried no firearms which might inbue my actions with unconscious aggressiveness; (b) I moved slowly, and used binoculars and cameras sparingly at the beginning to eliminate gestures which could be interpreted as threat; (c) I nearly always approached them alone, leaving my companions behind and out of sight at the point where the animals were first noted; (d) I wore the same drab olive-green clothes every day; and (e) I almost never tracked the gorillas after they had voluntarily moved out of range. This last point was, I believe, of special value, for at no time were they subjected to pursuit, an action which could easily frighten them as well as increase the chance of attacks. By adhering to my conditions I not only habituated six groups to my presence quite well but also was never attacked, even though I inadvertently stumbled into the middle of a group or nearly collided with animals several times.

Although naturalistic observation studies may at first sight seem less formal and rigorous than experiments, much scientific preparation is necessary in order to carry them out. What categories of behaviour to observe? At what time intervals? What are the important features of the natural setting? Will the animal (or child) be aware or unaware of the observer and will that affect what he does? Chapter 11 illustrates some of the very careful preparation and categorization that went into the Oxfordshire observation of children at play. However, naturalistic observations are not only a valuable methodological tool in themselves, they also enable psychologists to develop hunches which they can later test by experiment.

Case study

Some of the most famous case studies have been those produced by Freud (see Chapter 5). The case study approach is sometimes called the 'clinical method' (not to be confused with Piaget's clinical interview) because it is mainly used by clinicians and clinical psychologists when they are treating patients. The psychologist tries to reconstruct a history of the subject's past life on the basis of his memories, reports by other members of his family, and other records. It involves work rather like that of a detective in piecing together an accurate picture of past events.

The example of Anna O (see Chapter 5) is one of Freud's most famous case studies. From the detailed reconstruction of her past history and the significant events in her life, Freud was able to trace the source of her neurotic problems back to a traumatic event in her early childhood.

Case study method usually involves one subject although studies such as that by Anna Freud and Sophie Dann used several individual subjects. It involves no kind of scientific proof and cannot be completely objective, but it provides a particularly useful tool in the understanding and treatment of problem behaviour.

Survey

Everyone is familiar with the idea of a survey, such as those carried out for opinion polls. It is a useful method for collecting information from a large number of people in a relatively short time. Surveys usually consist of a carefully-constructed set of questions, which are presented either as a questionnaire or in an interview given to a large (and usually random) sample of people. The wording of the questions is important, since it may bias the way people answer.

Psychologists using surveys have to be careful that their samples really are characteristic, since they usually wish to be able to say something about the population as a whole. It is occasionally possible to carry out a census survey in which every single member of the population is questioned. Usually, however, the sample has to be restricted. Telephone directories and electoral registers are sometimes used to obtain a sample that is likely to be characteristic because it is random; even these, though, may produce a slightly biased sample (e.g. in favour of that part of the population that has a telephone and is not ex-directory). Obviously, surveys are useful to politicians and advertisers, but they are also useful to psychologists, particularly when they are investigating topics such as the effect of housing on reading performance or the various ways of disciplining children used by different ethnic groups. Although surveys do not establish cause and effect relationships in behaviour, they may produce ideas for further and more detailed investigation.

Correlational methods

When we say that there is a correlation between a person's height and weight, we mean merely that they are related: a positive correlation means that there is a positive relationship (the taller the person, the heavier) while a negative correlation means a negative relationship (for example, the more expensive the train fares, the fewer passengers, perhaps). Correlational methods aim to reveal events which are positively or negatively related to each other – though there is not necessarily any cause-effect relationship between them; if a correlation is found it does not mean that one event necessarily caused the other.

This fact would be very important, for example, if we were interested in the possible relationship between lung cancer and smoking. It would be possible to collect data from a sample of patients with lung cancer, and from a sample without and record whether they smoked or did not smoke. The data might look like this (these data have been invented):

	Smokers	Non-smokers	Total
Cancer	2,300	780	3,080
No cancer	4,650	6,520	11,170
	6,950	7,300	14,250

Table 16.1

Of 14,250 subjects, 6,950 were smokers and 7,300 were non-smokers. Of the smokers 2,300 had developed lung cancer, 4,650 had not. Of the non-smokers, 780 had developed lung cancer, 6,520 had not. This looks like a correlation but it sheds no light directly, of course, on the causes of lung cancer. Both smoking and cancer could be caused by something else, like anxiety or stress.

Although a high correlation does not indicate that one thing caused another, it does enable us to predict the likelihood of one thing occurring given the occurrence of the other. If two events are highly correlated, the presence of one means that the other is more likely. Correlations establish probable relationships. The correlational studies of smoking and cancer led to later experimental studies and now the link between smoking and lung cancer has been experimentally confirmed.

The Rutter, Tizard, Whitmore study on the Isle of Wight quoted in Chapter 3 looked at possible relationships between factors at home (broken homes) and later behaviour problems or delinquency. They were investigating the possible correlation between parental separation and later delinquency, though even if they had found a high correlation, this would not have meant that one caused the other. As is often the case with correlational data, there might be a third factor involved – in this case parental discord and quarrelling – linked to both factors and therefore responsible for the correlation.

Correlation is expressed by a number between −1 (a perfect negative correlation) and +1 (a perfect positive correlation), with 0 implying no correlation at all. Perfect correlations are very rare indeed, but +0·9 would be a high positive correlation and −0·9 a high negative correlation.

Some developmental questions can be answered by surveys or by observing what goes on in the natural environment. Many questions, however, especially causal ones, require animal experiment since it is often impossible or unethical to manipulate variables or control conditions when studying human development. For example, humane considerations would not allow a psychologist to allocate children into conditions of either maternal deprivation or normal mother, or to design an experiment to measure the effects of inhuman discipline on later development.

Collecting results

Having carried out the investigation (using experimental or non-experimental methods) the psychologist presents the results (data) which will either support or refute his hypothesis. There are various ways of presenting results, and it is important to give as much information in as clear and useful a way as possible.

Table

A table is an orderly arrangement of numerical information and is the simplest way of presenting results and the form in which most results begin. A complete table of all the individual results presents 'raw data' (called this because nothing has yet been done to summarize or interpret them). The table is clearly headed and labelled to show what the numbers refer to.

Subject	Condition A (violent television)	Condition B (non-violent television)
1	6	2
2	7	4
3	3	7
4	10	4
5	4	2
6	6	3
7	5	0
8	7	2

Table 16.2 *Number of aggressive incidents seen in each subject*

Table to show number of aggressive incidents initiated by boys who viewed either (a) violent television programmes or (b) non-violent television programmes (invented data)

What does this table tell us? It presents scores for the number of aggressive incidents initiated by 16 boys who watched different television programmes. It also tells us that the range of scores (lowest to highest) for condition A boys was 3 to 10 and the range for condition B boys was 0 to 7. On average, condition A boys initiated six aggressive incidents, while condition B boys initiated three aggressive incidents. This average is sometimes called the mean. Both the range and the mean are useful ways of describing and comparing data although closer inspection is necessary before any conclusions can be drawn. From this table it would be possible to conclude that the boys who had watched violent programmes initiated more aggressive acts on average than the boys who had watched non-violent ones. However, one difficulty with averages is that they are strongly influenced by single extreme scores; a single high score among lower scores will raise the average artificially.

Histogram

A histogram is a diagram which shows the spread of scores or measurements within certain limits. The blocks show the number of people in a sample whose scores fall within the limit defined on the horizontal axis. The figure below shows that (a) 5′ 2″ to 5′ 4″ was the commonest height and (b) 90 to 100 the most frequent IQ score. The histogram presents results so that it is easy to see at a glance the spread of scores; it gives a general picture of how data are distributed, and the proportion of subjects falling into each category (see Figure 16.4).

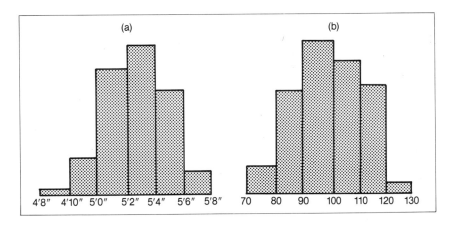

Figure 16.4 *Two histograms: (a) shows the distribution of height in a class of fourteen-year-olds; (b) the distribution of IQ in another class*

Graph

A graph is a line or curve formed by plotting numerical data on two axes.

Chapter 15 described the normal distribution which is a curve (or graph) showing the number of people of different (for example) IQ scores. (See Figures 15.3 and 15.4.) Histogram (b) is another presentation of the same data.

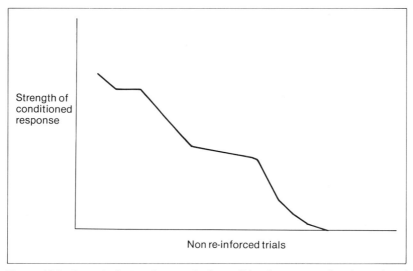

Figure 16.5 *A graph plotting the strength of a conditioned response against the number of non-reinforced trials*

Scattergram (or scatter diagram)

A scattergram shows the 'scatter' of individual scores (on two measures on the two axes) and presents data (usually correlational data) in an almost pictorial form, so that it is possible to see at a glance what kind of relationship or correlation exists between two sets of scores. If the points are scattered along a straight line, this indicates a high correlation, whereas if they are scattered all over this indicates a low correlation or no correlation at all. A scattergram presents the values of one set of scores on one axis (x) and the values of the other set on the axis (y). (See Figure 16.6.)

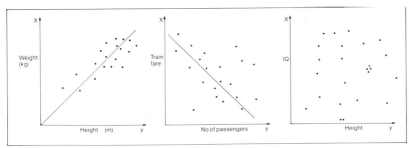

Figure 16.6 *Three examples of a scattergram*

Drawing conclusions from data

Psychologists collect data in order to support or refute their hypotheses. Assuming that they are usually observing only a sample of behaviour, how confidently can they generalize results to the population of humans or animals as a whole? Mention has been made of some of the techniques used to ensure that the study is as representative as possible – these include sampling techniques and controls. In addition psychologists use techniques of statistics with which they analyse data. These techniques have been developed to take into account the different types of data collected by psychologists, but basically they all set out to reveal how likely it is that a particular result is significant, and not the result of chance. For instance, suppose I have two groups of 100 children each, give them both the same IQ test, and find that one group scores on average 5 points more than the other. Is that group really better at IQ tests, or is this a chance result? Statistics can indicate the odds against a difference like this appearing between two *equal* groups. If they are very long odds indeed, we can safely assume these groups are *not* equal – that there is a difference in ability.

Statistical methods can tell psychologists how confident they should be that their results are not due to chance. We cannot pursue them further in this book, but serious study of psychology requires a sound acquaintance with them.

Method	Characteristics
Experiment	Form hypothesis. Manipulate IV, control other variables, measure DV.
Naturatistic observation	Select individuals and environment. Observe unobtrusively, record, analyse according to well-defined categories of behaviour.
Case study (usually one subject)	Record what subject and others remember, consult written records, reconstruct a history.
Survey	Administer questionnaire, or interview a large sample.
Correlational study	Collect data for two factors (or more) and compare to see relationship.

Table 16.3 *A summary of how different kinds of empirical studies are carried out*

How observation and experiment connect

Observation is the starting point for all psychological enquiry, and has been continually developed and refined as a method by psychologists. Many psychologists, particularly those interested in child development, believe that investigations should so far as possible always be in the 'natural environment'. However, although observation often suggests that events are related to each other, it cannot explain how or why. In the nineteenth century the philosopher J. S. Mill pointed out that although we may observe regular relationships between events, we cannot say anything about the relationship and certainly not that one event causes the other; otherwise we would be led to the absurd conclusion that night causes day and vice versa. So in their attempts to understand behaviour and their desire to find out what causes what, psychologists often move into the area of experimentation where it is more possible to isolate events, manipulate variables, and control the rest of the environment finely enough to pinpoint causes.

Summary

Return to the beginning of the text. All sorts of people have commonsense notions about children and ideas on how they develop and how they should be brought up. Often these ideas conflict with one another, and fads and fashions come and go. At one time parents were warned of the dangers of over-indulgence and spoiling the child, while a few years later they learned the horrifying consequences of a rigid discipline. One practitioner recommends feed on demand and comfort for the baby when he cries, while another emphasizes the routine of four-hourly feeds and ignoring his attention-seeking behaviour. How are we to disentangle the threads of truth from the web of commonsense and personal prejudice?

This is where the psychologist takes up the challenge of objectivity, and attempts to collect information in a scientific manner to establish facts about behaviour. But the boundaries between sound commonsense and science are not clearly defined, and psychologists too find themselves advancing with more or less certainty. Some methods are more rigorous than others, some facts more easily established than others, and psychologists use all available methods of investigation to push back the boundaries of commonsense and build a framework of scientific truth. Science also proceeds in fits and starts. Scientists may have a hypothesis which appears to fit the facts and provide the cornerstone for theory; this theory may be supported for some years until one day it is refuted by fresh evidence which sheds a new light and creates a more sophisticated theory. Psychologists are continually formulating and testing hypotheses about human and animal behaviour and gradually building the firm foundations and structure of a scientific theory.

Some of the 'giants' of child psychology, such as Freud, Bowlby, or Piaget, put forward grand theories to explain development, and justified these by quoting evidence derived from various methods and sources. Such theories provide fruitful sources for later investigations; later psychologists looked critically at some of those early studies, and usually collected evidence which pointed out the need for new, more sophisticated and complex explanations of human development. Chapter 7 shows how the theory of Piaget is continually subjected to test and rethinking.

We have looked at some of the theories put forward by psychologists investigating human and animal behaviour and considered some of the ways in which psychological theory has been applied to the practice of caring for and educating children. We emphasize the importance of methods used in psychology since an understanding and appreciation of methodology enables the student to go forward to criticize, evaluate, observe and investigate, and discriminate between, facts derived from common sense or hearsay and those established by the tests of science. The ideal is that research and practice should move forward hand in hand so that scientists inform practitioners and those working in the field feed back to the researchers. By this means; children can be better understood, and their lives enriched.

Glossary

When a phrase is divided by a /, both halves are to be found separately in the glossary.

ACCOMMODATION (Piagetian theory)
The process whereby a **schema** is modified to fit better with the environment. It is through accommodation that schemas become differentiated. (*See also* **assimilation, adaptation**.)

ACTION PATTERN (Piagetian theory)
A well-practised action which is guided by a **sensory-motor schema**, e.g. a child's striking at objects.

ADAPTATION (Piagetian theory)
Fitting in with – and thriving in – the environment. According to Piagetian theory, adaptation is achieved through the complementary processes of **assimilation** and **accommodation.**

AFFECT (Freudian theory)
Emotion, feeling or mood.

ALIMENT (Piagetian theory)
A new object (or idea) that 'feeds' a **schema** until it becomes more practised.

ANAL STAGE (Freudian theory)
The second stage of **psycho-sexual/development**, in which the child's main source of pleasure comes from expelling or retaining his faeces.

ANIMISM
Attributing feelings and intentions to non-living things. In Piagetian theory, children's thinking is characterised by animism in the years 2–6.

ASSIMILATION (Piagetian theory)
The process by which new information is taken in and incorporated into existing **schemas**. (*See also* **accommodation**.)

ASSOCIATION
A connection between two events. Associative learning occurs when a child or animal changes its behaviour after events in the environment have been paired. (*See* **classical conditioning, operant conditioning**.)

ATTACHMENT
The forming of a close, emotional tie between mother and baby. Some psychologists say that there is a **sensitive period** during which this 'bonding' must occur if the child is to develop normally.

BABBLING
The speech-like (but meaningless) sounds produced by babies.

BEHAVIOUR MODIFICATION
See **behaviour therapy**.

BEHAVIOUR THERAPY
A method of therapy based on learning theory. It uses techniques of **observational learning, shaping of behaviour**, and **reinforcement** to change behaviour.

BEHAVIOURISM
A branch of psychology associated with J. B. Watson. It defines psychology as the study of behaviour and limits its data to observable activities, thus leaving out thoughts and feelings.

BONDING
See **attachment**.

CHAINS OF THOUGHT
Sequences of ideas and memories that pour forth under the therapeutic technique of **free association**.

CHRONOLOGICAL AGE (CA)
Age from birth, or calendar age. (*See also* **mental age**, **intelligence quotient**.)

CLASSICAL CONDITIONING
Learning which occurs when a previously neutral *conditioned stimulus*, through repeated pairing with an *unconditioned stimulus*, acquires the response originally associated with that *unconditioned stimulus*. Thus: a dog salivates when food appears. Food is the *unconditioned stimulus* and salivation the *unconditioned response*. If a bell is made to ring whenever the food appears it will, after a while, cause the dog to salivate even if food is not forthcoming. The bell is the *conditioned stimulus*. The salivation is now the *conditioned response*. Note that the conditioned response is the same as the unconditioned response – it is just paired with a new stimulus. (This is also called Pavlovian conditioning.)

COGNITION, COGNITIVE DEVELOPMENT
Pertaining to the intellect, and its development.

CONCEPT
A mental category. The category may refer to *things* (such as chairs, objects, or dogs) or to *ideas* (such as truth, or infinity).

CONCRETE OPERATIONS (Piagetian theory)
Mental 'actions' that are characterized by **logic** and mathematics. When a child's **schemas** become logical (at 6–7 years) he is said to have entered the concrete operational sub-period of the **operational period**. (*See also* **formal operations**.)

CONDITIONED RESPONSE
See **classical conditioning**.

CONDITIONED STIMULUS
See **classical conditioning**.

CONDITIONING (learning theory)
The process by which conditioned responses are learned (*see* **classical conditioning** and **operant conditioning**).

CONSERVATION (Piagetian theory)
The realization that changing the physical appearance of things does not change their quantity, volume or mass.

CRITICAL PERIOD
See **sensitive period**.

DETACHMENT
Psychological withdrawal that occurs when young children are separated from their mothers for long periods of time.

DEVELOPMENT
The process whereby a person or animal grows and becomes more complicated. It is partly a genetic process (**maturation**) and partly a process of interaction with the environment. When the *mind* becomes more complicated, it is called cognitive development; when *feelings* get more complicated, it is called emotional development. When new *ways of interacting with others* appear, it is called social development.

EGO (Freudian theory)
The part of the personality that deals with the external environment in rational ways; it operates according to the **reality principle**.

EGOCENTRISM
Taking oneself as the sole reference point when thinking and perceiving.

EQUILIBRIATION (Piagetian theory)

A 'self-righting' kind of thinking or acting that helps the child to attain a new stage in cognitive **development** by resolving a contradiction.

ETHOLOGY

A branch of zoology concerned with the behaviour of animals, especially those actions that enable them to adapt to their environments.

EXTINCTION (learning theory)

(a) The 'unlearning' of a response.

(b) In **operant conditioning**, the experimental procedure of removing the usual **reinforcement** after the response. In **classical conditioning**, the experimental procedure of no longer pairing the conditioned stimulus and the unconditioned stimulus. In both cases, a reduction in response is the result.

FORMAL OPERATIONS (Piagetian theory)

Mental 'actions' that are characterized by *abstract* **logic** and mathematics. When the child's **schemas** become abstract in logic and maths (at age 10–11 years) he is said to enter the formal operational sub-period of the **operational period**. (*See also* **concrete operations**.)

FREE ASSOCIATION

Letting one thought follow another without censoring or judging. This technique helps to uncover **unconscious** thoughts and memories.

GENES

A chemical blueprint for **maturation**. Through genetic inheritance children acquire *traits* such as eye colour and *behaviours* such as sucking.

GENETIC INHERITANCE

See **genes**.

GENITAL STAGE (Freudian theory)

The fifth, *adult*, stage of **psycho-sexual/development** in which the main source of pleasure comes from mature genital contact.

GRAMMAR

A set of rules for linking words together in a meaningful way.

ID (Freudian theory)

That part of the personality where the impulses of the **libido** arise. Its functioning is characterized by the **pleasure principle**.

IDENTIFICATION (Freudian theory)

The process whereby an individual takes on (metaphorically) the identity of another (for instance the father or mother) as a way of growing and changing.

IMITATION

Copying the behaviour of others (a form of **observational learning**).

IMPRINTING

The process whereby young animals learn to follow an individual or thing, and as a result treat individuals of that species, or things of that type, first as a parent and later as a mate. If following occurs during the **sensitive period**, this learning is difficult to reverse.

INFANTILE SEXUALITY

The Freudian theory of childhood that claims that children have sexual impulses (**libido**) which – although not mature – are directed towards the parent of the opposite sex.

INFERENCE

Reasoning of the following kind: if X leads to Y and Y leads to Z, then X leads to Z.

INNATE

In-built, a capacity transmitted to the individual through the **genes**.

INSTINCT

An inherited need or action.

INSTRUMENTAL LEARNING
Change in behaviour that occurs as a result of **operant conditioning**.
INTELLIGENCE QUOTIENT (IQ)
A score used to measure intelligence, based on a ratio between **mental age**, as defined by an intelligence test, and **chronological age**.
INVARIANCE
A fixedness in the **sequence** according to which **development** takes place. Both Freud and Piaget believed that development followed an invariable pattern (though of course their theories proposed sequences of quite different kinds).
LATENCY STAGE (Freudian theory)
The fourth stage of **psycho-sexual/development**, in which the impulses of **libido** lie dormant until adolescence.
LEARNING
A change in behaviour brought about through **reward, punishment, association** or **observational learning**.
LIBIDO (Freudian theory)
The energy of the sex **instinct**.
LOGIC
A kind of reasoning that requires rules.
LOGICAL OPERATIONS (Piagetian theory)
Mental 'actions' that follow rules. When a child's thinking is characterized by formal **logic**, he is said to be in the **formal operational** sub-period.
MAKE-BELIEVE PLAY (Piagetian theory)
Play which includes elements of pretence or fantasy. It is particularly prevalent in the **pre-operational period** (2–6) and requires capacity for using words or objects symbolically.
MASTERY PLAY (Piagetian theory)
A kind of play seen often in the **sensory-motor period** (0–2) when the child is particularly absorbed by practising different actions.
MATURATION
The genetic process which causes physical growth and contributes to the acquisition of cognitive, emotional and social complexity. (*See also* **development**).
MENTAL AGE (MA)
A unit proposed by Binet to describe level of intellectual attainment. On standardized texts an average 6-year-old would have a mental age of 6, whereas a bright 6-year-old might have a mental age of 7 or 8. (*See* **chronological age, intelligence quotient**).
MENTAL STRUCTURES (Piagetian theory)
The **schemas** that guide motor action in babies and logical or mathematical problem-solving in older children and adults.
MORAL REALISM (Piagetian theory)
Judging an act to be right or wrong according to its consequences, and not according to the intention of the actor. According to Piaget, children are moral realists until 8 years or thereabouts.
OBJECT PERMANENCE (Piagetian theory)
Understanding that objects continue to exist when they are out of sight.
OBSERVATIONAL LEARNING (learning theory)
Learning by observing an adult or child and then imitating his or her actions. The person whom the learner copies is called the model.
OEDIPUS COMPLEX (Freudian theory)
The quasi-sexual love for the parent of the opposite sex (and hostility to the parent of the same sex) which is felt by children in the **phallic stage**.
OPERANT CONDITIONING (learning theory)
The strengthening of a response by presenting a **reinforcer** if and only if the response occurs.

OPERATIONS (Piagetian theory)

Mental 'actions' such as **conservation** or **inference** which do not appear in **development** until the sub-period of **concrete operations** (6–11 years).

OPERATIONAL PERIOD (Piagetian theory)

The third period of intellectual **development**, starting at about 6 years old, when thinking becomes logical. It is subdivided into the period of **concrete operations** (6–11 or so) when a child can manage e.g. **conservation**, and the period of **formal operations** (11 onwards) which includes awareness of one's own thoughts and mental strategies.

ORAL STAGE (Freudian theory)

The first stage of **psycho-sexual/development** in which the main source of pleasure is the mouth.

OVER EXTENSION

Including unconventional items within the meaning of a word. Some psychologists say that young children do this when they define a word by only one feature (i.e. they may define 'moon' by 'roundness', and then use the same word also to mean e.g. 'plate' or the letter 'O').

PHALLIC STAGE (Freudian theory)

The third stage of **psycho-sexual/development**, in which the main source of pleasure is immature genital activity.

PHOBIA

An irrational fear of an object, person or event.

PLAY THERAPY (Freudian theory)

Therapy which uses play as the means of communication whereby the patient reveals **unconscious** conflicts and desires, and works through his or her problems.

PLEASURE PRINCIPLE (Freudian theory)

The mode of functioning of the **id** which is characterized by fantasy rather than reality.

PRE-OPERATIONAL PERIOD (Piagetian theory)

The second period of intellectual **development** (2–6 years) in which the child's thinking is characterized by symbols such as language but not yet by **logic** or mathematics.

PROPRIOCEPTION

The sense dealing with the position of limbs in relation to each other and to the body.

PSYCHOANALYSIS

Therapeutic treatment invented by Freud for uncovering memories, thoughts and feelings that are **unconscious**.

PSYCHOLOGY

The *science* of behaviour, thoughts and feelings.

PSYCHO-SEXUAL

The psychological rather than reproductive side to sexual feelings and actions.

PUNISHMENT (learning theory)

An unpleasant event following an action (response) that makes less likely the occurrence of that response in future.

REALITY PRINCIPLE (Freudian theory)

The mode of functioning of the **ego**, which is characterized by rational planning and evaluating.

REGRESSION (Freudian theory)

A return to infantile ways of behaving or feeling.

REFERENCE

The relationship between a word and an object or event in the real world.

REINFORCEMENT (learning theory)

The process which increases the likelihood of a response. In **operant conditioning** the procedure of following response with the reinforcing **stimulus**.

REINFORCER (learning theory)
An object or event which increases the likelihood of a response occurring.

REVERSIBILITY (Piagetian theory)
A mental **operation** which brings something back to its original state. For example, if a child pours water from one container to another, differently shaped, container, so that the *amount* of water seems to change, he can prove to himself that it has not changed by reversing the operation mentally – i.e. imagining pouring it back.

REWARD (learning theory)
A pleasant event following an action (response) that makes more likely the occurrence of that response in future.

SCHEMA (Piagetian theory)
A **mental structure**. The baby 0–2 years has **sensory-motor** schemas whereas the child 6–7 years has **operational** (or logical) schemas.

SENSITIVE PERIOD
The time interval early in the life of an animal (or baby) in which **attachment** occurs.

SENSORY-MOTOR PERIOD (Piagetian theory)
The first period in intellectual **development** (0–2) years which is characterized by *practical* intelligence.

SENTENCE
A meaningful string of words organized according to the rules of **grammar**.

SEQUENCE
A series of stages according to which **development** takes place. The notion of sequence is important to both Piagetian and Freudian theory, though of course the sequences themselves are different for the two theories. (*See also* **invariance**.)

SEX-ROLE LEARNING
Learning the behaviour that a society considers appropriate for an individual because of his or her sex.

SHAPING OF BEHAVIOUR (learning theory)
Changing behaviour by **reinforcing** only those variations in response which move in the desired direction.

SOCIALIZATION
The shaping of an individual's behaviour and attitudes so that they conform to social conventions.

S-R PSYCHOLOGY
See **stimulus-response psychology**.

STAGE
A **developmental** period, usually part of a regular **sequence**. Freud said that children's emotions developed in **psycho-sexual** stages and Piaget said that children's thinking developed in **cognitive** stages.

STIMULUS
Any objectively describable object or event to which an individual responds.

STIMULUS – RESPONSE PSYCHOLOGY (learning theory)
A psychological view that all behaviour may be viewed as a response to a **stimulus** and that the task of psychology is to study the processes between stimulus and response.

SUCCESSIVE APPROXIMATION
See **shaping of behaviour**.

SUPEREGO (Freudian theory)
That part of the personality that contains the moral conscience. It often conflicts with the needs of the **id** and it is then up to the **ego** to find a successful (compromise) action in the real world.

SYMBOL (Freudian theory)
A word, image, thing, or activity **unconsciously** substituted for another which has been repressed.

THEORY
An organized body of **concepts**. Scientists lay great stress on prediction in the testing of theories: i.e. in demonstrating that if theory X is true then Y must be the case, and then testing to see whether it is.

TRAUMA (Freudian theory)
Literally, a psychological wound.

UNCONDITIONED STIMULUS (UCS)
See **classical conditioning**.

UNCONDITIONED RESPONSE (UCS)
See **classical conditioning**.

UNCONSCIOUS (Freudian theory)
Mental processes of which an individual is unaware, including those which have been repressed.

Further reading

Chapter 1
Bee, H., *The Developing Child* (3rd ed.) (New York: Harper & Row, 1981)
Bower, T. G. R., *A Primer of Infant Development* (San Francisco: Freeman, 1977)
Mussen, P., Conger, J. J. and Kagan, J., *Child Development and Personality* (5th ed.)
  (New York: Harper & Row, 1979)

Chapter 2
Dunn, J., *Distress and Comfort* (London: Fontana/Open Books, 1977)

Chapter 3
Clarke, A. M. and Clarke, A. D. B. (eds), *Early Experience: Myth and Evidence*
  (London: Open Books, 1976)

Chapter 4
Schaffer, H. R., *Mothering* (London: Fontana/Open Books, 1977)
Stern, D. N., *The First Relationship: Infant and Mother* (London: Fontana/Open
  Books, 1977)

Chapter 5
Maier, H., *Three Theories of Child Development* (3rd ed.) (New York: Harper & Row,
  1978)
Hall, C., *A Primer of Freudian Psychology* (New York: New American Library)

Chapter 6
Bower, T. G. R., *The Perceptual World of the Child* (London: Fontana/Open Books,
  1977)

Chapter 7
Bryant, P. B., *Perception and Understanding in Young Children* (London: Methuen,
  1974)
Donaldson, M., *Children's Minds* (London: Fontana, 1978)
Ginsburg, H. and Opper, S., *Piaget's Theory of Intellectual Development* (New Jersey:
  Prentice Hall, 1979)

Chapter 8
Blackman, D. E., *Operant Conditioning* (London: Methuen, 1974)
Rachlin, H., *Introduction to Modern Behaviourism* (San Francisco: Freeman, 1970)

Chapter 9
de Villiers, P. and de Villiers, J., *Early Language* (London: Fontana/Open Books,
  1979)
Clark, H. H. and Clark, E. V., *Psychology and Language* (New York: Harcourt Brace
  Jovanovich, 1977)

Chapter 10
Bryant, B., Harris, M. and Newton, D., *Children and Minders* (London: Grant
  McIntyre, 1980)

Garland, C. and White, S., *Children and Day Nurseries* (London: Grant McIntyre, 1980)

Tizard, B., *Adoption: A Second Chance* (London: Open Books, 1977)

Chapter 11

Garvey, C., *Play* (London: Fontana/Open Books, 1977)

Sylva, K. D., Roy, C. and Painter, M., *Childwatching at Playgroup and Nursery School* (London: Grant McIntyre, 1980)

Chapter 12

Parry, M. and Archer H., *Two to Five* (London: Macmillan, 1975)

Webb, L., *Purpose and Practice in Nursery Education* (Oxford: Basil Blackwell, 1975)

Bruner, J. S., *Under Five in Britain* (London: Grant McIntyre, 1980)

Chapter 14

McAuley, R. and McAuley, P., *Child Behaviour Problems* (London: Macmillan, 1977)

Axline, V., *Dibs: In Search of Self* (Harmondsworth: Penguin, 1971)

Chapter 16

Robson, C., *Experimental Design and Statistics* (Harmondsworth: Penguin, 1974)

Nadelman, L., *Research Manual in Child Development* (New York: Harper and Row, 1982)

References

Chapter 1
1. Opie, I. and Opie, P., *Lore and Language of Schoolchildren* (Radlett: Granada, 1977)
2. Skinner, B. F., *Science and Human Behavior* (New York: Macmillan, 1953)

Chapter 2
1. Freud, A. and Dann, S., An experiment in group upbringing, *The Psychoanalytic Study of the Child*, 1951, Vol. VI
2. Harlow, H. F., Love in infant monkeys, *Scientific American*, 1959, vol. 200, No. 6, 68–74
3. Harlow, H. F. and Harlow, M. K., Social deprivation in monkeys, *Scientific American*, 1962, vol. 203

Chapter 3
1. Bowlby, J., *Attachment and Loss*, Vol. 1 (Harmondsworth: Penguin, 1971)
2. Spitz, R. A. and Wolf, K. M., Anaclitic depression, *The Psychoanalytic Study of the Child*, 1946, Vol. 2, 313–42
3. Lorenz, K., *Studies in Animal and Human Behaviour*, Vol. 1 (Cambridge, Mass.: Harvard University Press, 1970)
4. Hess, E. H., Imprinting: an effect of early experience, *Science*, 1959, 130: 133–41
5. Goldfarb, W., The effects of early institutional care on adolescent personality, *Journal of Experimental Education*, 1943, 12, 106–29
6. Rutter, M., *Maternal Deprivation Reassessed* (Harmondsworth: Penguin, 1972)
7. Clarke, A. M. and Clark, A. D. B., *Early Experience: Myth and Evidence* (London: Open Books, 1976)

Chapter 4
1. Schaffer, H. R., *Mothering* (London: Fontana/Open Books, 1977)
2. Richards, M. P. M. and Bernal, J. F., An observational study of mother–infant interaction. In N. J. Blurton-Jones (ed.) *Ethological Studies of Child Behaviour* (London: C.U.P., 1972)
3. Stern, D. N., *The First Relationship: Infant and Mother* (London: Fontana/Open Books, 1977)
4. Macfarlane, J. A., *The Psychology of Childbirth* (London: Fontana/Open Books, 1977)
5. Ainsworth, M. D. S. and Bell, S. M., Attachment, exploration and separation: illustrated by the behaviour of one-year-olds in a strange situation, *Child Development*, 1970, 41, 49–67
6. Klaus, H. M. and Kennel, J. H., *Maternal Infant Bonding* (St. Louis: Mosby, 1976)
7. Schaffer, H. R. and Emerson, P. E., *The Development of Social Attachments in Infancy*, Monographs of Social Research in Child Development, 1964, 29, No. 94
8. Ainsworth, M. D. S., *Infancy in Uganda* (Baltimore: Johns Hopkins University Press, 1967)
9. Schaffer, H. R., *Mothering* (London: Fontana/Open Books, 1977)

Chapter 5
1. Freud, S., *Three Essays on the Theory of Sexuality. Standard Edition of Complete Psychological Works of Sigmund Freud*, Vol. 7 (London: Hogarth Press, 1962)
2. Freud, S., *Introductory Lectures on Psychoanalysis. Standard Edition of the Complete Psychological Works of Sigmund Freud*, Vols 15–16 (London: Hogarth Press, 1963)
3. Freud, S., *Analysis of a Phobia in a Five Year Old Boy. Standard Edition of the Complete Psychological Works of Sigmund Freud*, Vol. 10 (London: Hogarth Press, 1955)
4. Brown, R., *Social Psychology* (Chicago: Free Press, 1965)
5. Yarrow, L., The relationship between nutritive sucking experiences in infancy and non-nutritive sucking in childhood. In H. J. Eysenck and G. D. Wilson (eds) *The Experimental Study of Freudian Theories* (London: Methuen, 1973)

Chapter 6
1. Fantz, R., The origin of form perception, *Scientific American*, 1961, 204, 66–72
2. Gibson, E. and Walk, R. D., The visual cliff, *Scientific American*, 1960, 202, 64–71
3. Bower, T. G. R., *The Perceptual World of the Child* (London: Fontana/Open Books, 1977)
4. Vurpillot, E., *The Visual World of the Child* (London: Allen & Unwin, 1976)

Chapter 7
1. Piaget, J., *The Child's Conception of the World* (New York: Harcourt, Brace and World, 1929)
2. Piaget, J., *The Origins of Intelligence in Children* (New York: Norton, 1963)
3. Piaget, J., *Play, Dreams and Imitation in Childhood* (London: Routledge, 1951)
4. Piaget, J., *The Moral Judgement of the Child* (New York: Harcourt, Brace and World, 1932)
5. Ginsburg, H. and Opper, S., *Piaget's Theory of Intellectual Development* (New Jersey: Prentice Hall, 1979)
6. Piaget, J., *The Child's Conception of Number* (London: Routledge and Kegan, 1952)
7. Bryant, P E., *Perception and Understanding in Young Children* (London: Methuen, 1974)
8. Donaldson, M., *Children's Minds* (London: Fontana, 1978)

Chapter 9
1. Snow, C. E., The development of conversation between mothers and babies, *Journal of Child Language*, 1977, Vol. 4
2. Bruner, J. S., Learning how to do things with words. In J. S. Bruner and A. Garton (eds), *Human Growth and Development* (Oxford: Oxford University Press, 1976)
3. Bloom, L., *Language Development: Form and Function in Emerging Grammar* (Cambridge, Mass.: M.I.T. Press, 1970)
4. Clark, H. H. and Clark, E. V., Meaning in children's language. In *Psychology and Language* (New York: Harcourt Brace Jovanovich, 1977)
5. Brown, R. and Bellugi-Klima, U., Language and learning (a special issue of *Harvard Educational Review*), Spring 1964, 34, 135–55
6. de Villiers, P. and de Villiers, J. G., *Early Language* (London: Fontana/Open Books, 1979)
7. Cazden, C. B., Play with language and meta-linguistic awareness. In J. S. Bruner, A. Jolly and K. Sylva (eds) *Play: Its Role in Development and Evolution* (Harmondsworth: Penguin, 1976)

Chapter 10

1. Triseliotis, J. (1980) Growing up in foster care and after. In J. Triseliotis (Ed.) *New Developments in Foster Care and Adoption*. London: Routledge and Kegan Paul.
2. Tizard, B. and Rees, J., A comparison of effects of adoption, restoration to the natural mother, and continued institutionalization on the cognitive development of four-year-old children, *Child Development*, 1974, 45, 92–9
3. Tizard, B. and Hodges, J., The effect of early institutional rearing on the development of eight-year-old children, *Journal of Child Psychology and Psychiatry*, 1978, 12, 99–118
4. Mayall, B. and Petrie, P., *Minder, Mother and Child* (London: University of London Institute of Education, 1977)
5. Bryant, B., Harris, M. and Newton, D., *Children and Minders* (London: Grant McIntyre, 1980)
6. Garland, C. and White, S., *Children and Day Nurseries* (London: Grant McIntyre, 1980)

Chapter 11

1. Piaget, J., *Play, Dreams and Imitation in Childhood* (London: Routledge, 1951)
2. Garvey, C., *Play* (London: Fontana/Open Books, 1977)
3. Sylva, K. D., Roy, C. and Painter, M., *Childwatching at Playgroup and Nursery School* (London: Grant McIntyre, 1980)

Chapter 12

1. Bandura, A., Ross D. and Ross, S. A., Imitation of film-mediated aggressive models, *Journal of Abnormal Social Psychology*, 1963, 66, 3–11
2. Webb, L., *Purpose and Practice in Nursery Education* (Oxford: Basil Blackwell, 1974)
3. Smith, P. K. and Connolly, K. J., *The Ecology of Pre-school Behaviour* (Cambridge: Cambridge University Press, 1980)
4. Hutt, C., *Males and Females* (Harmondsworth: Penguin Books, 1972)

Chapter 14

1. Brown, R. and Herrnstein, R. J., *Psychology* (London: Methuen, 1975)
2. Watson, J. B., *Behaviourism* (Chicago: University of Chicago Press, 1924)
3. McAuley, R. and McAuley, P., *Child Behaviour Problems* (Macmillan, 1977)
4. Axline, V., *Dibs: In Search of Self* (Harmondsworth: Penguin, 1971)

Chapter 15

1. Brown, R. and Herrnstein, R. J., *Psychology* (London: Methuen, 1975)
2. Burt, C., *The Factors of the Mind* (London: University of London Press, 1940)
3. Gillham, W. E. C. (ed.), *Reconstructing Educational Psychology* (London: Croom Helm, 1978)

Index

Index